Making Tracks
Unique Recording Studio Environments

Jeff Touzeau

Schiffer® Publishing Ltd

4880 Lower Valley Road, Atglen, PA 19310 USA

Dedication

For My Dad...

...defender of my dreams despite their being improbable, impractical, and unprofitable.

Photo courtesy Donald Touzeau

FRONT COVER:
1) View of the Big Room exterior. Air, water, and light are fundamental elements throughout the facility and its grounds. *Reproduced with kind permission from Real World Studios Ltd. http://realworldstudios.co.uk. Photographer: York Tillyer. © Real World Holdings Ltd., Real World Studios Ltd.*
2) Allaire's SSL-based 5.1 control room, designed by Walters-Storyk Design Group (WSDG). *Randall Wallace*
BACK COVER:
1) The production room at Real World. *Reproduced with kind permission from Real World Studios Ltd. http://realworldstudios.co.uk. Photographer: York Tillyer. © Real World Holdings Ltd., Real World Studios Ltd.*
2) The John Harms Theater, viewed from the stage, is a meticulously restored 1,400 seat theater connected by an underground fiber optic cable to Bennett Studios. *Photo courtesy of Bennett Studios*
SPINE:
Side/rear exterior of Imaginary Road Studios at night. *Photo by John Cooper, courtesy of Imaginary Road*
TITLE PAGE:
Allaire Studio's Neve Room, providing unrivalled ambience inside and out. *Randall Wallace*

Library of Congress Catalogin-in-Publication Data:

Touzeau, Jeff.
Making tracks : unique recording studio environments / Jeff Touzeau.
p. cm.
ISBN 0-7643-2438-1 (hardcover)
1. Music and architecture. 2. Architectural acoustics. 3. Sound studios—Design and construction. I. Title.
ML3849.T68 2006
781.490973—dc22
2005031330

Designed by John P. Cheek
Cover design by Bruce Waters
Type set in Grenadier/Lydian BT

ISBN: 0-7643-2438-1
Printed in China

Published by Schiffer Publishing Ltd.
4880 Lower Valley Road
Atglen, PA 19310
Phone: (610) 593-1777; Fax: (610) 593-2002
E-mail: Info@schifferbooks.com

For the largest selection of fine reference books on this and related subjects, please visit our web site at **www.schifferbooks.com**
We are always looking for people to write books on new and related subjects. If you have an idea for a book please contact us at the above address.

This book may be purchased from the publisher.
Include $3.95 for shipping.
Please try your bookstore first.
You may write for a free catalog.

In Europe, Schiffer books are distributed by
Bushwood Books
6 Marksbury Ave.
Kew Gardens
Surrey TW9 4JF England
Phone: 44 (0) 20 8392-8585; Fax: 44 (0) 20 8392-9876
E-mail: info@bushwoodbooks.co.uk
Free postage in the U.K., Europe; air mail at cost.

CONTENTS

View of Allaire Studios atop Glen Tonche. *Randall Wallace*

Acknowledgments

There are many people who I would like to thank who helped me one way or another over the course of writing this book. First, I'd like to thank my children, Caroline and Ashton, and my wife, Kim. Writing a book takes a significant amount of time, and unfortunately it takes time away from those people you love the most. My family was extremely patient and supportive throughout the duration. Kim deserves substantial credit for taking many of the photographs that appear in this book and for helping me proofread and edit the manuscript. Thank you also to Bing and Marcy Carlson for watching our children during overseas trips and for helping accommodate many of these interviews by providing access to office space and facilities.

Second, I want to thank all the studio owners, managers, producers, and engineers who selflessly gave their time and effort to help make this book a reality. These people welcomed me into their personal recording spaces and contributed by helping with interviews, phone calls, photos, and emails. They were extremely gracious with their time and their passion and dedication shines through on the each of the pages that follow. Thank you especially to Randall and Jackie Wallace, who gave me uninhibited access to Allaire (Randall also shared his artistic talent by providing many stunning photos in this book). I would also like to thank the many people behind the scenes who helped me with factual content and coordination, including Sally Grossman, Chris Laidlaw, and Patty Merklin at Bearsville, Eric Carlinsky at BearTracks, Lucy Ward at Rockfield, Ruth Taylor at Sawmills, Gordon Rice at Roselane East, Victoria Andrew and Corin Nelsen at Imaginary Road, and many, many others who assisted in getting information to me. Thank you also to Fran Manzella for putting me in touch with the folks at Blue Jay and The Barber Shop Studios, and thank you to Nick Mason.

Third, thank you to Tina Skinner and Jeff Snyder, my editors at Schiffer Publishing, who embraced my idea from the outset and carried it through with quality and conviction. Thanks also to Terry Edelman for transcribing, and thank you to all the photographers who granted me permission to use their work throughout these pages. I also wish to thank Tom and Joseph Kiley at Katonah Image, who helped me develop most of the photos in this book.

Finally, there are a few other people I would like to thank who perhaps unknowingly influenced me in this endeavor. This book may never have come to fruition if I hadn't received support and encouragement as a writer from Larry Crane, Editor of *Tape Op* magazine. Last, and certainly not least, I would also like to acknowledge Linda Kummer, my aunt, who encouraged me to write about something I was passionate about.

The production room at Real World. *Reproduced with kind permission from Real World Studios Ltd. http://realworldstudios.co.uk. Photographer: York Tillyer. © Real World Holdings Ltd., Real World Studios Ltd.*

FOREWORD

Blue Jay Recording's control room through custom made PRG "di-view-ser" plexi-glass diffusion unit.
Photo by George Roos, courtesy of Blue Jay Recording

What are the factors that create a truly unique and great recording studio? Is it the console, the microphone selection, the monitors, the room acoustics? Is it the environment, the staff, the instrument selection? Or is it the sum total of all these tangible variables along with some harder to define, less tangible quality?

I have seen quite a few studios over my twenty-four years spent in this business filling a diverse number of roles, including technical engineer, touring sound man, recording engineer and producer, and, most recently, acoustic architect. I've listened to awesome sounding control rooms and recorded in horrible sounding live rooms. I've designed a fair amount of successful facilities as well as a few that haven't been able to stand the test of time. Through all this, I have found there is a definite "quality" to some of these unique studios that can be very hard to define. The best word I have found is "vibe".

Let's face it, that's what this "business" is all about: a great song, a great mood, some talented folks, and a comfortable place to capture a once in a lifetime performance. Get the performance on tape (or hard disc, whatever)! That was what I learned first as a recording engineer. Record everything. You never know when something will come out of the singer's mouth, or the guitarist's amp that everyone wants to hear again! I can tell you one thing, the ratio of "cool" stuff that comes from the musicians on any given session can be directly correlated to their level of comfort during the session. Making a studio a comfortable place, physically and emotionally, is what makes it a place that people will want to come back to.

This can be achieved through many widely varying approaches. Some studio owners will choose to hire an acoustic designer whose work inspires them and makes them comfortable. Some will try to do it themselves by sketching their vision out on a napkin. Still others will stumble blindly into a great space that is almost impossible to mess up! Throughout the last fifteen years of my career as an acoustic designer, I have endeavored to give all of my projects a unique "vibe" that might just make a talented artist comfortable enough to forget about the glass for a few minutes and achieve that once-in-a-lifetime performance.

Jeff has assembled a truly unique collection of recording facilities and studio professionals. These studios were selected without prejudice towards level of sophistication or capital investment. You are invited to experience the "all-elusive vibe" through Touzeau's own words, his collection of interviews and the breathtaking photographs that follow.

Francis Manzella

Preface

My earliest personal exposure to the world of recording studios came about in the early 1980s, when as a teenager I was offered an internship at House of Music, a studio that was based in South Orange, New Jersey. The tasks outlined in the position were routine and menial: pouring coffee, setting up mic stands, warming up the recording console, patching cables, cleaning the floors. After listening to the run down of the required tasks, I remember asking my interviewer about the history of the studio.

Suddenly, her face was aglow and the conversation turned magical. "Well, Meatloaf recorded *Bat Out of Hell* here...'Paradise by the Dashboard Light' was recorded right over there," as she proudly pointed to a section of the live room and continued to describe how the session went down in detail. From that point on, for me, House of Music and every other studio suddenly graduated to mythical status. The studio became a place where creative musical visions became realized. Who cares if I was asked to make coffee? My interest in recording studios became permanent and insufferable.

More recently, as a writer for *Tape Op*, *EQ*, and *Pro Sound News*, I have had the privilege of writing articles on many influential figures in the recording world, including acousticians, artists, producers, engineers, and many others. I have seen first hand how a special recording environment can enhance creativity, as in the case of David Gilmour's Astoria studio boat, the most technically advanced and aesthetically beautiful recording environment I have ever seen. Listening to the 5.1 mix of The Dark Side of the Moon at Astoria, where it was mixed, was a once in a lifetime privilege that I will never forget.

In writing this book, my overall goal was to uncover the passion behind these special recording environments by speaking with the people who have built them and worked in them. They are the voices behind the creativity, the people behind the places where the magic is assembled. "If these walls could speak...."

Introduction

There are, and have always been, many forces at work defining and altering the landscape of the professional recording studio industry. Rapid advances in recording technologies, combined with an ongoing sea-change in music distribution methodologies and evolving (or dissolving) musical trends, have created an exciting, if uncertain, market for manufacturers, producers, artists, and studios. Throughout the history of recorded music, the studios themselves have been on the front lines witnessing these changes first hand and adapting to them.

Over the course of an unrelenting change, some things have remained constant: the laws of physics governing acoustical properties, "best practice" recording techniques, the need for a high quality song/performance, and, of course, talented recording engineers and producers. Another constant is the passion which recording professionals bring to the field and to their respective facilities.

The studios spotlighted here are dynamic and creative, and have a diverse and colorful range of personalities, like their caretakers. It is for this very reason that I chose to write this book in interview format, which maintains the unique voice and perspective behind each recording environment and individual.

This book is not, nor was ever intended to be, a "studio directory." It is also not meant to be a "commercial guide" of any sort. Instead, it was created with the intent of highlighting unusual recording environments from many different origins and perspectives. Each facility has an equally interesting face behind it; people who arrived in their current stations by way of many different paths and backgrounds. Some were building contractors, some were respected engineers and musicians, and some owned highly successful niche recording labels.

The studios come in all colors and sizes and are used to record all conceivable genres of music. There are multi-million dollar facilities sprawling across acres of the most pristine landscape imaginable, and there are smaller, more esoteric facilities in urban environs. The buildings are converted barns, firehouses, railroad stations, churches, and sawmills. The environs are islands, lakes, mountaintops, beaches, vineyards, and the Navy yards of Brooklyn. There are studios in all stages of life: some are in their infancy and others nearing retirement. The single resounding element common to all these places is the timeless passion of the people behind them.

This book could have easily been an in-depth rundown on the history of recording studios; from Edison's lab in West Orange, New Jersey, all the way to the present day state of the art multi-track facilities. I chose not to take that approach because it seemed too static and one-dimensional. The individual histories of the places in this book and the people behind them are far more compelling, especially when told in the first person by the people who were there.

Woodstock: An Overview

Woodstock sits between the Catskill Mountains and the Hudson Valley of New York, comfortably due north of New York City. Since the nineteenth century, Woodstock has been a prolific artistic community consisting of craftspeople, artists, musicians, and writers. While the Woodstock event of 1969 put the town's namesake on the international map, the actual Woodstock event took place eighty miles southwest in Bethel, New York.

The artistic community that developed in Woodstock, particularly in the 1960s, drew many influential musicians and songwriters such as Bob Dylan, Jimi Hendrix, Van Morrison, Janis Joplin, The Band, Todd Rundgren, Eric Clapton, George Harrison, and countless others. The area manifested the classic "going up the country" mentality, serving as a retreat where musicians could surround themselves in an environment that was supportive, inspirational, and brimming with talent. The Woodstock event catapulted the music community that inhabited this region, as culture, music, and a sense of purpose all seemed to converge.

Indeed, the arts community within Woodstock still thrives; the region still counts among its residents many prominent musicians who still live in the area. Two of the studios featured in this book have their roots in the Woodstock region: Allaire Studios and Bearsville Studios.

Allaire surrounded by the autumn foliage of Woodstock. *Randall Wallace*

Statue of guitar in the town of Woodstock. *Photo by Kim Touzeau, courtesy of Hummingbird Media*

The Band poses for a picture during the genesis of Bearsville's Studio A. *Photo by Barry Feinstein, courtesy of Bearsville Studios*

A helicopter view of Bearsville Studio in autumn. *Photo by Stephen Green-Armitage, courtesy of Bearsville Studios*

Allaire Studios

Mark McKenna, Studio Manager

Allaire is situated on a magnificent twenty-five-acre mountaintop estate in the Catskills overlooking Woodstock and the Ashokan Reservoir. On a clear day, you can see into three states, New Jersey, New York, and Connecticut. Raymond Pitcairn, the glass tycoon who is the namesake of PPG, originally built the mansion in 1928 as a summer retreat for his deeply religious family. In 1998, the estate was purchased by Randall Wallace, a New York City-based photographer and musician, who spent three years and a vast amount of resources to repurpose it into a "no compromise" recording environment.

Despite the enormous scale of the facility, Allaire feels like home. Mark McKenna, Allaire's Studio Manager and one of the most respected studio managers in the business, often refers to Allaire as the artists' "home away from home". Allaire isn't just a no-expense-spared, technically marvelous facility set atop sprawling grounds of beauty and luxury, it is a place where artists, producers, and other professionals can attain the presence of mind required to help them focus and reach their creative peak.

The "family" vibe that the Pitcairns imparted many years ago still permeates the walls of this mansion. When you walk through Allaire, it doesn't seem distant or aloof; it feels warm, inviting, and hospitable. The Wallace family's passion for the grounds and facility are manifested everywhere; through Randall's photography (found on these pages) and immense guitar collection, Jackie Wallace's guest room décor, and the many other painstakingly detailed finishing touches found in every room. There has been an articulate, concerted effort to retain the overall beauty and integrity of the building and the estate.

Technically and aesthetically, Allaire has few rivals. This is the only facility in the world that was collaboratively designed by two of the most accomplished acousticians in the industry: George Augspurger and John Storyk of Walters Storyk Design Group (WSDG). The result is a sonic masterpiece: John Leckie, one of the world's great producers, called Allaire's Great Hall control room "The best I've ever worked in."

Following its opening in 2001, Allaire wasted no time getting records into the top ten of the Billboard charts. The list of bands and artists who have recorded at Allaire reads like a Who's Who of pop music: David Bowie, Natalie Merchant, Tim McGraw, Joan Baez, The Gipsy Kings, Norah Jones, Cassandra Wilson, and The Strokes. Allaire attracts the top talent in the industry today and, according to McKenna, most people who record there end up coming back.

The South Wing Sunset Porch, offering views of the Ashokan Reservoir and the Hudson Valley. *Randall Wallace*

Can you describe the history of these grounds?

Well, the Hudson Valley was originally inhabited by the Dutch. The family who originally developed this property was the Pitcairns and this was their summer home. Raymond Pitcairn was the son of the founder of PPG Industries. Like a lot of the industrialist families, the Pitcairns wanted to have a nice summer home in the mountains. The Rockefellers and the Vanderbilts chose the Adirondacks, but the Pitcairns wound up in the Catskills. They built this place in the 1920s, and it was really just a summer home. I think they had a caretaker year round just to keep an eye on the grounds and buildings, but they would shut most of it down during the winter.

Randall Wallace, the current owner, bought it around 1998. I think it was just a complete revelation to him. He weekended

Raymond Pitcairn, photographed during the original construction of Allaire in 1929. *Photo courtesy of Allaire Studios*

up here, and renovated little bits of it: first the gatehouse, so he could live somewhere while they worked on the rest of the place.

What do you know about Raymond Pitcairn?

Well, he was into building glass, auto glass, any type of glass. The plate glass throughout this facility is amazing and stunning. This place was built during the no income tax, "robber baron" period, the gilded age in the United States, I guess. The railroad families were making big fortunes, including the Vanderbilts, and people like that, contemporaries of his. The Pitcairns were very religious and this was very much a private family place, and they had all their kids and grandkids up here. They played a lot of music and spent a lot of time together.

What was special about the construction?

Architecturally, it's somewhat of an unusual design. It's like a Cape Cod meets Adirondack design with these steep pitched roofs, presumably to keep the snow from collecting on them. Raymond Pitcairn was a Gothic and Romanesque architecture expert and a collector of antiquities. He built a house outside of Philadelphia in Bryn Athyn, which is similar to this in scale, but it's all granite. It's phenomenal. Pitcairn was a medieval architecture expert to the point where he drew walls that were slightly out of square, kind of a hallmark of that type of design.

He had a real eye for it.

And he also knew a lot about the construction techniques. He had really good people working for him, using exquisite materials. They used huge Douglas fir timbers and native blue stone. All of that said, this place is modest compared to the place outside Philadelphia.

Preserving the flavor of the original structure and marrying the new design must have been a challenge.

I think we did a good job. We used craftsmen that Randall knew from New York to do a lot of the finishing work that really helps maintain that classy look. For example, all these doors were made out of Douglas fir, just like the rest of the wood in the Great Hall. It looks similar, but it's actually not the same; it has been stained to match the original wood. The floors also have radiant heat.

Can you give me a visual tour of Allaire in my mind?

Basically, there are two main wings to this place, the north and the south wing. The north wing contains the Great Hall Studio, and the south wing contains the Neve Room. In each wing there are a number of bedrooms as well. This is a lot more than a studio; it's like a hotel. There are about fourteen bedrooms and there's a kitchen that sometimes operates all day long.

With a full-time chef?

Yeah. It's a restaurant, a hotel, and a studio, so it's a lot more complicated than just a studio. The Great Hall is in the north wing and is an enormous room; I don't recall the precise number of square feet, but the main room is about 40' x 50' with a 45' ceiling with a number of isolation rooms off of it. There's the vocal booth, there are two sound locks, there's the Sunset Porch, there's the Sliver Room, and there's another room upstairs. So there are six

Aerial view of Allaire Studios. *Randall Wallace*

The Neve Room at Allaire with its "open air" environment. *Randall Wallace*

isolated rooms plus the Great Hall and then there's the control room, which is enormous. We also have a private lounge for Great Hall clients. Altogether, there's about a half a dozen or so bedrooms in the north wing, then there's this sort of courtyard which creates a natural boundary between both wings. When we have two clients in, there seems to be enough space that people aren't all over one another.

The Sunset Porch was originally an open patio that had operable windows with a blue stone floor. They had patio furniture out there and this is where the original owners could go to enjoy the day's end. They would raise these windows up and be virtually outdoors.

Connecting the north wing and the south wing is a little walkway. The south wing consists of a large studio, the Neve Room, and four bedrooms; soon there will be five. There's also a game room underneath the Neve room, which has pinball games, foosball games, Pac Man, and all that stuff. There's also a little studio upstairs, which isn't being used very much, but it's full of Randall's guitar collection. There are about 160 guitars in there.

Are clients able to use Randall's guitars from his collection?
Yes. Out of 160 guitars, there might be twenty that are off limits. We give the bands here like about ten or twelve guitars for free use, then the rest, there's a nominal fee, like thirty-five bucks for the day, which is minimal. There are about seventy guitar amps here as well.

Randall Wallace's instrument collection features a variety of amplifiers and over 160 guitars. *Photo by Kim Touzeau, courtesy of Hummingbird Media*

Is there a separate workshop or room where the maintenance is performed?

Well, Ken McKim has a nice shop downstairs. I actually share a space with him. It's under the Sunset Porch and it looks out over the mountains. He has all the test gear: a distortion analyzer, oscilloscopes, parts, everything you need to troubleshoot a state of the art studio.

Are there many outbuildings?

No, it's pretty self-contained. This is a big building and there are plenty of rooms that I don't even get to go in because I don't have time. But if you stretch it out from one end to the other, it stretches all the way down to the tennis court, which is 150 yards away from the swimming pool. The summit of the mountain is beautiful and within walking range.

Mark McKenna, studio manager, gazes across the Hudson Valley atop a porch off of The Great Hall. *Photo by Kim Touzeau, courtesy of Hummingbird Media*

How were you originally drawn to the Woodstock region?

I went to college nearby.

So you had known about this area.

You couldn't have not known about it. Back in the seventies, Woodstock was the oddity; a town of like 3,000 people that had Van Morrison, Tim Hardin, Paul Butterfield, Jimi Hendrix, The Band, and Bob Dylan all living here. It was unprecedented. There was such a concentration of people around Woodstock that you couldn't not notice it.

Did you arrive just after the Woodstock event?

Well, I didn't get here till much later, but in the late sixties, let's say from 1967, '68 through '71, '72, there was just this concentration of major musical talent. Eric Clapton and George Harrison visited Woodstock and fell in love with it. They fell in love with The Band. In fact, I'm told they wanted to have The Band on Apple Records.

How did you land in this crazy business?

I was a musician in my twenties and I was actually mixing live sound for this band called Orleans. My wife and I had a little boy named Flannery, and we wound up staying in Woodstock. Some of the people that I knew that were involved with Orleans were also involved with Bearsville Studios, and I was eventually asked to come on as an assistant engineer at Bearsville in 1979 or 1980.

An interesting time at Bearsville and in the music business.

Yes. Albert Grossman was the owner of that studio and had also been the manager of Bob Dylan, The Band, Janis Joplin, and Todd Rundgren. There was all this activity going on at Bearsville because of Albert and who he was. He had the Bearsville Records label and was in business with Foghat, Jesse Winchester, and many others. So we did a lot of records and it seemed like when I was there we were transitioning from being a modest, in-house production facility for Bearsville Records and Publishing, to a more commercial studio with many outside clients. After both of the studios were revamped, we started getting people like Bob Clearmountain, Jimmy Iovine, Rhett Davies, and these sorts of people coming in. That's when I became aware of the larger picture of recording.

Original fireplace inside The Great Hall, featuring "Glen Tonche" inscription. *Photo by Kim Touzeau, courtesy of Hummingbird Media*

The Sliver Room at Allaire, designed by Walters-Storyk Design Group (WSDG), serves both as a sound lock and a flexible recording room when needed. *Randall Wallace*

Bearsville got a much more prominent position on the radar as well.

Well, it did. Bob Clearmountain, who was already established by the time he came to Bearsville, helped us realize what we didn't know, which was a lot. I learned a lot there, and I was sort of tutored, if you will, by people like Eddie Kramer and John Holbrook, who was an in-house producer/engineer. You get to work with these people at close hand and they teach you what they know by osmosis.

While you worked for Bearsville, you made the transition from Engineer to Studio Manager. Why did you change roles?

I think I got tired of working eighteen hour days, or whatever it was. I was married and we had two little boys, and I thought, "Well, maybe it would be better if I weren't working around the clock, better for my wife, better for my kids." So I became Studio Manager and I got Albert Grossman to introduce me to many of the people he knew in the business that came up to Bearsville.

Were you doing maintenance at Bearsville at some point? You have all your bases covered in handing all the roles applicable in a studio environment.

Well, that has to do with training that was common at that time. As an apprentice, coming up in a studio like that, the regimen was that you were put in the shop initially. You had to come to grips with everything technical beforehand, and you certainly didn't go into the control room at a session until you at least knew as much as possible about it. You had to learn how to solder, how to fix things, how to align a tape machine, electronics. That was sort of the "old school" approach to becoming an engineer.

What happened after Bearsville and why did you leave?

After I worked at Bearsville, and after Albert Grossman died, I thought it might be a good idea to get out of town because Woodstock was beginning to shrink. I left and worked at A&M Studios, then brought my family out about three months later. A&M was another step up altogether. Bearsville was a good studio, but it was nothing like the environment that A&M had. A typical day at A&M would have Bob Seger in one room, Tom Petty in another room, Bruce Springsteen in another room; you know, there were times when we had U2 in all five rooms.

Was that exciting for you?

Yeah, it was great. Not just the hype of being around all these artists, but knowing how to conduct yourself in those kinds of circumstances and not be intimidated, which is important.

So A&M brought you up to a more professional level.

Yes. When you're dealing with people like Herb Albert and Jimmy Iovine you become immune to the pressure and realize what the priorities are. You have to elevate your game in a situation like that, or you don't survive.

When did you arrive at Allaire?

I came back East in '92, and ran Bearsville for a whole other segment. I spent six years in LA, a couple of them at A&M and about four as an independent engineer and producer, working everywhere. Then I finally came back to the East Coast to run Bearsville again. I actually ran Bearsville Theatre first.

Why the theater and not the studio?

I did the theatre thing to try to do something else with my life. But the theatre was too small to really sustain itself, so I wound up getting imported back into the studio. That's really when I did a much better job of turning it into a commercial success and when we had the Dave Matthews Band, Phish, Jeff Buckley, and all these other artists.

So that was kind of the resurgence of Bearsville if you will?

Yes. Then I left Bearsville once more, for the last time. I was working in New York and was called by Jay Unger, a musician, who said, "I have a really good friend who bought this beautiful property and he wants to turn it into a studio; we think he's getting bad advice. Would you go up and meet with him?"

So I met Randall Wallace, the gentleman who owns this place, and his wife, Jackie, the co-owner. They had an employee running the property, who I'd met with. Randall and Jackie both had a very kind of hands-off approach.

Were you already familiar with its existence?

I'd seen it from down below, and remember being amazed at what little I could see from afar. I knew some enormous structure was here, but I didn't know what it was. Anyway, I came up and sat with them, thinking that maybe it was going to be Randall's hobby and that he wasn't really looking to build a studio; maybe he just wanted some equipment. So they rolled out these plans, and I was like, "Oh my god. This is a huge commercial building." Having been familiar with a large-scale facility, like A&M, I knew it was serious. At A&M, all the rooms are built on the old Charlie Chaplin soundstage lot, taking up almost the size of a football field. This rivaled A&M in terms of the scope because we have this large, complex room, The Great Hall.

The courtyard inside the Allaire structure, with four car stone garage. *Photo by Kim Touzeau, courtesy of Hummingbird Media*

One of the many porches clients can enjoy to take in Glen Tonche. *Photo by Jeff Touzeau, courtesy of Hummingbird Media*

Allaire's Great Hall, combining beauty, ambience, and sonic perfection. *Randall Wallace*

What kind of construction issues were you dealing with?

The infrastructural issues were immense. In order to have proper sound isolation, they had to build a room around the Great Hall to protect it from outside noise and to keep noise from getting out, so they wrapped the whole building in scaffolding to do the work.

The fellows who were supervising the construction started calling me and asking me questions from afar. "Should we do this, or should we do that?" "People have told us we should have these monitors, what do you think?" I was answering questions for three months over the phone until they finally asked me to get involved in a more serious way. I drafted Ken McKim, who had been the very respected Chief Technician at Bearsville, since I knew that I couldn't tackle this thing alone. Ken and I basically walked the process through from the blueprints. They hired John Storyk, the renowned architect and acoustician, and I felt it was important to have George Augspurger involved, too. George's philosophy has seeped into just about every good studio in the United States. He's a really capable guy and has got it all together on the theoretical end and the practical end. He used to be a speaker designer at JBL, and he's the person responsible for the sound of the control room.

So you got the best of both worlds...John Storyk and George Augspurger.

It works, because John was in charge of the entire architectural operation. He has a big office with a very capable staff; there's a lot of detail in those plans. It contrasted Albert's approach, since when I worked for Albert, Albert would sit down...he wouldn't even sit down. He had a contractor or a builder working for him all the time, and he would draw something on a napkin and just say, here....and the guy would do it [laughs]. John Storyk's work was really specific, you know, with hundreds of detailed Auto Cad drawings.

You came in right when they were ready to start construction?

Just about. They had put the new exterior roof on the Great Hall, and they were just beginning. They had put the scaffolding up, and they were about to wrap the building and put the new siding on.

I can see how just getting up here with the trucks must have been difficult. It's not easily accessible.

I can only imagine what the scenario would have been like in the '20s when it was built.

What is the scope of your position at Allaire?

Ultimately it's sort of the Harry Truman thing, "The buck stops here." I'm responsible for everything. If someone doesn't like the food, they're going to come tell me, they're not going to tell the chef. But that doesn't happen, fortunately. There are all kinds of little things that come up.

How did it feel to be back in Woodstock?

When I started working here it seemed very positive, because the place was so unusual. I'd never been in an environment like this, and nor had anyone else, for recording. From the beginning we were fully booked. We started with the Neve Room, and everybody loved it. Our first client was Don Byron, second client was Norah Jones, third client was Natalie Merchant, fourth client was David Bowie, and the fifth I think was Guster. We were blocked booked for about seven months. There was hardly a day off. I thought, "This is going to be easy."

So the whole retreat philosophy was paying off. Did it feel like you nailed it?

Well, then came September 11th, and the entire country slowed down. Shortly after that, was the winter of 2002, and things got very quiet in the business. The music business started to shrink and things got a little scarier.

Were there nerves during those first few sessions, when the first few clients came in?

Oh yeah, I was scared to death. My whole philosophy with these studios, smart or not, has been "Let's just get it open." When I worked at Bearsville, we had a room, The Barn, which we expanded and built a control room onto just months before Dave Matthews came in, and that was our deadline. He was coming in on a certain date, and we had to have the room done. And it wasn't finished. We would go in with carpenters and build it from 7:00 in the morning till noon.

Did you have the luxury of time with Allaire, or was it kind of a race to the finish?

Well, it's always a race and I think you have to put a little bit of pressure on yourself that way. You have to start, you have to bring people in, or you'll never get it done. Before Norah Jones came in, we had no idea if they would like it or if it would work, it was scary.

Did the room emanate a certain kind of vibe?

Well, the artists told us it did. When David Bowie came in here, we were all a bit like "Let's not screw this up." It was just David and Tony Visconti doing a lot of the music, Matt Chamberlain was playing the drums, and David Torn played guitar.

How did Bowie find out about this place?

He found out from David Torn, another friend of mine for twenty years. If there wasn't a mountain in the way, you could almost see Torn's house from here. David knew about the place, and told Bowie "You should come here and check this place out because you're not going to see anything like this, anywhere." So he came up with Tony Visconti. Natalie Merchant was working here at the time with T Bone Burnett.

Natalie invited him to have lunch with them, which was interesting because there's a connection there. You know the *Ziggy Stardust* album? Well, *Ziggy Stardust* was based on a character called The Legendary Stardust Cowboy. And T Bone Burnett,

Allaire's North Wing in the winter. *Randall Wallace*

who was producing Natalie's record, did the *Legendary Stardust* album in Fort Worth, Texas, when he was a teenager [laughing]. So the two of them are having lunch, and I don't think it occurred to them that one was somewhat responsible for the other's persona! So that was a little cosmic synergy. Anyway, when David experienced this introduction to Allaire, he was enthralled and said "OK, let's do it!" He would just wander around the grounds and sometimes lay in the hammock. He was here in August and into September. In fact, he was here on September 11th.

Was David's reaction to Allaire typical of what most artists feel when they see it for the first time?

Yes. This kind of place, or a place like Bearsville, really forces a band to come together and really coalesce in a way that they probably wouldn't somewhere else.

Also without distractions.

And not have to deal with anyone else. Not having friends drop by, or having to drive their car down the freeway to the studio and run out every five minutes. It keeps you focused.

Did you spec out the Neve? You have very nice SSL and Neve consoles.

Well, we didn't really plan it, frankly. I suggested to Randall that we get a small analog console for the project studio. It would make a lot of sense because people could use the mic inputs and all that. And the fellow who was the supervisor at that time said, "Why don't you see if you can find a Neve?"

So you found one. Can you tell me about it?

It's an 8068 with 32 channels and it came from a commercial studio in Miami. We did it just as a very informal way to get things going before the Great Hall studio was ready.

So the Neve Room was always an 'open-air' studio with the artist and control room in the same room? Why did you take this approach?

It's just a really easy way to work, and you don't have to build a control room. One of the most interesting aspects of that development is that people would come up and have to adjust to it or relate to it. Some people are quite happy to do it. Steve Lillywhite and U2 and others have done it countless times.

But it's a new way of working for a lot of people.

Yes. The first record we did with Don Byron, the premier jazz clarinetist, and his engineer, Tom Lazarus, who's also fantastic, had never worked that way. Tom was like "This is never gonna work. How can I do this?" Don kept saying, "It'll work.

Allaire's SSL-based 5.1 control room, designed by Walters-Storyk Design Group (WSDG). *Randall Wallace*

The Neve Room, on a break from a session with John Leckie and Longwave. *Photo by Kim Touzeau, courtesy of Hummingbird Media*

Keep trying it. It'll work out." So Tom was skeptical, but after a couple of hours, he got it. He understood what he had to do to make it work, and they made a great sounding record. He was very happy with it.

Has this approach worked particularly well for certain kinds of artists?

I don't know, I don't think it's discriminatory in any way. Psychologically, it's nice because it doesn't feel so imposing; there are literally no walls. There's sort of a mythical and a real aspect to that. When you take the walls out, you do put the engineer at a slight disadvantage because they can't monitor exactly the way they might be accustomed to, but it also makes it easier to communicate. At the end of the day, you're trying to put some energy into the record and this approach just helps make the energy happen. All the electronics and all the recording gear is still really first rate: the Neve console, the API outboard, the really nice limiters and EQs and compressors and stuff like that are all there. We try to give our clients the best of everything.

How did you get Tim McGraw up here?

Tim McGraw's people called and I was like "I've got to get this guy up here somehow." We talked, and I described what was going on, that we had these two rooms, one operational, one not, and Robert Allen, Tim's Production Manager, said the Great Hall room is what they wanted. So I Fed Exed them a floor plan of the Neve Room, which was the only room available then and I said, "Here's how we can do everything that you want to do. You want all this isolation, here's how we can do it." I got a call the next day, and he said, "If you hadn't sent this thing, we wouldn't even be having this conversation now. Tim is going to fly up with Byron Gallimore, his producer, and we'll be there tomorrow." Tim has a private jet, flew up to a private airport in Poughkeepsie. I drove over and got them, brought them over here, and they walked around and they said, "This is it. We'll figure out a way to make it work."

So we had his musicians in all of the various rooms off the Neve room; we had a player in the basement, we had guys upstairs in the project studio, we had the drummer over here on the Sunset Porch. We stopped construction for two weeks so they could do the record and we hooked up video monitors and cameras everywhere so people could see one another.

So Allaire was all interconnected, like a single organism.

Yeah. And not only that, nothing went wrong, if you can believe that.

So it was really just getting them up here and then figuring things out.

Whatever it takes, just figure out a way to do it. And we did it. God must have approved.

Was that one of the biggest sessions you've ever had here?

Yes. Anytime Tim comes up it's a big deal because he brings about twenty some odd people, including his producers, first engineer, several assistants, management, and a few technicians. He made his last two records up here. This record, the one that's out now, is in the top five. It was number one for a while and it's going to be a big record.

It's like a mobile company.

Oh, it's more like an army. We always laugh about it. I call Robert Allen the General Patton of Rock 'n' Roll, because when he moves in....[laughs]

....there's all the logistics, it's almost like troops.

It is. It gets heavier every year. It's very much that way.

I can only imagine what their tour operations are like.

Oh, they have over 100 people on the road; it's outrageous. But they're great guys, and Tim's a sweet guy and has been very generous talking about how working here aided his work. He's mentioned this place countless times in interviews.

Clearly he's enthralled by it.

He thinks it's a great asset. It enables him to do something he can't do in Nashville.

I would imagine it's a relief to get out of a "music city" in general, to come out to the boonies and chill out.

I guess we're spoiled because we don't see the other side. We don't get to see David Bowie navigate New York and deal with all that. So yeah, he can dress down and hang out up here. They have nothing to worry about.

Joan Baez did her last record up here, and she spent a lot of time hiking the mountain trails. She's very much in tune with nature, more than most people. People can go mountain biking or cross country skiing in the winter if they want to. I mean most people don't have the time to take advantage of all that unless they're mixing and somebody's bored and they want to do something else.

More often than not, people are recording. The typical regimen here is that people get up around 10:00 am, they have breakfast till 10:30 or 11:00, go to work, sit down for lunch at 3:00, work some more, take a break at 8:00 for dinner, go work some more [laughs], then sleep! A lot of people don't feel the need to leave the mountain, but some people feel the need to escape to get a newspaper or something. John Leckie told me that he doesn't like to break up the focus by leaving.

Can anybody record here?

Yes, we're not discriminatory.

That's really nice...this place is so amazing that you could really be elitist and select about your clientele.

Well, the thing is that the music business is so small. People don't realize how small it is, and every kind act that you do usually comes back to you, and every time you are unfair or unreasonable, it just gets spread around.

Allaire's professional kitchen runs day and night to suit its clients' appetite. *Photo by Kim Touzeau, courtesy of Hummingbird Media*

Jackie Wallace has created an interior décor that is warm and inviting, as seen here in this guest room. *Photo by Kim Touzeau, courtesy of Hummingbird Media*

Ornate woodwork is present throughout the facility, as seen here in Allaire's North Wing foyer. *Photo by Kim Touzeau, courtesy of Hummingbird Media*

A misty sunrise over the Ashokan Reservoir, seen from Allaire's vantage point. *Randall Wallace*

Bearsville Studios

John Holbrook, Producer/Engineer

Bearsville's Turtle Creek facility as it appears today. *Photo by Kim Touzeau, courtesy of Hummingbird Media*

The legendary Bearsville Studios has woven itself into the very fabric of the Woodstock area and American rock, having been host to the likes of The Band, Muddy Waters, and Paul Butterfield. It was the vision of Albert Grossman, who moved here in 1964 and was manager of Bob Dylan and many other prominent artists during the sixties and seventies. Bearsville Studios was a natural growth and extension of Mr. Grossman's music business activities, serving as a place where artists he managed could comfortably record in a reclusive, inspiring environment in Woodstock.

In the late sixties, Bearsville was at the sweet spot of a musical renaissance that was occurring in the area. Woodstock had already served as a Mecca of music activity even before the Woodstock festival with the arrival of people like John Sebastian, Tim Hardin, The Band, and many others. Shortly thereafter, the studio was built and ultimately became the engine of the Bearsville Records label and a breeding ground for other Woodstock talent. Clients on the Bearsville Records roster included Todd Rundgren, Foghat, Paul Butterfield, and Jesse Winchester.

By the 1980s, Bearsville itself developed into its own little community within Woodstock, ultimately comprising of three recording studios, a theater, and a café. It had carved out a unique identity and solid reputation in the recording industry through the studio and record company operations, serving a wide ranging, international clientele.

Over the last three decades, Bearsville Studios has been a microcosm of what has been happening in the American popular music scene. During its first iteration, the likes of The Band, Janis Joplin, and Muddy Waters all passed through, leaving an indelible mark in the early to mid-seventies. In the late seventies, new wave and punk bands came through, and in the '80s, Bearsville saw the cavernous Studio A accommodating heavy metal acts such as Metallica and Tesla. Finally, in the late '80s and beyond, the Replacements, REM, The Dave Matthews Band, Phish, and many, many other influential recording acts have been drawn to the special wooded environment and indelible hospitality that Bearsville Studios has provided over the years.

Currently, in addition to its recently upgraded residences, Bearsville Studios consists solely of the Turtle Creek facility, an original structure on the property that is still dripping with the aura and vibe of a bygone era.

John Holbrook originally joined Bearsville in 1973 and was chief engineer there during the mid-seventies. He was resident producer there in the early eighties and remains connected with Bearsville as a technical advisor to this day. He has witnessed first hand the amazing iterations that Bearsville has experienced over the last several decades, and has witnessed the ebb and flow of the larger recording industry as a whole.

What did you do before Bearsville, and what drew you into recording?

Well, I grew up in England and I had two fascinations when I was growing up. One was my fascination with electronics, the other was playing guitar. Having dropped out of university, there was nothing else that I could think of doing besides combining my interest in music and electronics. So I applied at a number of different studios in London, and was fortunate enough to get entry into a studio as an apprentice. The main gig that they threw me into was stereo disc mastering. We called it disc cutting, where you did the lathe and you cut the grooves.

Do you remember the name of this place?

Yes, it was IBC Studios. This was in the late sixties, and it was one of the few independent, happening studios at the time in London. A lot of good music was recorded there, like The Who's *Tommy* and Cream.

What an exciting time.

So I was kind of the backroom boy because they threw me in the back [laughs] with a cutting lathe. "Here's the tape! Cut that onto the record!" On the weekends, I'd record demos with friends and that was sort of my beginning. Soon after that, I had a friend who had hooked up with this crazy person trying to start a radical rock group in France; initially, I signed

Bearsville was host to many classic acts in the 1970s, including Muddy Waters, pictured here. *Photo courtesy of Bearsville Studios*

on as the sound guy, then ended up being one of the guitarists. My crazy friend ended up getting married in the States, and through a series of coincidences, he met Todd Rundgren and Albert Grossman, who had set up Bearsville. So that was my entree. He gave them this big snow job: "Oh, I know the best engineer in England. You've got to get him over here!" [laughs]. He talked them into it and amazingly enough, they paid for my trip here and I stayed.

What year was this?

That would have been about '73. I had run a couple of sessions but was not a seasoned studio pro and was basically goofing around. They soon discovered that maybe I wasn't what I was put up to be, so they put me out on the road. At the time, Bearsville Records had various artists that were out on the road, including Todd Rundgren and Paul Butterfield. I ended up mixing front of house for Todd and his band for the next several years. It ended up being a great way to be introduced to the United States, traveling through the heartland.

It exposed you to the U.S. music scene pretty quickly, huh?

There were moments of it being like *Spinal Tap!* I got the experiences of seeing the American rock 'n' roll audience and live sound mixing, which is different, but has relevance to how things are done in the studio.

At this point, Albert Grossman was sinking his teeth into the studio business and got Bearsville off the ground?

At that point the studio had just started and only the one room was functioning. By the time I got done with touring with Todd, there had been a few years of active recording there by groups like The Band and various other artists. It continued to be only Studio B through the late seventies and then there was this other room, Studio A, which later became the famous room in the eighties. Studio A was just a huge, empty concrete shell. Early on, not being able to use it was sort of frustrating to me because we felt somewhat stifled in the smaller room. In fact, I had done a couple projects where we had gone out to another studio, which didn't please Albert much. Eventually, we set up a control room and turned it into a rough and ready studio; we put some blankets and stuff on the walls and started using it.

How did it sound?

I was lucky actually, because I had bought a book on studio acoustics and had a rough guess at the acoustic equations. I hung a bunch of mismatched packing blankets up, then hung up some diffusors on the ceiling and man, it worked! In fact, it stayed that way until the end. There were people who came in after me, like Bob Clearmountain, who said "If you change anything, I'm never coming back." It was a huge room, so as time went on people came up with strategies that involved separating it in different parts with curtains and using iso booths in different locations.

The handcrafted spiral staircase inside Turtle Creek. *Photo by Jeff Touzeau, courtesy of Hummingbird Media*

When did Bearsville reach its peak and become recognized on an international scale?

Well, there were different phases. The early phase, which was before and during when I first arrived, was the post-Woodstock festival influx. People were still around like Bob Dylan and The Band. Actually, Bob Dylan never recorded at Bearsville, but had been around up until the time it opened. The Full Tilt Boogie band, which was Janis Joplin's band, had also been around. All these people were living in the area and there was the whole thing surrounding Albert and Bob Dylan, and all the various artists that he was representing.

Did all these people being around serve as a catalyst to help Bearsville get on the map?

At the time there was a lot of stuff happening. People like Paul Butterfield, Jesse Winchester, and all the various other acts that Albert got involved in were thriving. The Bearsville label came into existence. As the '70s wore on, a lot of these people moved on and went their own ways. Then there was an in-between phase that had a sort of mish-mosh of people, like the new wave and punk stuff from England, for example. Then,

Exterior of Bearsville Theater, one of Albert Grossman's crowning achievements. *Photo by Stephen Green-Armitage, courtesy of Bearsville Studios*

the last phase in which things really started to take off was in the '80s, when Bearsville became known as this hard rock place. Studio A, being this huge cavernous room, was great for drums and it was great for the big, loud bands. There was space for bands to spread out and it was a great tracking and recording room. There was a great old vintage Neve in there and bands like Metallica, Tesla, and all those heavy rock bands often worked there. Also, R.E.M. made several albums at Bearsville. There's a long list!

Was it ultimately good for you to come off the road from doing live work and move into a studio environment?

Yeah, I think it was. I think I finally got enough confidence that I could finally pull it off, whereas before, I was this kind of novice who had been hyped up.

Did you get the sense back then that Bearsville was this unique retreat from the urban environments of New York, Los Angeles or London?

Definitely. That was the appeal from the beginning, and it applied to the whole Woodstock area. It was always sort of a retreat for New York artists, even back to the '20s or '30s. In the '60s, it took on this other element with the rock generation and the Woodstock festival. Then it was that funky sort of "Going up the country to get my head together man" kind of stuff. It wasn't this kind of "lifestyles of the rich and famous" thing that's so common now, which are more sort of deluxe hideaways. Bearsville was always associated with the Woodstock generation and was a bit more down home. Being in the middle of the woods was part of the appeal.

What would you say about the mythological appeal that Bearsville has, having been host to the likes of The Band, Muddy Waters, and all the other larger than life figures who have worked here?

The barn still has some of that, and it's quite funky. The main studio building had a more modern feeling on the inside, but had a sort of older feeling on the outside with its rough cut wood look.

How strong is Woodstock's cultural draw today, and has it been riding this Woodstock event wave the whole time?

It's weird now, because it's become more and more of a "Hamptons North", if you will: a bunch of rich people with weekend houses. The art thing is still there though. There is still an arts and hippie vibe, but I think it's more diffused.

Can you describe when and how Turtle Creek came about?

Well, Turtle Creek was an existing barn on the property. Albert already owned it, and they just insulated it and began using it as a rehearsal space in the early seventies. Then there were these guys who at the time had a remote recording truck. They struck up some deal with Albert where, when they weren't using the truck, they'd park it at the barn and there was a little walkway so you could get into the truck. So it was already a potential recording facility from very early on.

In the mid-seventies, the Muddy Waters *Woodstock* album was recorded there. Later on in the seventies, it became the home base of Eddie Offord, who had been the engineer for Yes. He had brought this recording rig that he put together which was all in road cases. He had this radical idea of setting up his recording gear in the same room as the band, one of the first people to do that.

That's quite amazing and innovative. There are many people doing that now.

More people became aware of it because Daniel Lanois espoused it at a certain point. But I can tell you that Eddie Offord was doing this way back.

The cavernous live room of Studio A, complete with moving mats on the walls, was ideally suited to heavy metal acts.
Photo by Stephen Green-Armitage, courtesy of Bearsville Studios

Turtle Creek pictured from the rear, with its unique woodsy environment.
Photo by Kim Touzeau, courtesy of Hummingbird Media

This enables the engineer to be more of a performer or a band member.

It breaks down the barriers, I guess. Eddie Offord had these very, very large playback speakers, the biggest speakers JBL made at the time. He had four of them and he would stack them up and use them almost as a PA stack. He could have a mix going through them at the same time he was recording.

The control room at Turtle Creek, featuring French doors leading into the live room, was added on in the late '80s. *Photo by Kim Touzeau, courtesy of Hummingbird Media*

Turtle Creek is an interesting looking room the way the ceiling is, or the way the loft is sort of cut out.

I think that just developed from the way the original barn was, because I guess there was a hayloft and they had to hoist things with pulleys and stuff. That was the way the layout of the barn was. I don't think they cut out that hole just for recording, but I wasn't there when they did the work on it. When Mark McKenna was managing Bearsville during the early '90s, the discussion came up that there was a need for a control room, so we added the control room on the back. This would have been while Studios A and B were really humming, because Bearsville was contemplating running three rooms simultaneously.

That was the peak, when Mark was still working there. It was a conscious decision to make the control room an extension off of the barn and just have French doors between the control room and the live room rather than simply having a control room window. It was all meant to be a little more informal. There's not perfect separation, but the theory was that a client could have the whole board moved into the barn if they wanted to. After that control room got put on, the Dave Matthews Band and Phish did a lot of records there.

The live room at Bearsville's Turtle Creek has a vibe unlike any other. *Photo by Stephen Green-Armitage, courtesy of Bearsville Studios*

quartet or something. Having said that, both Phish and Dave Matthews seemed to enjoy working there.

That's interesting; because there's an example of two artists who could have recorded anywhere they wanted, presumably.

I believe Trey Anastasio ended up building his own version of the barn on his property in Vermont!

What a good endorsement! But what was the real draw of Turtle Creek?

I think it was about being out of the city, where time is money. It felt like you were out in the boonies when nobody was paying attention. A band like Phish, they never sold that many albums, but they still had the money because they made it on the road. They would hole up at Bearsville and take as long as they wanted.

The rear racks in the control room at Turtle Creek. *Photo by Kim Touzeau, courtesy of Hummingbird Media*

That extension looks very natural, and looks as if it's been part of the barn for years.

That was sort of the idea. The concept was, "Let's not make it look like a modern thing stuck on." We also put a French door to the outside world, so you got daylight into the control room. I'm a big fan of control rooms that have daylight in them. I think, partly, it was a reaction to the original Studio B at Bearsville, where I spent too many hours. Studio B was really a bunker in which there was no daylight in the control room or the studio. When you closed the door, if the lights were out, it was pitch black; sort of like the padded cell. For me, if I had anything to say about any control room, I'd say "Put a bloody window in it!!" [laughs].

Bearsville has stayed in business for many years despite all the recent highly publicized studio closings. What do you attribute Bearsville's survival to?

When Mark McKenna was there and there were three rooms going, there were two or three technical guys, a bunch of assistants, and all these people on staff. Now that the recording business is changing, it was probably a smart thing for them to scale back. The thing with running a studio, if a room's not booked, it's just money going out the window. The barn, in this environment, has been more manageable and has made better sense.

It almost sounds like Turtle Creek has always had the nicest aesthetic feel among all the studios on the grounds. Is that a fair characterization?

Yes. Definitely for somebody who was concerned about the ambience and vibe. I mean, Studio A had a vibe, slightly different, but it was more of the hard rock thing with the exposed concrete. It wasn't comfortable or anything, but there was a bit of daylight in it.

In your experience, has any particular genre of music worked best at Turtle Creek?

I think it lent itself to slightly more intimate, acoustic kind of stuff, singer songwriter kind of things, like Cassandra Wilson, who did one or two records there with Craig Street. Or it's good for a live

The main studio at Bearsville. *Photo by Stephen Green-Armitage, courtesy of Bearsville Studios*

Interior of Bearsville Theater, which provides an intimate environment for performers and listeners.
Photo by Stephen Green-Armitage, courtesy of Bearsville Studios

Just walking through its doors, one feels a nice aura in Turtle Creek.

I hesitate to use this word, but there is an organic nature about it. Part of Albert's legacy and aesthetic was to try and create something that was an organic atmosphere. There was that whole aesthetic with The Band that was old Americana. At the time, there were a few other residential facilities starting up, such as Caribou Ranch in Colorado and Longview Farm in Massachusetts, of that trend, and Bearsville was the granddaddy of them all. Plus it had the association that when you walked into any one of the studios at Bearsville, you walk into this history. I don't want to get too cosmic [laughs], but it's in the grain of the wood; the residue of the vibe of the people who worked there.

When did you move on from Bearsville and what did you do?

I kind of drifted away in the early eighties. I guess I just felt like I had to have a change. I ended up moving to New York City, doing freelance engineering. Then I did some writing and recording of TV commercials, a phase that took me through the late '80s.

It seems like during your tenure at Bearsville, you came across many people, like Bob Clearmountain, who helped you grow professionally.

I think that period when I became the defacto staff engineer and producer there, it was a great time to spread my wings a little bit. I started producing. I had more to prove and I could of thrown my weight around a little bit in the studio. I got to work with lots of interesting people and it felt like my home away from home. I had a fairly supportive group of people around me. Looking back, it was a pretty good time.

What kinds of things do you miss?

[Laughs.] Well, I'm sure everybody goes through an age thing. I certainly don't miss late night sessions and working through 'til the morning hours. Now, I wouldn't even dream of doing that. I got booked on a session recently for somebody to come in and engineer for one day. It turned into this ridiculous marathon. Eventually, I just said "I'm sorry, I'm leaving."

Good for you. So many people get sucked into that draining, bleeding mentality of working around the clock.

And it's unfair. It's kind of always been that way with younger engineers. If people can get away with it, they'll exploit them. They say, "Well, we've got to get this done. Keep working." You end up doing like a sixteen-hour day, and it's horrendous. That's the one thing I definitely don't miss as a young engineer.

It's not good practice to exploit one's passion for engineering.

Yes. You talk to anybody who is rational about these things, and they'll agree, that after like eight or ten hours, it's pretty much downhill.

It sounds like you have created borders and a nice balance around your work.

Well, at one point, I was working so much that I made myself ill. I had to check into a hospital for a couple of weeks because I just wore out and had a minor breakdown. You can't do that day after day after day, I mean, not eating or sleeping well....you've got to find a balance. It's a funny thing too, because in England, mixing engineers are called Balance engineers. And it's actually this great metaphor for finding balance in life. Not only must you find balance in your music, but also in your personal life and in everything.

Bearsville has been known for its unwavering service to its clients, always putting their needs first. Is this a culture that has always permeated Bearsville?

Well, as an engineer, we always strived to provide whatever the artist needed to get where they wanted to get. I think that's true of most studios, but at Bearsville, there was definitely an atmosphere of being supportive of the artist.

Having spent all this time at Bearsville, and seeing the industry from your vantage point of years and experience, can you characterize any changes that you have seen in the artist community? Is the sense of community still evident that was there in the early seventies that Woodstock helped propagate?

Bearsville was one of those places that develop into music communities. There was the whole Seattle thing, Athens, Georgia, or even the Memphis/Stax and Detroit/Motown thing if you go back a ways. They just seem to pop up at different times. It's when a musical community suddenly finds some kind of critical mass and something comes out that hits the mainstream.

Woodstock still has a music community; there are still musicians around, but the "scene" isn't what it was. More recently, bands that come in to Bearsville to record may not have as much attachment to the community as before. They just come in from wherever, record, and then leave. The nature of the business has changed somewhat, too. It used to be more freewheeling, easy to get budgets for albums, more craziness. The labels at that time were more about trying to support the artist. The bottom line wasn't necessarily the immediate priority and it was about "Let's just try to get the best artist and make the best music." Now it's more about running the business and the bottom line, which is ludicrous to me in the case of music, because you can't predict how many albums somebody is going to sell! It ends up causing "product" to get formulaic and predictable. Then people get surprised when something that's different is successful.

Even with evolving recording mediums, the recording industry seems to have gotten it wrong every time. They slammed the cassette and came out with the whole "Home Taping is Killing Music" campaign, now there's the resistance on adapting to a standardized digital distribution methodology. It seems the labels are always the last to adapt!

That's the thing. Who knows where it's going, but one thing is for sure: things seem ripe for digital distribution. The labels only handle artists that are above a certain threshold and everyone else is just trying to find their own ways to deal with it. The major labels are now just vehicles for the mega-platinums; but it wasn't always this way. Back then, you'd be happy to sell fifty or a hundred thousand records. They'd let somebody like Todd go off and make three albums, or Jackson Browne, or whatever. They'd let them develop their craft and grow. Having said that, it's still encouraging when you see bands like Green Day coming out with a politically charged album, still being able to sell a lot of copies.

The Turtle Creek apartments. *Photo by Stephen Green-Armitage, courtesy of Bearsville Studios*

Interior of residence.

The Barber Shop Studios
Mark Salamone, Co-Owner

Exterior of The Barbershop Studios, built inside a century old burned out church. *Photo by Jeff Touzeau, courtesy of Hummingbird Media*

The Barber Shop Studios is a converted nineteenth century church in Lake Hopatcong in New Jersey, only minutes away from New York City. On the outside, the structure has a classic limestone appearance, as it stands proudly on "The Lake of Many Coves" beside a restaurant and marina, both of which are contained within the studio complex. Inside, the facility is modern, professional, and slick, reflecting the pinnacle of acoustic design and client-oriented amenities.

For its owners, Scott Barber and Mark Salamone, The Barber Shop Studios is the result of long career paths that finally resulted in the two great friends achieving their dream of creating a world-class recording environment for gifted artists to create music. This dream began along two parallel paths which ultimately converged once they both decided to go all-in. No expense was spared; The Barber Shop Studios was designed with an exceptionally high standard in mind, to demanding acoustic and technical specifications.

Mark and Scott called in Fran Manzella of FM Design to design the facility, who had always wanted to design a studio in an old church. He ultimately helped turn their vision a reality, evolving napkin drawings into a set of professional plans that would make for a sonically superior and aesthetically beautiful recording facility.

Of all the places featured in this book, if there was any place that was "meant to be", this would be it. Many things seemed to fall in place for Scott and Mark (both of whom are religious people, by the way). Of all the people I interviewed, Scott and Mark seemed to be among the most confident and certainly had the strongest sense of purpose. To begin, both men knew they wanted a unique structure on the water, and were drawn to a dilapidated and burned out (literally) old church that seemed perfectly suitable. Importantly, they felt a strong sense of gratification that the church, which previously had been through some dark and dreary times, was being given a new purpose and a renewed "communion" of musicians and artists within its walls. The local community was just as excited to see the structure being acquired and taken care of by Scott and Mark.

Now, after much planning, designing, building, and promoting, The Barber Shop Studios is open. Of all the facilities in this book, this is the youngest and one gets the distinct feeling that wonderful things are going to happen within its walls. For Scott and Mark, the excitement is palpable as they gaze across the lake in anticipation.

The Barbershop Studios is adjacent to a marina, overlooking Lake Hopatcong, the "Lake of Many Coves." *Photo by Jeff Touzeau, courtesy of Hummingbird Media*

Mark, how did you get to this place in your career and what led you to wanting to open a commercial studio?

Well, I've been a musician for all my life. I studied jazz performance at Berklee School of Music and was always interested in recording. I always had some kind of home studio set up. Then my father passed away so I came home to be with my mom in Levittown, Long Island. When this happened, I began to view the world a little bit differently; I got more into classical music and began to study classical composition at William Patterson, a college in New Jersey. At around the same time, in 1987, I built a recording studio in the garage called Turtle Recording. It was an oversized garage but I built it right.

So this was before the home studio boom which happened in early '90s.

We used it to record my band and a lot of other clients. I had an 8-track Tascam analog and I used to do a lot of bouncing down to CD or 1/4". Then I would take the two tracks back to 8. Kind of a lot of like *Sergeant Pepper* mentality! I got some great sounds and I really learned the fundamentals of recording. I learned how to do punches and I learned how to communicate with artists to get the best sound and to make them feel comfortable. It was always a challenge for me as a producer to get the best possible performances out of musicians.

So you were born and raised on analog.

Right. It's the way I loved it, and I still love the sound of it too. Whenever I hear it, it just makes my body go [relaxed sigh] even though Pro Tools and digital is so much easier to work with.

How did you hook up with Scott and how did The Barber Shop Studios come about?

Well, Scott and I knew each other. In fact, he's my brother's brother-in-law. I used to, and still do, have Thanksgiving meals with Scott and the rest of the family all the time. We would share our music with each other and talk about how we were going to open up a recording studio one day. We always laughed about it.

However, I went one way, he went the other. I toured a lot as a musician, wrote a lot of songs, made a lot of records. Scott wrote a lot of great songs and did a lot of demos for himself on an 8-track with other musician friends.

Did you ever seriously pursue him with a studio idea?

Yes. I gave him an almost formal proposal for a rehearsal and recording facility. He laughed, and was like "We're going to lose a ton of money! It's going to be great!" [laughs]. The numbers were like, "Well, we can't really make a big living out of that." But the music always added up between Scott and me, and then suddenly Scott had a very successful business and I ended up being director of sales at EMTEC, the tape manufacturer, for about seven years.

A real corporate environment.

It was a great company to work for with great leaders. With digital though, it was very hard for them to find their niche in the marketplace. I was in charge of archives, working with clients like the Library of Congress and NPR. We archivists had a particular love and passion for preserving music and film. I made sure that they made an educated choice in choosing the tape. I did an analysis with the Library of Congress on how long tape would last and documented everything with them. I was also involved with the government. They took me in all these secret hallways because not only was I involved with analog but I was also involved in LTO [linear tape open] and AIT [digital tape storage] technology. Eventually, EMTEC just went under worldwide. My old boss just called me up and said "today's the day," and that was it. So I moved to Jersey from New York where I used to work at home. We moved nearby Scott, who would be my future business partner.

Live room and vocal booth, featuring refined stonework and woodwork. *Photo by George Roos, courtesy of The Barbershop Studios*

Where were things with Scott at this point?

Well, Scott is a very successful businessman, so he sold his company for a lot of money and was able to open up a studio. So he came over and said, "What do you say? Let's open up a world-class place."

So he kept his passion for recording alive even while he was a businessman?

Absolutely: we both did, and now we had the funds to do it. I explained to him as much as I knew about the big recording business because I had a good idea of how it works; how to treat clients, the basic technology and what goes into it. I said to him, "It takes millions of dollars to do it right and if we're going to do it, we can't afford to do it any less than world class if this is what we want to do for a living." You have to get the big clients that spend big money, and that's what we're looking for: to cater to clients like Aerosmith and Alicia Keys, for instance.

It sounds like you were both philosophically on board with where you were going with it from the outset. You didn't want to be mid-tier.

That's right, and we wanted a special location: we had our heart set on that. Scott said "It's got to be on the water," and I said "If we can do it, it'd be really cool if we could find a church." So we found a church on the water! [laughs]. It was like a blessing from God, it really was.

So tell me why Lake Hopatcong? Was it just a coincidence?

Well, Scott was finishing up with his old company and I was finished with EMTEC, so each day I went out looking for a location, working on the business plan and educating Scott so he knew what he was getting into. I went out one night with a good friend of mine and he said "I think I know the lake, Mark. If Scott's looking for water and you're looking for a church, I know the lake. We should go around and see if there are any churches." We found a couple of different buildings. I knew what I wanted: a real rustic old stone building. Then we found this abandoned church that attached to a beautiful Italian restaurant and a marina with 120 boat slips.

So the Italian restaurant and the marina were still active but the church was out of commission?

Exactly. It was an old church that had been converted into a famous dance club called The Lighthouse. It used to be mobbed in the '70s and people like Twisted Sister, The Ramones, and all these local bands would play there.

So the place had a rock 'n' roll lineage. How much time did you actually spend hitting the pavement before you found it?

A month.

Long view of the SSL XL 9000k. Note custom stained glass window. *Photo by Jeff Touzeau, courtesy of Hummingbird Media*

The control room at Barbershop, featuring a 72 channel SSLXL 9000k. *Photo by George Roos, courtesy of The Barbershop Studios*

The lounge area is adorned with historic photos of the Church's original construction in 1911. *Photo by Jeff Touzeau, courtesy of Hummingbird Media*

Do you remember the day you first saw it?

Scott and I pulled in the parking lot and we both were in silence just looking at this giant church that was abandoned. We looked at each other and said "This would be perfect!" I go into the bar, which is attached to the marina and the barmaid says to me "Can I get you something?" I said, "Can you tell me who owns this place and if it's for sale? She goes, "As a matter of fact, the owner just put it up for sale." Scott and I looked at each other, smiling. We were like "Really? What's for sale?" And she said, "The church, the restaurant, and the marina. But the church is not really worth anything. It's a disaster in there, all burnt." And we're thinking "Perfect," you know? So that was it. We contacted a real estate agent and Scott negotiated the price.

And what state was the church actually in when you found it?

It really was terribly burnt; a complete disaster. When we first walked in, we had to use flashlights. There was debris everywhere and it was dusty and smelly. The stairs were rickety and everything was sealed up. All the stained glass windows had cinder blocks keeping them up. But I still remember, it was the most amazing thing when the light shined through for the first time. We just knew this was the place and we saw the potential not only in the studio side but in the real estate side.

So despite all these unpleasant sights and smells, you remained optimistic?

Yes. And when we went to the town and we asked them permission to do what we want to do, they were so happy because they found something that was perfect for that building that was a disaster. We were going to bring the town back to life.

The hallway leading to the technical areas has an electric, classy vibe. *Photo by Jeff Touzeau, courtesy of Hummingbird Media*

The Barbershop Studio's kitchen/lounge area, directly adjacent to the entrance/reception area.
Photo by George Roos, courtesy of Barbershop Studios

Can you tell me about Lake Hopatcong?

All these famous comedians would come to Lake Hopatcong from the city. There were beautiful houses and giant hotels; the economy was booming and it was an extremely affluent area. Back in the '40s, Abbott and Costello used to perform here, the Rat Pack used to do gigs here. The area is gorgeous. It's all set in the mountains with beautiful, multimillion-dollar houses all around the lake. There are twenty-two miles of shoreline. For a geographic reference, I think it's about forty-seven miles from the George Washington Bridge. There are all kinds of sailboats and motorboats. Lake Hopatcong is called "the lake of many coves," since it is full of these intricate coves with lots of bridges and islands.

So you enjoy having all the amenities of nature, without being out in the sticks.

Yes. There are nice hotels nearby, antique shops, and restaurants all along the waterline. At night the lights are on all around the lake and you dine while looking out onto the water. There's a real cool vibe to it all.

Since the place was burned out, you presumably had a flexible palette on which to build. How did you move forward?

We didn't want to go too rustic and that's why we hired Fran Manzella on a whole bunch of people's recommendations. They all said it's going to sound awesome. And then when we looked at all the studios he has done, we said "They look awesome too," and you know what? He's given 120% to this project.

Fran is very passionate about his work.

Absolutely. If every single detail isn't perfect, he has the guys rip it down and does it again. He's somebody who wants it done right. He fell in love with the place too. When he first saw it he was like "Guys, people are going to flock." He said, "I've always wanted to do a church. This would be an incredible opportunity for me too."

Opposite Page:
The live room at The Barbershop Studios, with its wood and stone craftsmanship, is adorned with a huge stained glass window. *Photo by George Roos, courtesy of The Barbershop Studios*

So we came up with our vision of how the studio might look. Scott and I went on a piece of paper and started drawing where we thought the control room would be and then when Fran came in it was like completely opposite [laughs]. He was like, "You guys have no clue. How are you going to get from here to here?" We believe that Fran knows what he's doing. He's a pro and the two of us let him do his thing.

How has the overall construction process been?

It's been quite a bear. I can't say it hasn't been stressful. There are so many permits and things. We also had water problems and had to put all French drains all the way around the facility. And it still leaked, so we hired the basement doctor. We had to dig up the foundation and put down pipe with gravel, then we had the outside pointed between the stones to stop the outside leaks.

How deep was the foundation?

I think it was like four feet at the edge and then the floor was like six inches or a foot deep. The building itself was just a giant shell with steel beams going across it because the structural engineer didn't want it to fall down as we were building. The thing is going to be around forever, it's not going anywhere. We ended up putting four floors in it.

So the basement has regular eight-foot ceilings?

Yes, except for when you first walk in the reception area and the lounge is a little lower. Then the second floor is the main control room. Then there are two vocal booths in addition to another vocal booth off the main live room.

Now if I know Fran, the thing that he was probably mainly concerned about was the control room, right?

Absolutely. Size of the control room was very important. It's big, the perfect control room. You wouldn't want it any bigger or smaller, it's exactly the way he would want it. I think the ceilings are like ten feet or so.

When you were designing the rooms, did you want each room to be a certain flavor?

It's so funny. I pictured it like every room being a different country. The control room is Africa, then you go into England and then you go in another country. There'd be all these significant artifacts stating that: a different cultural feel for each room. I told Fran this and he thought it was a terrible idea [laughs]. He's like laughing "No, we're not going to do that." I had all these visions, the most important being to have as much light as possible. Fran just basically shakes his head and says "Okay, I can try to get that done, I'll do the best I can." He ended up creating pipe organ windows. They're rectangular ones signifying a pipe organ for the church.

And obviously you maintained the stained glass features?

Yeah. We wanted to keep the original but Fran suggested something more contemporary. So Scott and I drew up something with a little different flavor, had the stained glass folks make it and Fran loved it. Sometimes the light hits it just right into the main tracking room. It looks magnificent.

The way Fran envisioned it, if you look one way it's got a little contemporary feeling, but as the sun goes over the place and you look the other way, and this is on the inside, it becomes more rustic. There's this mix of contemporary and rustic throughout the studio. He did a really good job blending the two so it sort of has a corporate feel to it as well.

How has it been going through all this with a business partner?

It's been excellent. Today we were just laughing about it because Scott and I are like brothers. We really get along really well and we've spent a lot of time in the same office together.

What type of projects do you want to get in and where are you going in terms of the flavor?

We'll take whatever comes our way; all we want is class. We care more about the people than the projects. We hope that the people who come to our studio have morals and bring a good positive vibe with them. As our client, you're going to come and you're going to get treated with elegance and the environment is going to be just perfect for creating music. We've bought all the best equipment in the world. I mean our outboard gear selection is incredible. If Phil Ramone comes in here, he won't be disappointed; he would probably never leave.

The Barbershop Studios exterior, taken July 2005. *Photo by Jeff Touzeau, courtesy of Hummingbird Media*

BearTracks Studios

Jay Beckenstein, Artist/Studio Owner

BearTracks Recording Studio is located in a century old barn constructed entirely of fieldstone.
Photo by Jeff Touzeau, courtesy of Hummingbird Media

Jay Beckenstein is best known as a founding member of the famous jazz group Spyro Gyra. Having had an immensely prolific career with over twenty-five albums and tours since 1974, Spyro Gyra has built a loyal following of music lovers all over the world, and has provided a lifelong, passionate vocation for Jay.

After some of Spyro Gyra's initial success through touring and record sales, Jay and his then business partner Richard Calandra decided to find a rural retreat near New York City as a hideaway where the band could write and record. They were able to locate a stunning estate on five acres in Suffern, New York, twenty-five miles from the city. The complex consisted of several turn of the century structures built entirely of fieldstone, including a huge two-story barn with vaulted ceilings. The property was hard to beat, as it is adjacent to the Harriman State Park, consisting of over 40,000 acres of wilderness and access to the Appalachian trail.

Back in 1981, a dedicated artist project studio was not a mainstream idea by any stretch of the imagination. For one thing, professional tape decks and recording consoles were still very expensive, costing tens of thousands of dollars. ADATs hadn't yet revolutionized the pro audio market, and at the time, recording artists often lived in very different worlds from producers and engineers.

To justify the investment required in a major facility, Beckenstein and Calandra immediately realized that the studio would not only need to serve as Spyro Gyra's home base and primary recording vehicle, but it would also need to cater to other artists as a bona fide commercial facility, so they brought world-renowned acoustician George Augspurger on board to assist in the design and construction.

Once the facility was designed and retrofitted, a project that cost several hundreds of thousands of dollars, BearTracks allocated a top drawer collection of equipment, including a rare (i.e. one of ten in the world) Focusrite recording console, two Fairchild 660s (the rare mono version of the 670, by all accounts the more sonically pleasing), Pultec equalizers, and many other interesting esoteric pieces, making this one high end project studio. Once the studio was complete, groups like Dream Theater, Bruce Hornsby, and The Goo Goo Dolls became regular clients and BearTracks soon became known as one of the world's top residential facilities.

The landmark of BearTracks' entrance, the BearTracks Bear playing sax. *Photo by Kim Touzeau, courtesy of Hummingbird Media*

Can you describe your early experiences with the sax, and how you got into jazz?

Well, my parents were very musical. My mom was an opera singer, my father was a real jazz lover, and I grew up in a household that had a lot of Verde and Charlie Parker going on. My father, who was a pianist/clarinetist, was particularly in love with Lester Young, Parker, and all that bebop stuff from the early fifties. So when it came time for me to play an instrument at the age of seven, they gave me a clarinet for the school band. My father said "Go and ask them for a saxophone," so that's when I started.

Jay Beckenstein, founding member of Spyro Gyra, stands beside BearTracks' entrance. *Photo by Jeff Touzeau, courtesy of Hummingbird Media*

Not many people can point to having fallen into their vocation so early on, but it's clear that you took this early interest and developed it into a passion and career that would last your whole lifetime.

In addition to remembering having an instrument at seven, I remember them giving me braces at eleven, because I had buck teeth. The orthodontist insisted that I switch from saxophone to trumpet, because the tendency of trumpet is to push teeth in and the tendency of saxophone is to push teeth out. I refused. So I already had some form of commitment at the age of eleven. Some kids have a fantasy about playing shortstop for the Yankees, and mine was to be a jazz musician.

It seems like you had a great environment at home that supported that.

Absolutely. But when I went to school and started taking music courses, my parents were mortified. They hadn't realized that they inculcated this jazz fanatic. It was supposed to be fun and broadening, but not my vocation!

And then you were in all the marching bands in high school, right?

You know, I went to four different high schools. In my junior year, I met Jeremy Wall, who has been a creative partner with me since high school, this entire time. Jeremy had formed up some nice little ensembles in high school and I played with them and that was my first chance to play with bands. But then my senior year, my family moved to Germany. While living in Germany, I had the opportunity to play with American soldiers that had bands over there. Those were my first sort of professional gigs, playing with three sergeants in Nuremburg, Germany, for NCO clubs and officer club parties.

Would you say there was a strong jazz interest over there?

Actually, what I was getting over there at the time was Hendrix and "Sittin'" ("on the Dock of the Bay") by Otis Redding, because that's what we were playing. That was my first opportunity to play music that wasn't jazz oriented. Then I went away to college, back in the States, and studied a lot of classical saxophone and classical piano, regular music degree stuff.

So you had committed to music full-on at this point, going for the career? You knew you had the proficiency to make it?

I was quite sure I didn't have the proficiency. I just really loved it, still a fantasy. I certainly don't recall thinking "Hey, you're the shit man, you got this made!" [laughs].

Well to go after a college degree in music, while not necessarily risky, you've got to be proficient and competent to go after it.

My parents were mortified. I didn't start that way; my intention was to go for pre-med or something, then I devolved down the academic evolutionary scale, from pre-med, to psychology, to English, to music! [laughs].

By my sophomore year, some of my teachers who were involved in avant-garde classical music brought me into their ensembles because they liked the way I played soprano saxophone. Between that stuff and the classical music I was studying, I was pretty hungry for some "feel good" music. On the outside, I was playing in blues bands to make money on the side. Also, I got involved with a city gig after school called the Buffalo Jazz Ensemble and got to play a lot of jazz during that period of time.

When did your own style start to evolve? When did you mature in that way?

Here I had played classical music in college, I had been brought up on jazz, and now I found myself making a living in Buffalo, New York, playing in blues and R&B bands. I was playing a lot in horn sections, backing up singers. As it turned out, we had one day off: Tuesday. So I found a club that was willing to let us play for the door on Tuesdays, and formed an all instrumental, no singers invited jazz jam every Tuesday night. About this time, we started to write our own music. It was natural to combine all these styles: R&B, Jazz, funk. John Coltrane and Earth, Wind, and Fire!

What year are we in at this point?

Early '70s. The Tuesday thing turned out to be the hottest night in town. Then we started playing Tuesdays and Thursdays, then Tuesdays, Thursdays, and Fridays, then the club owner pressured us to come up with a name and I gave him this silly name Spyro Gyra.

Were you surprised that there was such a hunger for this music and a positive reception?

I wasn't thinking at all! I was drinking a lot of Jack Daniels and having fun. It was a blast, the music was very, very good, and the people involved went on to nice music careers. Some of them are still with me, like Tom Schuman. It was surprising that a non-vocal thing should catch on, though.

When did Spyro Gyra finally decide to record?

I had previously met a drummer: his name was Richard Calandra. He had been working in one of these R&B bands that were playing around town. Richard had the misfortune of getting into a very bad auto accident. Some woman had a heart

BearTracks' 47' x 30' live room features a 27' ceiling and motorized acoustic panels to adjust the room acoustics to taste.
Photo by Kim Touzeau, courtesy of Hummingbird Media

Side view of BearTracks. *Photo by Jeff Touzeau, courtesy of Hummingbird Media.*

attack coming on the other side of the bridge and hit him head on; completely out of the blue kind of thing. He was really busted up bad. Because this woman was so at fault, he received a decent amount of money to patch himself up. He could no longer drum, at least not well. So Richard came to me and had this idea of forming a production company. There was a lot of talent in Buffalo, a lot of different sorts, and we thought that maybe we could make some records.

The two of us formed a business, and we found a recording studio in a little town outside of Buffalo that was going to let us buy studio time, like ten days a month for a little bit of money. We embarked with the little money I had saved and the money he had gotten from his accident, and started recording all sorts of things. We did a disco record, we did a country-ish record, we did an R&B record, we did all this.

Just drawing from regional talent?

That's it; just drawing from our friends. The last thing we thought that was going to make our fortune was jazz. Because we were buying time by the block, there would always be this leftover time, and I would always have my guys on call and we would run in and record. Despite shopping these recordings around to lawyers and everything in New York, nothing happened with it. We lost all our money. We put a couple of things out locally that did okay, but we were looking for the big time, and it didn't work out. We took our last few thousand dollars and spent it on pressing what we had left over: the Spyro Gyra recordings. The band's future looked in doubt, because all the band members were talking about leaving town, you know, "I'm going to Los Angeles," "I'm going to Nashville," etc. If we did this last project, it would give all the band members a farewell present. Also, we thought we could make a little of our money back.

So you did a small pressing?

I think we did 500. And we took that to the local radio stations, and low and behold, they picked a song off it and started playing it. We had been going around to local record stores, dishing out five and ten copies on consignment. Then there was a local distributor who took 150 copies from us. We got a call two weeks later, and he wanted 500 more. We got a call two weeks after that, and he wanted 2,000. The next call was "I want to sign you guys to a record deal." He was smarter than we were, because he had his ear to the ground. A big radio station in Miami had picked up the record, and a big station in Cleveland had picked up the record, all without record promotion, totally word of mouth. At that point, everything changed and he got us a deal with MCA records. Suddenly, we found ourselves with a lot of resources, a good deal of money coming in, and this runaway success going on which was our first record.

So you had enough money to build up the infrastructure of the band?

Well, most of the band members were still involved at that point. We were doing our first tour and everything was going very nicely. But Richard and I both decided that this was an opportunity to get out of Buffalo and move our entire dream to

New York. In my case, it was as the leader of Spyro Gyra, but in Richard's case it was being the record producer, to have more record success. That's where BearTracks Studio comes in.

The two of us lived in Manhattan for a while, but the entire time, while I was on the road with early Spyro, Richard was looking for a property outside New York that had a nice house and a big barn, with the idea that he was going to build a recording studio. Our production company would use the recording studio to produce different records of different types and form our own little industry. At the same time, with the money coming in from our second record, which had "Morning Dance" and went platinum, we needed a good place to put some of the money for the business, rather than just throw it all into taxes.

So Richard found this absolutely magnificent old barn with a house attached from about 1900. It was just a big old gutted barn, but unbelievably sound, and the two of us embarked on building a recording studio.

This was the late seventies?

This was 1981. It took from 1981 to 1983 to do the construction and build the studio. We had the proximity of being close to New York City, only twenty-five minutes out, versus say Woodstock, which was two hours and twenty minutes out.

The silo at BearTracks now serves as a second reverb chamber for the facility. *Photo by Kim Touzeau, courtesy of Hummingbird Media*

But one definitely gets the "rural" feel out where you are. You're "far enough" away.

Particularly with this property, because it butts up against the Harriman State Park, which consists of like 40,000 acres. The Appalachian Trail runs through the back yard. I like horses and we've had horses here too. It has afforded me an entire lifestyle. I can be a recluse mountain man if I so choose! [laughs].

What kind of effort went into repurposing this place into a studio? Clearly you had a beautiful structure and unique ground to start with, but what went on?

Well, Richard oversaw construction. I was out on the road making the money and he was here spending it. His vision of the studio right from the beginning was no expense spared. They went to great lengths. The flooring in the place has so many layers so there's no conductivity in the floor. Every drop of equipment we bought was the best. He went pretty nuts. And we ended up with an awfully fine facility. We made some of it back by renting the studio out. We had many, many clients during the '80s, and it was a fabulous place to make Spyro Gyra records obviously because I could take my time.

Unfortunately, Richard died in 1986, and the studio came into my hands solely at that point. Richard, if he had anything to say about what was meaningful in his life and what he accomplished, I suspect that this studio would have been at the top of his list.

What a legacy and a special place he has left behind.

This place is like a Buddhist monastery, it has such a great vibe. It was our home base. So many good projects have been done here and so many people have come through and said this was a peaceful break in their lives to work here.

You have probably one of the most unique recording consoles I have ever seen. Can you tell me about it?

Well, it wasn't the first board we ever had in the facility. We started out with an SSL, which was a good console, but not automated at the time. After ten years of that, we had to make a decision on a new console. SSL was making it very attractive to buy another SSL, but another small company in England, called Focusrite, began building consoles designed by Rupert Neve. We have serial number 9 of 10 of these that were produced in total. It's an astoundingly good sounding console. Despite the fact that we're in digital, most people who record here prefer to go through the console because it has such a nice warm sound.

Can you give me a mental tour of the facility?

Well, the studio is a 36' high stone barn. The bottom floor of it is the reception area with a little kitchenette and office space; very roomy. Then you go up the stairs to this large room with movable ceiling panels so you can change the acoustic nature of it if you want.

BearTracks control room houses a rare Focusrite 72/72 console with flying faders, serial number 9 out of 10.
Photo by Jeff Touzeau, courtesy of Hummingbird Media

Is there an acoustic flavor to it? How would you describe the room sound?

Well, when we were building it, we were working at Power Station a lot. If there's a room that it reminds me of, it's that room. The size of the room afforded us the luxury of being able to record all at once in a live setting, with very little leakage. And we have movable baffles. We can go anywhere from recording an orchestra to recording an acoustic guitar in there and pull it off.

Have Spyro Gyra records typically been recorded live in here?

There is no typical production technique for Spyro Gyra records. In fact, we've made twenty-seven CDs, and we're always looking to do the next CD a little different. One of the ways to do that is to vary the production technique. We might do live, or layer things in sequencing. It depends, and it's one of the ways we vary what we do. For that matter, on the record we're making now, we're doing charted out live playing, we're working sequencing out at home and adding things, we're also doing jams, where the band splits the writing. We just jam in the studio and then cut it up to make songs out of it. So we try to capture something spontaneously. All three of those techniques are being utilized on this record.

Can you tell me about the unique reverb chambers you have?

Well, the place had a big silo and a nice ice house, so at various time we would try all sorts of things. In the silo, we had a speaker on a wire and a mic down at the bottom and created a delay in this long 60' silo. Same with the ice house, which was a big concrete bunker. It was great and we could change it. We would put stuff up on the wall, move the stuff around and try to get some ideal sound.

Back then there was this whole audiophile mentality: doing it right, experimenting, and whole recording process and technique. So much of that has disappeared now, because with digital recording techniques, everything is easier to use. Nobody has to splice tape anymore. That's an interesting thing about the last twenty-five years of being in the studio business, the technological changes are amazing. When we think back to the way we did recordings when we first built the studio, it's absolutely hands on primitive. But there was something quite nice about it.

And you were making great records back then, too.

Frankly, from a pure sonic standpoint, it was better then than it is now. A certain degree of sonic quality has been sacrificed for convenience: for convenience of price, for convenience of working with an elastic medium. But there was something extremely beautiful about the old method of recording.

Spyro Gyra often uses the live room at BearTracks to rehearse for its extensive worldwide touring.
Photo by Jeff Touzeau, courtesy of Hummingbird Media

In the old days, it was hard to fake. These days, it's very easy to fake. So now, someone who is attractive, charming, and has the right smile, can be made into a singer. That didn't used to be the case, so you had a lot better singers. The way people would record back then, because of the limitations, there were many more "all at once" live recordings; a "gotta get it now" kind of urgency, intimacy to the music that has been utterly replaced. Everybody can use Garage Band, and everybody can make a mediocre performance sound competent now. In the long run, I think it's downgrading people's abilities.

What things can distinguish artists these days?

There's still always going to be creative people doing creative things. It's the human condition. In whatever environment people find themselves, really fabulous creative things will be done. In the digital world of cut and paste, there are great cut and pasters. For me, the old guy that I am now having gone from Charlie Parker to 50 Cent, I kind of like the people that sound like they are doing it for real, like John Mayer. I like artists that really do it, where the lyrics are from the heart, not about how cute they are. I'm still a huge fan of singer/songwriters: Alannis Morrisette, Beck, instead of the cookie cutter type artists like Britney Spears, or Mariah Carey diva-style artists. To me, those are like "stock" artists and no matter how great someone's voice might be, I really don't give a damn.

I wonder if you were starting out right now, whether you would have found this industry as appealing. It seems with the lack of FM freeform and the quagmire of digital distribution, we're dealing with a really broken machine. Who would want to get involved in that from a career perspective?

Well, if you remember earlier in our conversation the idea that we put out a single in Buffalo in New York and other stations spontaneously picked it up around the country. Today? Impossible. You'd have to literally pay them. I try to avoid the cliché of the old artist complaining how rotten it all is. Like I say, there are still people that, no matter what the environment, still manage to say something that's meaningful.

What makes the control room special at BearTracks?

Well, to begin with, George Augspurger designed the speakers and the whole studio, including the live room. He was very hands on throughout all of it, and kept making adjustments while he was doing it. He was living in L.A., constantly visiting us as we were under construction. Over quite a few years of making records and mastering records, and finding out what the room sounded like, it was slowly adjusted to be a very, very neutral room. What you hear is what you hear at mastering most of the time.

You have some amazing outboard and a first class set up, including two mono Fairchild 660s.

When we first put the studio up in the early '80s, we bought a lot of what was vintage gear then. Pultechs, the Fairchilds. So we've held on to it, and we do have a nice selection of vintage stuff. We did it right when we did it.

Can we talk about the new Spyro Gyra album? Where are you now?

We're midway through cutting it. We're going to do some more recording sessions at the end of this month. It will be coming out in 2006. Another in a long string of CDs that we've made.

After putting all these records out, and still touring and recording, it's clear that you've maintained a strong passion for all of this.

There's two sides to that. Sometimes, if you do something as your passion professionally, it can get tainted. You can lose some of that passion, because you can associate it with things that aren't associated with it, like "How are you going to feed yourself!" Sometimes I envy people that do something that they are passionate about, but it's only their hobby. I do still love it a lot, but I have grown to hate airports. I love stages.

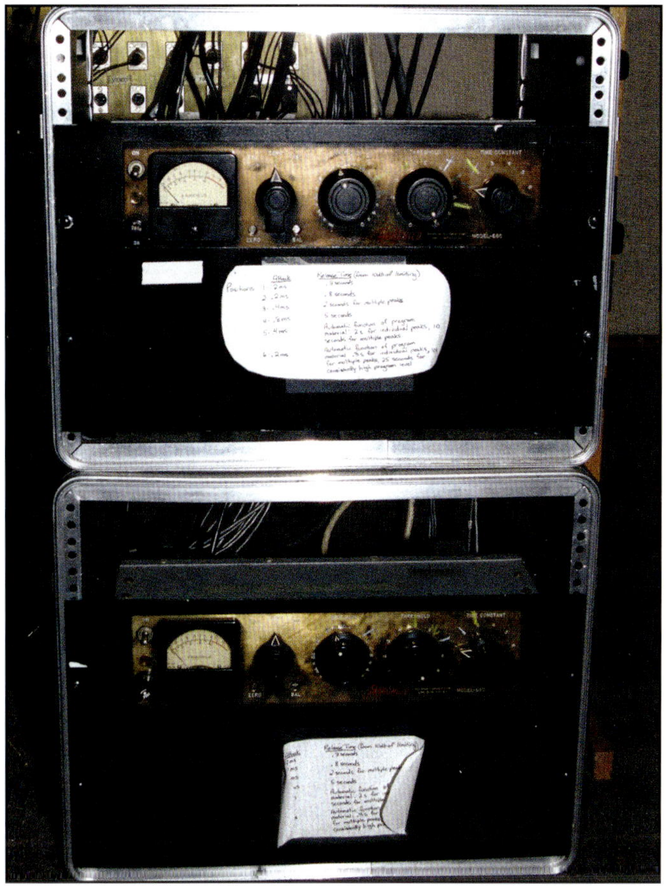

BearTracks counts two mono Fairchild 670s among its prized outboard collection. *Photo by Kim Touzeau, courtey of Hummingbird Media*

Wide view of BearTracks' control room. The wooden horns in the large monitors are a signature of Augspurger designs. *Photo by Kim Touzeau, courtesy of Hummingbird Media*

Across from the rear of the barn is this ice house that has been converted into one of the facility's two reverb chambers. *Photo by Kim Touzeau, courtesy of Hummingbird Media*

Can you actually pick up a sax and just enjoy it when it's not a professional thing? Can you really relax like other people can read a book?

Yes, especially on piano. Not so much on saxophone.

Do you find that you have time to do that, or are you a workaholic?

I have to find time to do that, because that's how I start writing. My writing always starts by having fun noodling around, then noticing "Ah, that was interesting. Let's develop that."

Has jazz taken you all over the world? It seems like there are less international barriers for jazz than there might be for pop music.

Yes. I would agree with your statement. We've been fortunate enough to go everywhere. Russia, Indonesia, India, South Africa, Europe, Japan.

Can you think of any particular instance where you introduced your style of music to folks that hadn't been exposed to it already?

Well, this style of music has been around a while now, and in the band's history, I think we've been very influential in a lot of places. But there's one story that has recent relevance to that comment. The first time we played South Africa was four years ago. We had been invited during the '80s, and for obvious political and social reasons, we passed. Finally, we got a recent invitation and now that the place is straightening itself out, we decided to go and we played in front of a crowd of about 4,000 people in a big auditorium in Cape Town. We go into one of the hits from the early '80s: "Catching the Sun". No lyrics, just an instrumental melody. And the entire audience sang along with it. So we're totally in shock that all these people are singing along. As it turns out, during some of the worst days of struggle in South Africa, our record was very popular. People made an association between our record and the struggle to beat down apartheid.

That is very powerful and must have totally floored you.

Oh, it was awesome. But I've also had an opposite effect. I remember being at a party with a bunch of Israelis, and somebody played "Morning Dance", one of our earlier hits. People said, "No, no, no. Please take it off!!" I said, "What was that about?" Well, apparently during the Lebanon incursion, Israeli military radio would start the day with "Morning Dance" [laughs]. So people would have a negative association of it!

It just goes to show the power of music. It's such an obvious thing to say, but it's one of these things that all of us feel that you can't put into words. It has such a strong emotional...

...yeah, and a memory thing too. It's associated with time. You can associate where you were during a particular place in your life by hearing a song.

Are you touring this summer?

Yeah, we tour every year. People can go to www.spyrogyra.com to find out where and when. One of the beauties of having a career that is a slow burn is that you can't afford to quit!! [laughs].

I think it's healthy for you though.

Damn right.

Live room view towards the control room; above is the loft, bottom right is the iso booth.
Photo by Kim Touzeau, courtesy of Hummingbird Media

Bennett Studios

Dae Bennett, Owner

Located in downtown Englewood, New Jersey, Bennett Studios was built in a turn of the century Victorian railroad station. It was this view that inspired Bennett to build a world-class studio on the site. *Photo by Dave King, courtesy of Bennett Studios*

The first thing you should know about Dae Bennett is that he has thrived in, and contributed substantially to, his community of Englewood, New Jersey. He built his first studio, Hillside Studio, about two decades ago in his basement and has since opened Bennett Studios, one of the best music and post facilities on the East Coast. With its fiber optic connection to the John Harms Theatre that enables 64 channels of audio and four channels of video direct from the theater's stage, it is also very likely one of the world's finest places to do a live, on-location recording.

For Dae, operating a successful business was only part of the equation though. He has given back substantially to his community by opening up an audio education program at the local Dwight Morrow High School and by building an engine to help spark Englewood's performing artist culture.

The second thing you should know about Dae is that Bennett Studios is the result of hard work and persistence. Bennett opened up on September 6, 2001, only five days before the World Trade Center terrorist attacks and in the throes of the difficult economy that would directly follow. Located only five minutes from the George Washington Bridge, this became Bennett Studios' first challenge; opening a studio in a very uncertain business climate at a time when our entire country was experiencing a great deal of pain and realigning its values.

Bennett Studios is a converted Victorian railroad station that is in the heart of Englewood, a charming "main street" town built in the 1920s with lots of character and great restaurants (over forty within four blocks!). If a converted Victorian railroad station isn't cool enough, the facility is connected by an underground fiber optic connection to Harms Theater, a beautifully restored 1,400-seat theater that has been host to an impressive roster of performances.

As one of Tony Bennett's sons, Dae has a keen sense of performance in his blood. While never boastful of his bloodlines or of the sheer beauty of his facility (Dae is one of the most down to earth and humble people I have ever met), Dae is quietly aware and extremely sensitive to the needs of the artist. He built Bennett Studios strictly as a vehicle for the artist, opting for a "conservatory" feel versus the more typical, self-absorbing "gold record on the wall" mentality.

On entering Bennett Studios, one is struck by a feeling of "creative spaciousness". The layout is inviting and professional, radiating with light, high ceilings, and ambience. The technical facilities are advanced, efficient, and purposeful. Dae's own demeanor is knowledgeable, warm, and hospitable. For artists, it is easy to see how all these elements add up to make a synergistically rich experience.

Dae Bennett, owner of Bennett Studios, behind the SSL in the South Studio.
Photo by Kim Touzeau, courtesy of Hummingbird Media

Can you give me the 10,000 foot view of Englewood?

Well, it's literally five minutes from the GW bridge, so we're very close to Manhattan. I can be in midtown in twenty minutes. It's a town of about 50,000 and there's a big main street with really nice restaurants and shops. It was one of those towns that got devastated when all the big malls opened up. Since then, they did a lot of economic development and it eventually turned back into a downtown. The theatre brought a bunch of really good restaurants. We really have a New York-esque selection of food here. It's a good place to be.

Let's talk about your early influences in recording. As Tony Bennett's son, you probably could have taken the performing or musician route but you chose the recording route.

Actually, I've done quite a bit of all of that, really. My earliest memory was my parents building a home here in Englewood, New Jersey, very close to where Rudy van Gelder's studio is. A lot of entertainment people live out in this area and it kind of started with Rudy's place being here because it's just a short hop over the bridge. In those days, it was just woods here [laughs]; you were really going into the country. It was kind of like Central Park, with the big jutting rocks and all that. When they built the house, Rudy actually put a little McIntosh system with an Ampex 2- track, probably as big as an A-80 [laughs]. It was like a small studio in the lower level of this house. Of course, they were on the road all the time, so my brother and I would be down there messing around. That's where we learned to play, so we kind of grew up with the equipment around.

I imagine it got your curiosity going.

I really have vivid memories. It started out with "Hey, you kids get out of there!" A few years down the road it was "Hey, how'd you get that piano sound?" [laughs]. So it was kind of an evolutionary thing.

Your father is a very gifted singer and performer. What was it like growing up with him and what kind of perspective did this give you on performance and recording?

My dad was on the road all the time, so it was kind of like growing up with a traveling salesman. When he was home, we'd spend days together and of course he did the "Sullivan" show many times. I was at a lot of those shows and even as a kid I thought they were fascinating. They'd be blocking out the show and all hell is just breaking loose. They'd have the guy with the hoops, and there'd be dog acts, comedians, singers, and they had an orchestra in the booth. Then they had a sound booth, a lighting booth, and a video booth. Even as a kid, you're sitting there thinking, "It's never going to come together. It's too disorganized." Of course, they break at 6:00 for dinner, come back at 8:00 and it would go off every time. I was very impressed, even as a kid.

Amongst all the chaos, you marveled at everyone pulling it together.

Yeah, and I think that I got my first visceral feel of professional equipment. Through the years, these guys get to know you and eventually they'd be riding you around on the booms and the cameras, stuff like that. It was pretty cool.

How early on did you take an interest in having your own studio?

Well, I've always had basement studios going. The first viable commercial location I had built up was called Hillside.

And that was in Englewood as well, right?

That's right.

And that introduced you to the commercial aspect of recording?

Yes. I kind of just took the chops that I already had. I would say I learned the real technical side from a guy named John Nagy in Boston, who is a very good engineer and a great guy. He used to have a place called Mixing Lab in the basement of his house, very similar to what my Hillside studio ended up being. He had an old Peter Troisi console, which was a great sounding desk. I actually still have some Troisi gear in my new place as well. Mixing Lab is where I got my technical chops up to a professional level. At that point it was only the business aspect that was missing. I had the technical know how, and really just had to upgrade equipment. I started Hillside, half personal and half commercial, with a Scully 280 eight track.

That was the 1"?

Yeah, and we had a guy come in and modify it so you could punch in. But it made a little sound, when you punched in and out, that sounded like Shemp from The Three Stooges, so it became the nomenclature, "Hey, Shemp me in over here and Shemp me out over there." [laughs]. It was pretty funny. But when I decided to get serious about a commercial facility I got a package from Studer with the A-80 24-track and 2-track machine and just kind of slowly went from there.

What kind of natural aptitude did you have? A lot of people really struggle to learn the technology. Did it come easy for you?

I'm definitely one of those people with a mechanical knack. In particular, I could always do a lot of my own maintenance. My hobby is restoring cars, so maintaining Studers and the mechanical aspect, which is usually the expensive part of having a studio, came easy for me.

Did Hillside give you a chance to grow as an engineer/producer? What were some of the experiences that brought you up to the next level?

I think you can sum it up in two words: Teddy Riley. I met Teddy Riley when he was about sixteen or seventeen. This was at a time when we had a lot of racially mixed people out here. The Sugar Hill is from town here, and a lot of acts came out here from Harlem and I met Teddy on one project. It was just one of those things; I don't know what it is, but I know what it is when I see it. This kid was just dripping with talent. It was an early period when computers weren't in the studio yet and synthesizers and sequencers were just coming on line.

It's funny, because at the time we were creating the techniques that we still use today, yet you don't think of it as being pioneering or anything. We had this song by Rob Base called "It Takes Two", one of the very early hits using a two bar sample as a loop in the rhythm section. At the time, we were using the really early versions of Performer or Vision just to get it done. That was a lot of fun, because all your experience as a musician really came into play. We were kind of like computer hobbyist hackers before they came to the studio, so as soon as the high end software became available, we were all over that.

And having these powerful sequencing tools obviously made a lot more production techniques available to you. Right?

Well, that's the thing. Most people could put a loop together, but the challenge was to put it together so it really swings, so people can dance to it. Because we had a couple of hits like that out of there, that led to a couple of records with Teddy and Naughty By Nature. The one with Teddy to me is like a classic record. We made that in about a month. Teddy would show up at like four or five in the afternoon and he'd have a sequence on a Korg DD-1, and we would lay that pattern down. Since we didn't have sequencers, he would just set up a keyboard and a couple of samples. We'd set up a bass sound then we'd punch our way through the bass track; the whole album is essentially Teddy playing live. After that, people were saying like "I just can't get that Hillside sound." It's like, "Dude, it has nothing to do with the sound, it more has to do with whose playing!"

Entrance to Bennett Studios. *Photo by Kim Touzeau, courtesy of Hummingbird Media*

How did the rooms sound at Hillside?

The control room was small; it was kind of like a pseudo live end/dead end type thing. It was really like a near field situation, and the recording room was tiny. We ended up doing a lot of jazz there, because we had a really nice Bosendoerffer 7'4" piano. At the time, it was a low rate studio and we got a good sound out of it; we had good mics.

Were you into the high end stuff as far as equipment was concerned at this point?

I was mostly working with Neumanns and had a couple of Coles lying around. I think that just progressed over time. We really built a good reputation up there for jazz, and today, that's really the mainstay of our business.

At what point did you feel cramped at Hillside and see an opportunity for Bennett Studios, where you are now? I imagine there is a pretty long period in between Hillside and Bennett.

There is. It's a period of about eighteen years. For the last four years of it, it was just a little frustrating, because you get to a point where you're like "I know I can do it better." I would get projects for a big band or something and I'd have to go somewhere else and record them.

And the console you had at Hillside was probably limited in its size.

Yeah, but it was a good sounding desk actually. It was that re-branded Quad-8 desk by Mitsubishi, very low maintenance, with a good EQ section. I think over time we'd gotten to the point where it was frustrating. Over the last six or seven years, I was doing primarily location and post recording; my feeling at the time was like, "I only have one room, and there's only twenty-four hours in a day" so I obviously needed to diversify.

Do you still do on location recording?

Yes. I've been doing the Newport Jazz Festival for ten years. It's one of my favorite things; we go out for four or five days. We just did the anniversary one last year.

Why did you choose to remain in Englewood when it came to building Bennett Studios?

I still liked the location out here; I felt that some of the clients really enjoyed getting out of the city. I think the area is pretty well established with Rudy's studio being out here, the Sugar Hill being out here, and House of Music being out in Orange. The area goes almost all the way back to Thomas Edison' lab for Christ's sake. So I felt confident about the location because I live out here.

Tell me about the facility.

This train station was an actual passenger station up until 1964, when it was converted into a restaurant/banquet type of place. The first one of those lasted ten or twelve years, then it became like a revolving door of restaurants. One would open, and then it would close after a year and a half. So the first time I had got the inclination to do this, the restaurant had closed. The city owned the building, so I went down there to see what the deal with it was, and actually went into a city council meeting on it.

And did they think your idea was nutty?

No, but the place had a restaurant fixture in it. But five or six years later, another two or three restaurants later, one of the building people slipped me a request for proposal under my door at Hillside. In the request, it said they were going to consider other uses. The restaurant fixture there had gotten old and it needed replacing.

The enclosed platform side of the Studios. *Photo by Kim Touzeau, courtesy of Hummingbird Media*

It seems like it would have been a very large restaurant.

Well, that was one of the problems. There are lots of restaurants around here, like twenty or so, but no really big ones. So I figured I would go back and think of a more synergistic thing that was more meaningful to them. I ended up offering to do an audio education program to the Dwight Morrow High School, which would be part of their performing arts center. What really works great is that you are teaching the technology, but also recording the students. Everybody gets a project that they worked on at the end of the day.

And you never know how many kids you are inspiring who will go on to do something special someday.

Well, you have to understand that with most music professionals, their hair caught fire on it between the ages of eight and thirteen! The school I am doing this with is actually my old high school.

That's really nice that you found a way to give back to the community and worked with the board on getting this deal through for your studio.

That's right. Another thing is that there is this crown jewel of the town that used to be an old movie house. It started life in the '20s as a vaudeville theatre, so it is a pre-amplification hall. It has that oval oculus on the ceiling; they've done some renovation work in there and opened it as a performing center. It's called the John Harms Theater because this man went door to door and literally collected money to buy this theatre, since it was facing destruction. He really did a major restoration and it's beautiful. Sadly, though, they took down the old beautiful marquee that had all the sequenced lights. When they saw how rusted out it was, they realized they couldn't restore it. The inside of the hall was really nice; they extended the balcony to add a couple hundred seats. When I did the initial proposal to the board, in addition to the school, I told them I would be hooking up the studio to the theatre. We have a 64-channel fiber optic connection set up between this hall and the studio, two buildings that are a city block away from each other.

Your interest in on-location recording must have inspired you to do this, right?

Absolutely. Something I learned early on from on-location recording is that you get something there that you don't get from a studio. I don't care how hard you try. For me, as techie as it gets sometimes, I'm still more of a performance-oriented person because that's what makes the best record. If somebody asks me what makes the best record, I say it's all about the songs and the performance.

That probably comes from all your early experiences from the Ed Sullivan theatre, and growing up around the performance aspect.

I think so. I don't think it's just a gut feeling. I know when we do rock stuff down at the theatre and there's ambient drums coming out of a PA system, there isn't a digital reverb on earth that's going to get that [laughs]. There's a certain edge to it.

And also the vibe coming off the performers, right?

Yeah. I think that's also the case with jazz. We do it in real takes. We don't sit around and punch it in. It's all about the performance. In jazz, we actually do a lot of live-to-two, and then edit. Some of the better records I've made are more spontaneous and there's just something there that you can't process. You know?

Yep. So the board was in agreement at this point?

They were thrilled about the theatre and delighted that I had a vision for the whole thing. If there was any hump I had to get over it was that many of these folks don't take the entertainment industry seriously. But I brought up some demographics and explained that this is one of the biggest industries in the country. If you grow it, you may as well put a car factory in here; it's the same type of thing. They grasped that and after the first couple of big productions we did here, they realized that we filled up all the restaurants. I walked around the streets and people were like hugging me! [laughs].

Did you have an eye on this place for a long time?

Yeah, I had a while to ponder it, let's put it that way; especially in those long periods where it remained empty. I'd keep seeing it, thinking "That big waiting room in there would make a nice...."

So finally, you are the one who is faced with restoring to your needs, not a restaurant's. Can you describe the kinds of things you faced to make it a workable space?

I had a bunch of thumbnail sketches that described the kind of facility I wanted, how I wanted it wired, and its overall capabilities. The premise, one of the things that I got from on-location recording, was that I wanted a studio where everything terminated on a panel. Whatever gets thrown at you, you can just rig it up. That's essentially what I have done here. I made a central machine room that just has racks. Everything is modular eight, on Elco's and whatever gets thrown at us, we can have it patched up in about five minutes. All the microphones come up on panels, all the consoles, all the machines.

How did you rationalize buying this space, which was considerably larger than Hillside?

For the type of work we're doing, basically I was going to invest all the money that I'd made up to this point in my life [laughs]! It was a pretty important decision in what I was going to do with that, and where I felt was the safest place to put my money. After thinking about it long and hard, I really felt that there would always be performing arts and there was always going to be recording. There are just fewer and fewer places with the aesthetic and the acoustical treatment inside where you have good sound. A big room where you can put a big band is not what a lot of people are building right now.

The John Harms Theater, viewed from the stage, is a meticulously restored 1,400 seat theater connected by an underground fiber optic cable to Bennett Studios. *Photo courtesy of Bennett Studios*

So you knew you needed a big room.

Yes. I felt that between a big room and the theatre, where we could do large format stuff, I had it covered. I mean, recording a sixty-piece orchestra in New York City is a nightmare. I know, because I've done it before.

How did you choose your designer?

Well, without naming names, I spoke to all the ones you would consider to be the major players. After speaking with a number of them and actually going through proposal stages with four of them, I ended up deciding on Andy Munro from England. He seemed to be on the same page with me right away in terms of what I was looking for. I had done some work in Europe before and I thought studios over there were a little thicker; I just wanted something a little different.

The John Harms theater, in conjunction with Bennett Studios, has led to an artistic resurgence in Englewood. It was originally built in the 1920s as a Vaudeville theater. *Photo by Kim Touzeau, courtesy of Hummingbird Media*

The interior of the John Harms Theater, which has served as the recording venue for several of Bennett's CD and DVD projects, including John Fogerty and K.D. Lang/Tony Bennett. *Photo courtesy of Bennett Studios*

The North Studio used to be the waiting room of the train station. Bennett wanted a "conservatory" feel in the live room.
Photo by Dave Kowalski, courtesy of Bennett Studios

He's worked on some pretty heavy hitters' places in Europe. David Gilmour, Paul McCartney....

And I've worked in his rooms and liked the sound of them. With the acoustic treatment and aesthetic that I wanted, I just felt most in tune with him right away. I felt a lot of people were like "Oh yeah, that sounds great" and then they would show me their ideas, and it was their ideas instead of mine. And it's not as if I was insistent on my idea, but there was just a certain feel I was going for and he understood what I was talking about. When he took out the pencil I knew this guy was good.

During the design phase, did he influence your decisions in any particular way? What stands out?

Not really. I've been doing this for a long time and I knew what I needed business-wise. Machine room, two mid-size studios, and a Pro Tools room for when I do the post work. I don't like using acoustical control rooms for that, that's a waste of space. I already knew I could do that in a closet size space from working at Hillside [laughs]! It's a small room, but a large revenue earner. It's a nice little room with a surround system in there, so I can cut audio for DVDs.

Can you describe how the meetings with Andy went?

When I sat down with Andy, he was like "What are your main objectives? What do you need to accomplish?" I told him I wanted it to be much more of a domestic feeling place, particularly in the large room, lending much more of a conservatory feel than say a modern architecture thing. I wanted to keep the aesthetic of the building but have all the acoustical treatments hidden. I didn't want all of the zagged wood. I didn't want to do the gold record thing on the walls. There was going to be artwork and photographs.

I was really going for all the stuff that was lacking when I had to leave my Hillside place. A lot of studios leave you with a cold feeling or are a little to "office spacey" looking; even some of the nicer studios. Architecturally, when you first walk in they are great. But after a while it's like being in the funhouse or something. We have a lot of daylight here, too, and that was one of the revelations with Andy. I thought I was going to lose these big windows in the waiting room. We discussed it, and he said, "No, no, you can keep them." I said, "I'm just paranoid that someone's going to go by outside and they're going to hear it," because there are shoppers in the street right outside. I asked Andy "What if someone drives a Harley by?" and he said "What model?" [laughs]. "So if you feel that comfortable about it," I said, "fine." "But if it's not quiet, I don't have a recording studio."

It seems that light is one of the basic needs for many people to feel comfortable working.

It totally works with the idea of having a creative space and it works really well with music, because the scene is always changing. You get different times of the day, you have different weather. You have snowstorms, you have lightning.

I know your father is an artist. Do you have any of his paintings on display?

I do. He was sitting in the park across the street one day and did a pen and ink drawing of the building. I have that hanging here. Most of the other artwork is by a friend of mine, John Merlino.

When you were designing these rooms, did you have a particular genre in mind from an audio perspective?

No. The thing that I learned from Hillside is that a room should be able to be used in a variety genres; it should be wired and ready to go. You can post a surround session for a DVD in any one of these rooms, as well as record an orchestra in the theatre within five minutes of each other. Everything is organized so that different things can be accomplished in different rooms. Nothing is superficial; everything is hard-wired in, ready to snap and go.

Another criteria I had for Andy was that I needed to be able to sit in the middle of my console and use Pro Tools. I was getting tired of having that handle on a cart that had been my main squeeze for four or five years. I like to run Pro Tools in conjunction with an analog console and I kind of use it as a tape machine. I have the console automation follow time code as it's coming out of Pro Tools. This way I can have the best of both worlds. For mixing, I still prefer to have the audio channels coming up on a console. Some automation things are faster on a console and some other Pro Tools type things you can't do on a console. So I just kind of have everything going on at the same time.

During the construction process, what consideration was given to retain the integrity of the original structure? What condition was it in and what kind of work was required?

What had happened was that over the years, every restaurant had added stuff over the prior one, so everything was just kind of layered on top. Three ventilation systems, five data systems, it was a mess! I had the power company come over and shut the place down and three or four guys with bolt cutters kind of cut everything out. That's where we ran into our first major disaster.

The main hallway of Bennett Studios, actually the enclosed passenger platform of the old train station. *Photo by Dave Kowalski, courtesy of Bennett Studios*

Once we had gutted the ceiling over the big room and tore the plaster down, we saw that the joist going across from one side to the other was in two pieces joined in the middle. These two pieces of wood, instead of being one piece going across, deflected downwards in the middle. That was something that was unexpected and something that we couldn't have seen on inspection of the place; so we were really up shit's creek.

We ended up refabricating a series of metal plates that went into the roof rafters above the deflected joists. We put these brackets in, hoisted up engineered lumber which went all the way across, bolted the queens posts coming down to the engineered lumber and when that was all secured, we cut away the old rafters. It worked out great and we actually ended up getting an additional foot of ceiling in the room as a result of doing it. You could drive a tank up there now; it's totally solid.

Bennett's natural reverb chamber was originally an old underpass tunnel under the tracks. *Photo by Kim Touzeau, courtesy of Hummingbird Media*

Is there a basement in your facility?

There is. That was actually one of my favorite discoveries. There used to be some walk in fridges down there which we disassembled and hauled out. It was loaded with years of junk. We cleared it out, and finally came to a doorway. I'm like, "What the hell is this, a closet or something?" As it turns out, there used to be an underground walk-under under the tracks that had been closed off on the other end. So we actually have an 11' x 21' cement tunnel that we use as a reverb chamber here.

How cool is that? You could have used it as a secret entrance for famous recording artists.

Yeah [laughs]. I'll tell you though, it's a great sounding chamber, just awesome. That was like the only "free" thing that happened during the whole construction process, which was all basically frustrating. Building this studio was kind of like giving birth to a John Deere tractor; I often refer to this place as "my last studio."

Can you describe any interesting architectural details on the building?

One of the interesting things is that in what we call our North Studio, the console actually sits in what was once the entrance from the platform to the waiting room. I was looking for a 60 channel Neve VR for this spot, but I had to find one with the remote patch bay so it would fit in there without too much trouble. Everyone was like, "You could just put a hole in there". I was like, "No, not after my roof experience!"

Don't want to go there.

I just said, "Let's use what we have." And it turned out great, it looks custom made. It's nice.

Can you take me through the facility room by room?

Well, when you first come in, there is a little reception area. There is a large kitchen area where the bathrooms are. It's all paneled in mahogany styled wood that's about waist high. Again, it's very domestic feeling. There's a nice, small, tiled PJ Clark restaurant style kitchen. There's glass running from one end of the building to the other, and we've kind of frosted it about halfway up, so people can't really look in. But no matter where you are it is really nicely lit and you have a nice view of the trees and sky and all that.

Then the lounge area has a pool table, a bunch of couches, and a big TV with a surround system. Then you walk down the corridor, which is right along the railroad tracks, and the first stop is the North control room, which is where we do the larger format stuff like big bands.

It's surprising how loud bands like that can get. It's usually when a band gets loud that the characteristics come out in a room, good or bad. And I really wanted a nice, even sounding room. The sound of this room is fantastic and artists feel good in their instruments. This room has three isolation areas, one that functions as a sound lock between the studio and the main room, then it has a full size drum booth and another one for piano. On the other side we have a lounge that has windows into a control room, where you can monitor on headphones from if you like. We tend to record bass guitar in that room occasionally. No room is left unused and we have a mic in each of them!

Our main room is 25' x 40', with 13-foot ceilings, the big windows, and nice woodwork. It's angled, almost octagon shaped on one side and almost flat and a parallel on the other. The main room was the original waiting room of the train station.

Can you describe your typical approach to recording drums?

If it's my call, I like having them out in the room. We get great results when we have everybody recording in there without separation. That's something we do a lot of here.

Are you somebody who prefers less mics on the drums?

I am, particularly with jazz. With rock, I'll use a full complement of mics. Whether I use them all or not, I don't know until I mix. My job is to really get what the drummer is hearing, though. For a jazz drum kit, I usually use a 57 on the snare, which doubles as a hat mic, a couple of overheads, either 414 or Coles; I'll just go light or dark with those. I use a lot of ribbon mics, just because with digital recording, they help. For kick, either a FET 47 or RE20, depending on the drum itself; then maybe a room mic with a little compression on it just to get a little more action.

How about distance?

Again, it depends. If somebody's doing a lot of brush stuff, I'll get them down low. And if they're not in the room, I generally tend to run the Wes Dooley mics, the R84 for the room mics. For live jazz, these work well as room or surround mics, because sometimes we shoot and record at the same time for DVDs.

The "open air" client lounge, just beyond Bennett's reception area. *Photo by Kim Touzeau, courtesty of Hummingbird Media*

How did everything work out with sound isolation? Are these train tracks active?

That was actually was one of my biggest concerns when we started. They are active, but it's like a couple of cars come by early in the morning, then again later in the day. We haven't lost a take yet, and we're starting our fourth year. It's kind of funny, because it runs right by that window I told you about, and when it comes by, everyone always runs over and wants to have their picture taken with it [laughs]!

So it's an unexpected ambience. Can you tell me when you were finally ready to open after all this preparation? How did the first session go?

I was really stressed out when we opened, then on that fourth day, just after Labor Day, I walk in and I see that plane hit the Trade Center. We opened on September 6, 2001, and then came September 11th. I remember weeping to some extent just from the sadness of the whole thing, but after that it was like, "You know, we tried to think of everything." It just hit me really hard, because I knew the effect it was going to have on the economy and everything else. My kids were in school, some of their friends had lost family members, it was a disaster. With all of this going on as a backdrop, we had to keep on working. We had no time to rest on our laurels at all. It was difficult for me, because as they say in "Celebrity Poker", I went "all-in" on this. It was a tough pill to swallow. But I had a good core of people around me, and we worked very hard. That first year was critical.

You've since built Bennett Studio's reputation and now you're definitely on the map; the John Fogerty project you did for A&E was huge and got rave reviews.

Yes. The last two years were pretty impressive. Actually, five records won Grammys out of here in our second year of business. We were virtually sweeping the jazz category. The first big project we did was the Philip Bailey record for Heads Up/Telarc records. That was done in the period between the 9/11 disaster and the holidays; it was very helpful to get the project in at that point.

How did the John Fogerty project feel?

When you're doing live production, you don't even want to think there might be problems or unknowns. You can't mess up. It was a big milestone, because that was the first really live broadcast. John was amazing of course; we got all nice phone calls the next day from the production staff. This was the biggest thing we had ever done in the theater. Now we have others planned, even bigger. Once the first one goes well you have a track record, and I don't even have to pitch it! I can just show them the DVD.

The North Control Room where the Neve V Series sits in an opening that used to be the main entrance from the platform to the waiting room.
Photo by Dave Kowalski, courtesy of Bennett Studios

Bennett Studios' P.J. Clark style kitchen. *Photo by Kim Touzeau, courtesy of Hummingbird Media*

When did your vision become reality with respect to the theater?

Well, I had done some research and I felt that the best way to connect the studio and the theatre was via underground fiber. For one thing, it didn't have any computers involved; it was actually a fiber splitter, which was really what I wanted. I got a bid for digging the trench between the locations, went down to City Hall to speak to an engineer, and they helped me out by digging the trench because they said I wasn't allowed to own anything in the street. Then we pulled the fiber. We have 24 strands of fiber, of which we have used six so far. It's basically like a 64 channel splitter and we have a side-car for Clearcom production communications that is terminated in our machine room and it comes up on an Elco 90 panel next to our mic panel inputs. We just need to take these Elco 90s off and plug it in.

What project was the first to fully utilize the functionality of this?

The real potential was achieved in doing these Live By Request projects for A&E. We've used it for album recording; the first album we recorded using this was by my father and K.D. Lang. We did that one with T Bone Burnett, and he was really getting off on the fact that we weren't using any artificial reverb on the record. We only used the dynamics of the space.

How did your father and K.D. Lang enjoy singing in an empty theatre used as a studio space? Did this enhance their performance?

They just loved it. They are both performance-oriented people, so that is really the best way to catch them.

Having been around "stars" your whole life, has this enhanced your ability to take care of clients and look after them?

Maybe because I might have a better sense of what makes them feel uncomfortable. I think growing up in that environment, more than anything else, you just kind of learn that people are people. When you're a kid, you just know who is an idiot and who is nice. As a matter of fact, at one of the "Ed Sullivan" shows, they sent me over to the piano bench with Duke Ellington just to get me out of the way! You don't think about it then, he was just a nice guy. Maybe there is some perspective gained there, but I don't have the other side of it so I don't know. I do know I am very comfortable around people. I've never been good at the business side of music, I'm not a good schmoozer. A lot of what we do here is being brutally honest with people in a really nice way, to keep the creative flow going. That honesty is an important part in the creative process.

The South Control Room. *Photo by Dave Kowalski, courtesy of Bennett Studios*

Blue Jay Recording

Will Sandalls, Chief Engineer

Blue Jay's control room through custom made RPG "di-view-ser" plexi-glass diffusion unit. *Photo by George Roos, courtesy of Blue Jay Recording*

Blue Jay Recording is owned by Kevin Richardson, a member of The Backstreet Boys, and writer/producer Marcus Siskind. The studio is located in Carlisle, Massachusetts, an area that was originally settled by colonial farmers. Up until this day, the region maintains an agrarian, rural feel and is dotted with many towns and villages dating back to the late 1600s.

Blue Jay is literally an underground bunker, entirely made of steel reinforced concrete on the bottom, top, and sides. It was built by Bob and Janet Lawson in the mid-seventies to serve as a recording studio during an early trend to create non-urban recording spaces in rural environs. According to Will Sandalls, currently the chief engineer at Blue Jay, they had decided on an underground bunker to save on heating expenses; an unexpected and unanticipated benefit of building underground was that they had attained an extremely low noise floor, making Blue Jay's technical areas among the quietest in the business.

Eventually, the Lawson's decided to sell and move on, believing that Blue Jay's best days had already come and gone. However, in 2001, Marcus and Kevin decided that the studio would make a perfect facility for their own productions. Their own work, combined with the commercial potential of renting the studio to outside clients, fit their needs like a glove. Will was asked to stay on and run the facility day to day, and this particular studio escaped the bulldozer and was given a new life.

The rooms were acoustically re-evaluated by Fran Manzella, who completely redesigned the interior to take Blue Jay into the next decade. For Marcus and Kevin, who would often require use of the facility when not on tour, a dedicated production room was built off the "commercial" areas, enabling the facility to become truly dual-purpose and flexible. Despite the continued prominence that Blue Jay enjoys, it remains entirely accessible by local musicians who continue to use the facility to take their careers to the next level.

Blue Jay is located in a not-so-obvious underground bunker in Carlisle, Massachusetts. The 60' x 40' steel reinforced concrete outer shell was buried into the hill in 1979. *Photo by Jeff Touzeau, courtesy of Hummingbird Media*

Carlisle, Massachusetts, is an old New England town originally settled in the 1700s. *Photo by Jeff Touzeau, courtesy of Hummingbird Media*

Originally hired as an intern under its previous ownership, Will Sandalls has worked his way up through the ranks to Chief Engineer, a position in which he must wear many hats. He was educated in Music Technology at Berklee School of Music in Boston, and also on the front lines as an assistant engineer. However, he maintains that he has learned mostly by applying his instincts and pushing himself to learn inside his own defined frameworks.

Can you briefly describe the history of Blue Jay?

Well, to begin with, it has always been a studio. Bob and Janet Lawson, the original owners, wanted to build a recording studio in the country. At the time there was sort of a movement to get out of urban environments with recording studios. They were looking at underground homes because of the oil crisis during 1975 or '76. When they found this property in Carlisle, the light bulb must have gone off. They thought that they were going to save some money on heating, but the more important benefit was the fact that it provides the facility with an extremely low noise floor. There is no interference from the outside whatsoever, electric or acoustic.

What about the natural sound isolation? Have you ever had to worry about airplane noise?

Not once. If you're in the lounge you can sometimes hear the UPS trucks if they're right in the driveway, but never in the technical or audio areas.

How did they treat the room?

When they built it, there was no science to building a studio at the time so they tried to do a lot of the treatment themselves. I have seen some pictures of some very strange acoustic devices on the walls. I think they were half barrels stuffed with egg crates; it looked like a ship [laughs]. Ultimately, they opened as a 24-track facility and I believe they had an MCI board. So it always had a respectable set up and they always had good clients coming in.

Could you describe Carlisle? What is the topography like?

It's pretty hilly and there is a lot of farmland, but not like the cornfields in Iowa. It's farmland in a sort of more traditional sense. A lot of these towns outside of Boston had rules about the amount of acreage you had to have if you were going to build a residence, as Carlisle probably did. Everyone had these huge plots of land.

So how many acres is Blue Jay on?

We're on a third of an acre lot. We don't have a hell of a lot of space but we do have a fairly decent backyard. Also, we don't really have any neighbors.

Is it sort of inconspicuous? Do people even know that there is an underground studio there?

A lot of people didn't know about it until Marcus bought the place. Then there was all this press with the Backstreet Boys and suddenly everyone knew. That kind of put us on the map as far as the local interest is concerned. There were some people that would wander down saying, "Hey I heard there's a recording studio down here" when we were in the middle of a session. It wasn't really convenient.

However, we also have encounters with people wandering down on their bikes or horses not knowing that it's a business. I was working on a project with Marcus once and I noticed from the control room that there was this giant horse standing in the backyard. It turned out that this giant horse had taken a giant crap next to Marcus' very expensive BMW. Marcus ended up having to talk to the guy who was riding it. I think he encouraged him to clean it up, so to speak. We always try to be nice to people but I think that's the one time we've not been so nice to our neighbors.

Can you describe the rooms?

It's probably easiest to start with the dimensions of the facility. It's a 60' by 40' concrete block that was buried in an excavated hill.

The rear of the studio, with its atrium and stucco covered concrete walls, was installed during a 2002 renovation. The concrete retaining walls replaced twenty-year-old railroad ties. *Photo by Jeff Touzeau, courtesy of Hummingbird Media*

So it's underground?

Yes, it's pretty bunker-like. There is steel reinforced concrete on the ceiling, ground, and walls. The studio is pretty much divided into thirds and the back third under the hill is the live room.

There are two isolation booths. There used to be only one iso booth and the room was divided into a live side and a dead side. When we renovated the place, we wanted to modify the room to suit our purposes, so we added the second isolation booth on the dead end side, which is floated and made the main space mostly live. Having one of the iso booths floated allows us to run overdubs from the A room and the B room. The live room's walls and ceilings are mostly redwood. There is a stone alcove, which predates the new ownership. The floor is acid etched colored concrete. It looks like marble in photographs.

Then there's a sound lock between the live room and a hallway leading to the control room, which can also be used as another iso booth, usually for bass or guitar. The control room and the machine room pretty much occupy the middle third of the facility, and the remainder is the lounge and Marcus' production room. Marcus' production room is floated so he can do his production work and not bother any commercial clients working in the A-room.

How did you get involved with the acoustician Fran Manzella?

Marcus bought the place primarily for his production work. He wanted to build a place in Massachusetts, but the building costs were astronomical. He had actually worked at Blue Jay as a producer on a previous project, and when he heard through the grapevine that Bob might be selling the place, Marcus realized the potential.

After he bought it, Marcus wanted to update the look so we started interviewing different acousticians and designers. We wanted to talk to Fran because he had done Sound Station Seven in Rhode Island. Marcus and I had taken a trip down there, and it looked great and it sounded nice. Some guys we interviewed made grandiose statements about what was wrong and what we should do, without ever doing an audio or a physical measurement. When Fran came up he measured first, then told us what to do. He had stuff on paper for us very fast. Everyone was on board with Fran as soon as they saw his plans, because they all knew we were operating at a much more professional level.

And his track record is just incredible.

It's phenomenal. Acoustically, Blue Jay is marvelous to work in; but Fran is also talented as a designer too. Marcus was insistent that he come up with some different ideas, and one of the results is that we've got this ceiling cloud configuration made out of corrugated aluminum that you simply wouldn't expect to see in a recording studio.

Yeah I saw that, that's beautiful.

The metal itself is sixty-three percent porous, so it's more porous than it is reflective. It was a way to tie the three audio spaces together. The control rooms are filled with absorptive material, so they act as traps. In the live room, they just cover the diffusion in the ceiling. The speaker towers that hold the UREI 813's into the wall are also coated in metal with the same stuff they put on bowling balls. The guy who did the coating said that you can actually shoot a bullet at these towers and it would not crack the finish.

Blue Jay's UREI 813 monitors sit in a classic-designed sheet-metal encasing, designed by Fran Manzella. *Photo by Jeff Touzeau, courtesy of Hummingbird Media.*

You've grown substantially in your career path since you've been here. You started out as an intern and now you're Senior Engineer?

It was pure circumstance. Four months after I took the job, Bob Lawson, the original owner, told me that they were probably going to bulldoze the place.

Really?

And I was like "Great; you guys made me commit to a two year sort of deal and now you're telling that the place is going to shut down." The two senior engineers ahead of me had both been with Bob for a very long time. They had expressed an interest in moving on. Without their main guys, it didn't make much sense to Bob and Janet to try and keep it open. Bob seemed pretty convinced that he wasn't going to be able to sell it. But in 2001, after one prospective buyer walked away from a deal, Marcus and Kevin, the current owners, came along.

And they have an association with the Backstreet Boys?

Well, Marcus has done production work for the Backstreet Boys and Kevin is in the Backstreet Boys. They're partners from a publishing perspective, I believe.

Once Bob had a potential buyer for the place, he decided to keep it running and suddenly I was the Staff Engineer. It was trial by fire for me in a lot of ways. Suddenly, I was solely responsible for the daily management and performance of the facility after only being on staff for about a year. I was pretty overwhelmed at first. I spent a lot of the time when I wasn't assisting gigs trying to update paperwork or figure out why all the gear had been wired the way that it had been. The selling process ultimately took about year, so I had the confidence I needed when the new ownership took over.

What kind of clients were Blue Jay attracting at this point?

I was inheriting some clients from my predecessors. There were a lot of young bands that wanted to mix here because of the gear that we had, including the SSL. There were also people who wanted to take advantage of our analog environment, since many people were starting to use ADAT's and Pro Tools. I did a few EP's and a couple of full-length records. I was mixing more than I was recording, though. It wasn't until Marcus bought the place that I actually got a handle on how the room works for cutting drums. He gave me a lot of space in terms of experimenting with set-ups when we were working on his projects.

But you guys have also catered to the local scene a lot, unlike many other commercial facilities.

We have to. The local scene has always been and continues to be Blue Jay's bread and butter.

How has Blue Jay's association with the Backstreet Boys influenced who works there? Does it really benefit you by having prominent owners?

It does and it doesn't. Any time a studio goes down for an extended period of time like we did during our renovation, you're going to lose a fair amount of your regular clients. In the time that you're down, they're going to look for other places to go and develop new relationships.

These aluminum "clouds" are found in the three main audio rooms in the facility. They serve a different sonic purpose in each room, while tying all the rooms together thematically. *Photo by Jeff Touzeau, courtesy of Hummingbird Media*

Marcus Siskind's production/writing room, off of the lounge area of Blue Jay. *Photo by George Roos, courtesy of Blue Jay Recording*

What is it like recording The Backstreet Boys? Do they insist on singing together? I would imagine they're not really into overdubs to preserve the harmonics and overtones live performance offers.

Well, it depends. It starts with whoever is the lead and that stuff gets laid down. It depends on who's arranging it too. Let's say Nick is singing the main part of the hook. He'll go through that and then he'll double it, triple it, whatever seems appropriate for the song. Then they'll get Howie to come in and do the high harmonies. It ends up being this constant revolving door of them going in and doing their parts. Whoever is doing the arranging will then say, "Ok, we need so and so to do this." They all know their ranges, their strengths, and their weaknesses.

Do these guys just nail the harmonies every time, or is there a lot of work?

There's a lot of work whether they nail it or not. You have to work just as hard to get it right, even when the technology is on your side.

When you're recording such vocal talents as the Backstreet Boys, what are your typical mic choices?

We have a fantastic C12 that has recently been refurbished. Previous to that, we used a really nice Telefunken 251 that everyone loves. Now we put the C12 and the 251 up against each other and it's always the C12 that wins out. I always start with the same thing initially though, because that gives me my frame of reference.

Will Sandalls, chief engineer of Blue Jay Recording. *Photo by Jeff Touzeau, courtesy of Hummingbird Media*

You have to start from a known position to move forward. Do you rely on dynamics going in?

Generally I don't. I try and stay away from compressing to tape as much as possible. I compress vocals to tape. Bass usually gets some treatment. Guitar does too. Really, it all depends on the player and the instrument.

How do you like working on the Neve VR?

The mic pres on this console are extremely clear. The pres were one of the things that were modified by the guy who commissioned it for us. On occasion, they have beat out the vintage Neve gear that I own. However, for vocals and big heavy guitars, I usually use the 1066 Neve pres.

Will, how many years have you been at Blue Jay now?

I've been here since '99, so just over five.

How did you ultimately land in the studio business?

Well, like a lot of people I started out as a musician first. I played bass, but only as an amateur.

Always in the Boston region?

In high school, yes, and then I started playing in bands when I was at Colby College in Maine. However, I didn't actually see music as a potential career until my junior year in Ireland. The school I did the exchange with had pretty decent jazz program and I ended up gigging a lot, being the only electric bass player. I fell in love with the possibility of making a living doing music.

The head of the jazz program had gone to Berklee College of Music in Boston and encouraged me to look into the programs there. I thought I would major in Music Technology so that if being a professional bass player didn't work out I would have a fall back. Little did I know how silly that was at the time! The summer after my return, I had gotten an internship at a small studio in Boston called New Alliance, which basically entailed hanging around and getting sandwiches for everyone. I loved it though, even though I didn't know what was going on.

By the time I ended up in the Music Production and Engineering major at Berklee, I realized my strengths were in the studio. More to the point, Berklee did a great job of teaching me where my limits were as a bass player. Being on the other side of the glass gave me a chance to participate in much more of the music creation process, which I enjoyed more than just being the bass player.

So was this a masters program at Berklee?

Nope, in fact it wasn't even a Bachelors degree. I graduated with a Professional Diploma, which means I took Berklee's core music requirements and the classes for the music production major.

Blue Jay's control room provides direct sightlines to the live room and several iso booths. *Photo by George Roos, courtesy of Blue Jay Recording.*

Did it feel like a risky thing to be getting into since you spent so much time in sociology and were suddenly headed towards music production?

I didn't know what the risk was. I knew that I wanted to do it, and that I was going to take it step by step. The first step was just school. It ended up working out because while I was still at Berklee I met a guy named Ed Goodreau, Berklee's Studio Manager, who was also the first Chief Engineer at Blue Jay. He was the one who let me know about the potential change at Blue Jay and encouraged me to get on the intern staff.

At this point, I was working as a night-time supervisor at Berklee. I helped the kids with technical problems in the rooms, mostly with time code and signal flow. I was also working at Genelec, the monitor manufacturer, testing speakers for them and taking care of their consignment inventory.

Was it hard to make ends meet when you're going through this period?

At the time, no. I had really cheap rent [laughs] and very little debt at this point. I had absolutely no spare time though, as you can imagine.

Would you say that you really cut your teeth at Berklee or as an intern at Blue Jay? Where did the real guts of knowledge come from?

It was here at Blue Jay because I was exposed to a slew of other engineers. Blue Jay was one of very few studios in Boston that had a staff assistant that could facilitate the room to outside engineers. In 1985, we became the first studio in New England to have 48-tracks of Studer and an SSL. This was a big deal at the time because there weren't even that many SSL's in New York. It kind of put us on the map and Blue Jay became a destination for engineers that wanted to get out of the city to work on a project but still wanted state of the art. This meant that we had to have the service to match the gear; that tradition was alive and well when I came on board.

I got to work with people like Phil Green, Jeff Glixman, Mike Tucker, Jimi "Bonzai" Caruso, Jim Farber, Bill Sheniman, Carl Beatty, Bill Winn, and Paul Hager. I like to think that I got to learn from a few of the top engineers in the business.

The live room is finished almost entirely in redwood, giving it a distinctive look and sound. *Photo by George Roos, courtesy of Blue Jay Recording*

It sounds like you got yourself into the eye of activity, moving from Berklee to Blue Jay, surrounded by competent professionals.

It was pretty intense. There was a high expectation of performance on my part. I was trying to learn as much from the other engineers as I could, but I had to keep doing the assistant gig right. The first two months of this were sleepless. I had been well prepared by my predecessor, but there were just things that I had to learn on my own.

Were there times you had to pull out all the manuals and just start digging?

I did a lot of that in the early days. Engineers would ask to use certain pieces of gear that I wasn't that familiar with and I would have to bone up on it very quickly. That was a good education too, because I learned to think about things in terms of a framework; what is this thing supposed to do and what are you trying to do with it? It's a very top down sort of thinking. Once you understand the framework, it's just a matter of filling in the blanks. The procedure is simple as long as you understand the principle behind it.

You've witnessed many changes in the last five years alone at Blue Jay. What state would you say that the studio industry is in now?

When things inexplicably slowed down for as long as they did, everyone blamed it on 9/11. After March of 2002, you have to start finding something else to blame it on. One thing is for sure: things have never quite picked back up. Studios are closing in New York left and right. All these mainstays and heavyweights are closing. Boston wasn't immune to the shift in the industry. I think a lot of people that used to support us as outside engineers had to go New York or Los Angeles just to find work.

Is this all happening due to the proliferation of home studios?

I don't know. I think there are some recording musicians that do a fairly decent job. Recording studios provide a service. For some people now it seems a recording studio is just a box you can buy. And if someone is convinced that $3,000 is better spent on a home recording package than at Blue Jay, then I'm not sure what to think. However, I am sympathetic to people who feel that they are paying by the minute.

It hasn't been easy for us to compete locally. We realize that we demand a high rate for the area but we made a decision very early on that we were going to keep our rate at a respectable place, not only for our livelihood, but also to keep the market priced fairly for the other studios in town. We have to be sensitive to what our peers are charging.

If you had to go back and do the whole Berklee thing again, would you? Or would you put all that money into gear in hindsight?

I think that the experience at Berklee was phenomenal. But I think I had such a good experience because I knew how to study. I was prepared to absorb a high quotient of information very quickly. But, I also met some people in the industry who I'm still very close to with.

Does a certain personality fit at Blue Jay?

Yeah. I'd say you have to be very flexible with what's expected of you, because sometimes you show up for a gig and you think that you're this but it turns out you're that. So you have to keep the studio's interest as your best interest, and that takes a certain type of personality. And you also have to be a good hang without being the main personality in the room.

If you're too alpha, then you are going to get in the way and you will make the client's experience a little stressful. They are here to work on their music, not be entertained by you. So it's important that people who work here have that sort of balance between knowing when to be visible, especially in a small room like this, but also be able to fade into the woodwork when necessary. That takes a certain degree of maturity. Generally I think the hardest thing to do is to get over yourself. Once you do that, everything comes a little bit more naturally. For me, I just try to listen, listen, listen, listen. I compare and take notes to try and figure out what I can do better the next time. It's definitely a process.

Blue Jay's live area provides a wide range of surfaces on its walls and ceilings, creating an extremely diverse palette of room options. *Photo by George Roos, courtesy of Blue Jay Recording*

Compass Point Studios

Terry Manning, Producer/Engineer

Compass Point Studios building, viewed from the front walk. The ocean is across the street. *Photo by Jeff Touzeau, courtesy of Hummingbird Media*

This book could have easily been just on Terry Manning; he has more interesting anecdotal stories and has had more interesting audio production encounters than anyone I have ever met, by far. He was reared in El Paso and Memphis, arguably the recording capital of the world. He was a first hand witness to Stax (and worked with Al Green), Sun (knew Sam Phillips), and Ardent Studios (recorded Big Star) when they were doing their most groundbreaking work. He has also been an engineer at Abbey Road Studios in London and now runs the world famous Compass Point Studios in the Bahamas, along with his wife Sherrie. Terry's ears and masterful engineering skills have been behind some of rock's most influential records: from Al Green to Ike & Tina Turner to Led Zeppelin.

Despite having a discography many people simply dream about, Terry is extremely humble. As far as his work ethic, if there is one word that I had to use to describe Terry, it would be focused. He is so serene and has so much integrity in his work that he never lets himself get caught up in reflection or nostalgia. He is utterly determined to get the session done right, to the utmost of his abilities. The sense of duty that he had as an engineer in Memphis at the tender age of fifteen still permeates his daily routine, no matter who he is working with.

Terry says that being at the right place at the right time was a critical factor in moving his career ahead. In fact, his friend Lenny Kravitz once likened him (much to his chagrin) to Forrest Gump. Clearly, however, he maintained plenty of talent and drive to help him achieve the level of success that he has today.

Terry and his wife began managing Compass Point in 1992 following the tragic death of Alex Sadkin, its previous resident producer and lifeline to the outside world. By the time Terry and Sherrie came aboard, Compass Point had reached the deepest part of its valley. The facility and the business itself nearly died with Alex, and the Mannings, along with partner Chris Blackwell, had to build up both the facility and the business to the professional, internationally renowned level that it had been during the 1980s.

Compass Point Studios, originally the home of Island Records founder Chris Blackwell, is located in a "rural" section of New Providence Island, Bahamas. It is west of Nassau, right beside a place called Gambier Village, a freed African slave village and the oldest settlement in the Bahamas. The world famous Compass Point Resort, along with some of the world's most pristine beaches imaginable, is directly across the street.

Compass Point's recording legacy is second to none. First, it's where one of rock's most all-time successful albums was recorded, AC/DC's *Back in Black*. Others who have found inspiration in this island retreat include Bob Marley, The Rolling Stones, Brian Eno, Bryan Ferry, Robert Palmer (who lived across the street), The Cure, Roger Waters, Talking Heads, and so many others. In fact, one of the isolation booths was specified by none other than Sir Mick Jagger.

Compass Point Resort is located across the street, directly on the beach. *Photo by Terry Manning.*

Some of the colorful bungalows at Compass Point Resort. *Photo by Terry Manning*

I know that you worked at many locations over the years, including Ardent, Abbey Road, and now Compass Point. How did you get going in this game?

I would hear sounds on records from a very, very early age, as a nine-year-old boy. I would fall asleep with the radio under my pillow listening to Elvis Presley, or other early rock songs, just wanting to do sound.

Almost subconsciously?

Music and sound. How did they get this all together so it became this one thing that came out of this little speaker? I started in El Paso, Texas, when I was in high school playing in local bands; I got hold of a couple of tape recorders. Me and some guys in my band The Wild Ones would put them up in our back house rooms. I even tried to use my father's church; he was a minister. I used makeshift studios to start recording. Among my good friends in Texas was Bobby Fuller, who later had the Bobby Fuller Four, with "I Fought the Law", a big hit. I played with him a few times, playing rhythm guitar, singing. At the time he had a great home studio, much closer to a pro studio.

This is one of the earliest home studios I've heard of.

He was way ahead of his time and was very popular locally. Bobby had very good recorders and boards at the time; I don't remember exactly what they were, but they were much better than what any of us other young guys had. He was also putting out local records on his own label and he had his own club. He was quite the entrepreneur and I just thought this was all so great, to be able to make sounds, get them on your own tapes, somehow get them onto these records, and get them out and onto the radio. He had a local version of "I Fought the Law", quite similar to the hit version that was recorded in Los Angeles. The LA version was played better by slightly better professionals. Bobby was also into Buddy Holly, as we all were at that point. Buddy was, of course, from west Texas.

Fine white beaches and crystal clear water are typical scenes in The Bahamas. *Photo by Terry Manning*

The world-famous D&D Fruit Stand, another one of Compass Point Studios' neighbors. *Photo by Jeff Touzeau, courtesy of Hummingbird Media*

Was he more popular than Elvis in that region?

Elvis was certainly a huge influence on everybody, but Buddy Holly was right up there, if not more so. Locally at that time, Buddy was "the guy." He was from a nearby place, and he recorded just up the road from us, in New Mexico, where Bobby also went to record a couple of things. Then there was a time when Bobby decided that he couldn't really make it nationally from El Paso, so he went to Nashville; but things didn't really work out for him there. He came back very depressed and didn't know what to do. One of the last times I saw him was at a bowling alley in El Paso. We were talking about what to do to get out of there, because we knew that nobody could really make it past the local market from El Paso. He decided that he was going to go to Los Angeles. I couldn't, because I was too young.

My father, as a minister, was moving every two or three years to different places. One of the options that was eventually presented to him was Memphis, Tennessee. I just instantly jumped on that. I was saying, "Oh, I've been getting all these great records on the Satellite label, like *Last Night* by the Mar Keys."

This was while the Stax label was in motion?

Yeah. It had already started by that time. The Mar Keys record *Last Night* was a big record for me. I bought it for $.79 or $.89 and just played it till the grooves wore out. Then I bought *Walking the Dog* by Rufus Thomas, and I just thought that was the greatest thing.

I don't know if that was why my father ended up going to Memphis, but I showed up in Memphis when I was fifteen years old. I went to Stax Records at fifteen, carrying a guitar, went up to the front door, knocked on it, and got invited in. I remember it was a movie theatre type entrance, which was closed in later years. I told the secretary there that I had come to work. She said, "Well, what do you do?" And I said, "Well, I sing, I write, I engineer, I produce, you name it!" I was just a punk kid; today if someone came to my door like that, I'd probably turn them away immediately!

So they said, "Okay, we'll put you to work." So I started sweeping floors and making tape copies and things like that. There was a tape copy room with all these machines for sending tape duplicates out, and I said "I can operate all these machines." So I began doing that. Simultaneously, a friend of mine in high school had a band and their keyboard player had quit, so I said "I can play the keyboards." And I couldn't, really. I had seen keyboards at my father's church in El Paso, and one time we recorded and practiced there. So I said to my Dad "I'm in a band now, and I've got to have a keyboard." So he took me down to a local music store, and we picked out a Wurlitzer electric piano, and I started playing.

Did you get any gigs?

We got on a TV show called "Talent Party"; the MC, George Klein, was one of Elvis' best high school friends, one of the leaders of his posse. He had his own TV show and he was a DJ on WHBQ-AM 56, which was the station that had broken Elvis.

The demo tape we used didn't sound great. So the band's manager took it to John Fry, who had a home studio he called Ardent, which was more or less a garage. He had very good Ampex 440s, well maintained, and a really nice Altec radio board. He was "high tech and into it" for the time. So John Fry ran the band's demo tape through some limiting, EQ'd it a bit, got the levels a little hotter on the tape. We then took it down to George Klein, and we got on "Talent Party". That started a music relationship between me and John Fry. I said, "Ah-ha! This is the place for me, right here." I loved being around equipment and recording; I just thought it was the greatest thing. So when John decided that he needed a pro facility, I was right there. He talked his dad into bankrolling it, putting in a real, higher level studio.

Because he was getting busier?

Well, it wasn't busy yet with people coming there to rent, but that's what he wanted to do because he loved the music. He didn't really want to go out into the business world. So we went out and found the building, which was on National Street. Not the greatest area of Memphis, but it was a new building, built by a man who had put in a Bible bookstore and wanted to rent out the other half.

How big was it?

It was a nice big studio, big control room, with room in the back for a small tech shop. I was there at the very beginning of that and helped with the wiring. I became more or less the first employee of this commercial venture.

He was kind of mentoring you the whole time.

Yes. John was a genius engineer in my opinion. He would teach me what he knew about engineering because he didn't want to be the only engineer there. I showed some interest in this and he mentored and taught me how this higher level of equipment worked. So we got this console built by a local man named Welton Jetton. These were very, very good sounding boards. In fact, Ardent had them for many years until it went with the more featured, better known consoles.

So you could hear the improvement in quality?

Well, it's hard to hear a sonic leap from an Altec Tube radio board, because you're starting at an amazing sonic level. These boards were not tube, they were discreet transistor boards, great for their time; we also got Scully multi-track tape machines, which were top of the line for the time. We had a great system in place. Stax at the time was not at that sonic level; they still had radio boards, non multi-tracks. So they would bring things over for us to boost to a higher level or to mix. Simultaneously, I was doing other things over at Stax: there was Hi, which was Willie Mitchell with the Al Green type stuff, there was Stax, which was Booker T. and the MGs, Isaac Hayes, Otis, and Rufus Thomas. Then of course the Atlantic things that they would bring down, like Wilson Pickett.

What was it like getting exposed to all these artists so suddenly, presumably who you knew from your days in El Paso, albeit from afar?

It felt as if I knew these people already, such as Rufus Thomas, the Mar Keys, Booker T. and the MGs. That was a big thrill to me, but there was work to be done. You know the music is great and that you're at a professional level, but you

A pool at Compass Point Resort. *Photo by Terry Manning*

never look at it from a historical perspective. It's just "what I'm doing today." Maybe it will be historically significant; maybe it will fall off the map. Bottom line is, you've got a job to do. In those days, it was much less of a technical, big production. It was much more like "There's a drum kit, there's a couple of mics. Get 'em on there, get 'em in the board, get a sound quickly; the people are here to play."

Years later, people will come to me and say "Wow, I've got to get the bass drum sound of Isaac Hayes." They will try to get you to search for hours and hours, putting up different mics, putting them in different places, using different mic pre's and all this, but that's not the way you got the sound back then.

It was a lot more intuitive, wasn't it?

Yes. It was much more about "There's a book about how recording is done, you go by the book until you can't, and then you make adjustments. You get it down on a tape, and then you can change it if it needs to be." We pre-mixed a lot then, because there weren't that many tracks. There were first just three or four tracks. They would bring something from Stax to mix. It would have drums and bass on track one, keyboards and guitars on track two, vocals, maybe even with the backing vocals on track three, and then track four would be for "extras", maybe horns. The horns of course might have been mixed into the guitars and keyboards, they might be on a track by themselves, or they might have something totally wacky like vibraphones mixed with something else on track four. The mix was taking pre-mixed things and doing your very best to make it all sound like one cohesive unit, which believe it or not, is harder with fewer tracks than it is with many tracks. On some of the recordings, you're thinking "What in God's name do we do with this to make a stereo mix out of it?"

A few years later, we thought that the Beatles' stereo, with all the vocals on one side and all the rhythm tracks on the other, was ridiculous. So we weren't going to do that, we were going to try having it panned a little bit, have echo returns on other sides, and do things that made somewhat more of an acceptable stereo mix. The Beatles themselves on their early stereo mixes were not involved. In fact, I don't believe even George Martin was that involved. The Beatles would go in and work very hard on the mono. Then they would say, "Ah, the work is done." And then the staff would later say, "A stereo mix needs to be done." And they would put it together quickly.

Isn't it funny how you hear some of these early records with, say, the bass panned hard left or something like that? All of these things that we look at now as sort of the standard practice simply weren't done.

Right. We thought that heavy, hard panning of bass and vocals really didn't work in stereo. At least on my part, I was trying to create the wideness, which may not have worked in some ways, but may have worked better in other ways.

So at this point, you and John are running the place, you are getting a high degree of technical proficiency, and you're getting exposed to all this different music and different recording techniques. Where does it go from there?

Well, more and more sessions came in, and people would bring things in from all over the South. We quickly got the reputation as being the technical and sonic leader of the recording field in the South: certainly outside of Nashville. Nashville was looked at as "country." And as much as I respect so much of what Nashville has done, at the time, it was quite a rivalry. Memphis and Nashville did not really mix and get along that well. Memphis was seen as the "rock" and the R&B," the "soul" side of it, whereas Nashville was seen mostly as the country side of it.

That rivalry was probably pretty healthy at the end of the day, wasn't it?

Well, it probably was. As the years went by, there was much more of a co-mingling, and a coming together so to speak. But in the early days, we would get all the sessions that wanted "high tech" let's call it. Things would come in from all over. For example, Ike & Tina Turner's "Rolling on a River" came in for finishing.

You recorded the horns on that one, right?

Yes, and I mixed on it. I remember even Peter Asher would bring in things like James Taylor all the way from California, because he wanted part of the Memphis sound. Our heroes at the time, as much as we loved the Memphis sound, were The Beatles and the British Invasion things. We were trying to do technically what Abbey Road was doing. The philosophy of course was "There is a recording manual, you do it by the book." You had to be perfect technically. You had to have your machines aligned just so, you had to have a good quality microphone in just the right place.

Was there any kind of reciprocal interest in the U.K. in what you guys were doing in Memphis?

Well, I have since found out that there was. When I was based out of Abbey Road working with a lot of my heroes, I found out that they were all listening to the Stax records. They were also listening to the Sun things that were happening with Sam Philips of course. When we recorded "I'll Take You There", we were sitting there trying to be Jamaicans. Years later, I met Sly and Robbie and they said, "We were listening to Stax and The Staples, and trying to copy that!" I thought, "Wow, the world is so small in music."

When was the first time you worked with Jimmy Page? Was he in the Yardbirds at the time?

Simultaneous to all of this engineering, I was playing in bands. My band was opening on a tour that was called "The Dick Clark Caravan of Stars." On this tour, one of these acts was the Yardbirds. I immediately sought out Jimmy Page, because he was one of my idols. Eric Clapton had already left the Yardbirds, but Beck and Page were still there. Can you imagine that band with Clapton, Beck, and Page all in it at the same time? Good Lord!

Shortly thereafter, the Yardbirds did another tour and I saw them again. On this tour, just before I arrived, Jeff Beck had quit in a huff, just walked out. He had been playing lead guitar and Jimmy had been playing bass at the time. Keith Relf was singing. Anyway, I had just gone out to see them, and on the same day Jimmy had learned that he was going to have to take over lead guitar. This is hilarious now, but then, everyone was worried; "Is Jimmy going to be able to handle lead guitar?" And of course, we look now and say, "Yeah, he could handle it!"

Did he have the chops that night?

He did just fine. So I would hang out during two or three other shows when they were playing these mid-range colleges around nearby Kentucky; then they had to go to Memphis to fly to somewhere else. I said to Jimmy, "Instead of going with the band, would you just want to ride with me?" and he said "Oh, yeah." So we took off through the night, probably leaving at two or three in the morning and drove for three, four, five hours, whatever it was. We went straight to Ardent Studio in Memphis. I showed him around, I got out some guitars and amps and we did different things. The guitar he was playing was Beck's Esquire. I brought out one of my guitars, a '52 Telecaster. He played that and said "Oh, I love this. The action is great, I'll trade you Jeff's guitar for it, what do you think?" So I'm sitting here looking at it, going "Hmmm. Do I take Jeff's guitar? Do I keep mine?" So I finally decided it just wouldn't have been right. That cemented the whole friendship with Jimmy, and the whole relationship. He had seen Ardent Studio, knew what we had technically, and knew what we could do. I sort of introduced him to our whole scene in Memphis. We talked about Stax, and all these other things.

After he left, we corresponded quite a bit; I knew all about where the Yardbirds were touring and what was going on. He finally called and said "I'm tired of the Yardbirds, we're not going anywhere. I'm going to make a new group." He was going to name it "The New Yardbirds." In one tiny minute, he said "Maybe you could play keyboard and rhythm guitar." And I said, "I've got a good bass player here, too." I was just helping him think through options. But of course that wasn't going to really work out, and to be honest, I'm really not that good a player!

He of course ended up with the people he went with, which was a fairly good move! The first singer was another friend of mine, and a friend of Jimmy's, named Terry Reid. He was to be the singer in the New Yardbirds, later Led Zeppelin, but was not allowed to by his producer/manager, Mickey Most, who was one of the big producers around the London scene at that time. Terry was the one who suggested Robert Plant, who was a friend of his he had seen singing in another band, called the Band of Joy. That's where the Bonham and Plant connection came in.

Because Bonham was their drummer, right?

Yeah. It was again, the stars working the right way. Then, Jimmy decided he wanted to put a studio in just for them that they could also rent out in the U.K. I was asked by Jimmy to leave and go do that, so I began putting together equipment lists and everything. I finally decided that things were going awfully well at Stax/Ardent, so I said "No." He had looked at the figures and quite wisely also decided no, because a commercial studio wasn't going to be a big enough money maker, but rather more of a worry, because they were getting bigger and there was more touring. He did say, "Will you be available to engineer for us if I need anything done? Because we're beginning to record a second album, and there'll be more to come." I said, "Sure, anytime."

So Led Zeppelin was getting quite prolific by this time.

Yes. They were getting quite prolific and were moving pretty fast. So when they had done some recording on the third album, but not all of it, and had a tour booked to promote that album that was still unfinished, there was panic. Jimmy called up and said, "Can you help me finish this album while we tour?" And I said "Sure." So they came in to the old Ardent studio in between shows for short periods. We did everything we could to get the album finished on a crazy schedule. I actually mastered it myself locally. Atlantic never heard, saw or knew a thing about the record, until the pressing plants received the parts. They never heard a rough mix, a song, anything.

To me, that shows a lot of integrity that Led Zeppelin actually wanted to deliver the master parts themselves to the pressing plant.

When I did the mastering, I went to Jetton's mastering studio called Audiotronics in Memphis, and we locked the door. Jimmy, myself, and the engineer there who ran the equipment sat in there and did the whole thing. I inscribed the sayings on the grooves and then took the master parts. We found out how many Atlantic needed and boxed them up carefully for shipment to the plants. I put them in the trunk of John Fry's car and drove it to Nashville, where the last gig was on their tour, and hand-delivered them to Peter Grant, Led Zeppelin's manager, who then hand-delivered them to the plant. So it never even got outside of Led Zeppelin's domain at all. They were fanatical about it, and I think history has proven that was the right thing to do. They maintained their integrity all the way.

Did you actually record any of the basics for *Led Zeppelin III*, or was it mostly overdubs and vocal parts?

We recorded some tracking but not a lot. We did a lot of overdubbing and a lot of mixing.

John Bonham was a special drummer. Do you remember recording him?

All I can really think back to is that there was very, very minimal mic'ing. John was the master controller of everything. Any engineer could have sounded good with him, because he controlled everything. If the toms needed to be louder, they wouldn't mic them separately. He would play them louder. If something needed to be softer, he would play it soft. They were all masters at what they did in every way. Every one of them a complete genius to the nth degree, planning and doing everything they wanted to do, the way they wanted to do it.

That's interesting. One common theme in the recording world today, at least one that everyone agrees on, is that you must have a really good source. It seems like John Bonham was a pretty good source.

Exactly. Another example is "Since I've Been Loving You", which has one of my all time favorite rock guitar solos. That was all done on one take, on somebody else's amp which was just sitting around the studio from some other session. Jimmy just plugged a guitar in, there was no mic'ing "technique", no warming up. Just stick it in there, play it, go. He took a second take, but it wasn't as good as the first. No messing around with anything, no planning what you're going to play for days, just being a complete genius and master of what you do and doing the right thing once.

Can you tell me about the Beatles pressing mystery?

One day in 1967, there was a Stax session at the Ardent studio on National Street. The night before, I had been the last person to leave, as I often was after a session. Because I would not only do engineer work, I would also clean up the control room, sweep the floors, empty the coffee cups, help type out the bills. There were very few of us, and we all did everything. I left late at night, probably between midnight and 2:00 am, I'm guessing. As I always did, made sure the back door was locked, and walked out the front door so I could double lock the deadbolt. I turned around, gave it that one last "Is everything okay?" look; lights are all off as they need to be, everything is set for the night. I remember looking across the front desk, which would have encompassed my viewpoint. I remember nothing special being there, everything was as it always was.

I was also the first person to come in the next morning, except for our maid, who let herself in the back door. She would vacuum and do the things that she needed to do. As I came in the front door, I immediately saw an acetate disk inside one of those brown Kraft paper sleeves that they used to be in, sitting on the front desk, right in the middle of it; couldn't miss it. I remember immediately thinking "This wasn't here last night, what is this?" So I immediately asked the maid, "Did somebody come and drop this off? What is this? Something for the session?" She said "No, nobody came. Nobody left anything. The front door has been locked the whole time." I thought that was very odd; I know this was not here last night. I wanted to see what it was. It wasn't labeled, as I recall. But I knew I had to get the equipment on, get ready. It was about 10:00 am, something like that, maybe a little earlier. I knew I had to get everything ready for the session. There were a few tube things that needed to warm up, I had to make sure the gear was on, make sure that nothing broke during the night. So I quickly got all that done. Since no one was there yet, and we still had turntables in those days, I put this disc on. It started with an acoustic guitar playing, strumming. I thought, "This is odd, this is nothing I know. Doesn't sound like it's going to be a Stax thing." Then a voice started singing, "I read the news today, oh boy..." which of course we now recognize as "A Day In The Life" by The Beatles. It took me a verse or two before I thought, "Boy, this voice sounds familiar. This certainly has Beatle-esque quality to it. It sounds like John Lennon, but in no way did I immediately think "It has to be The Beatles," because it was way too far-fetched.

There were groups out there who had done Beatles knockoffs. There were people who could come fairly close for short periods. But this really didn't sound that Beatle-y, for it wasn't like their other music. I wasn't immediately sure of what it was. Then when the bridge came, and McCartney's voice came in, what I now know is McCartney's voice, "Woke up, got out of bed, dragged a comb across my head..." I thought, "Oooh, this is too Beatles."

Then the bell went off.

You could immediately hear that this was the Paul addition to this song. The piano comes in and takes over the chord changes to the different kind of thing he would do. So I just started thinking this sure sounded like The Beatles, but there could be no explanation why it was there. John Fry was the next person to come in before the session; I played it for him, explained where I found it. He was also completely bewildered by what it was, but agreed that it certainly sounded like the Beatles. Then Rick Ireland, our tech guy came in, and I played it for him. He was quite a sarcastic guy, and said, "There's no way it could be this, but it sounds like them a little bit."

The garden area just outside reception at Compass Point Resort. *Photo by Terry Manning*

So we're all pretty convinced by now that it's either the greatest knock off group we ever heard, or that it was The Beatles. John grabbed a reel of Sony quarter inch tape, wrote "Beatle" on the back and I dubbed the acetate to the tape. Then I took the acetate and hid it in John's bookshelf inside of a book cover. I then took the dub and locked it up in the tape vault. Finally, the session finished and I remember thinking, "Can't wait anymore, we're calling Abbey Road Studio. We're speaking to somebody and finding the truth about this."

I called information and got the phone number, which I still recall to this day; it was a name and four numbers. I called up Abbey Road, and the secretary answered the phone, and I explained the whole story. She was quite used to getting Beatle calls from fans who would call in from all over the world, asking to talk to Paul or George or Ringo, whatever, so she just immediately wanted to hang up. But I said "Please, please. I'm not a fan...well, I am a fan, but this is not a fan call. This is a professional studio, and I think I have a Beatles song that I shouldn't have." So she finally got someone from the Beatles organization on the phone. I explained it to him, and he just laughed and said "I'm sorry. The Beatles are recording and I believe you are a professional in a studio, but I don't think this is possible." So I said, "Okay, stand by." And I just sang "I read the news today, oh boy, about a lucky man who made the grade..." By the time I got to "lucky man", he said "Hold on." I kept holding and I could hear music and voices in the background. Then suddenly there was George Martin on the phone. I explained to him what was going on, and he said "There is no way. We are recording a new album, but there is no way you could have anything like this." So I again, boldly, and I wish I had a recording of this, I sang the song to him, my version of "A Day In the Life", and he just said "Oh my God. That is one of the new songs we have recorded just a few days ago."

And you had his attention.

Boy, did I have his attention! Now I have not spoken to Sir George about this, even though I have met him a couple of times since. To me, at the time, it was one of the biggest things that had ever happened to me, but to him it was probably just a minor inconvenience. It was like a fly and he had to swat it. I would be embarrassed because he wouldn't even remember it. It certainly, for the moment, was a big enough deal for him to just say "This is true and you should not have gotten this. How in the world did you get it?" And I had to say "I don't know how I got it." And he said, "Would you mind sending it back to me?" I said "I'll do my very best." We just hung up, befuddled about what could have gone on, not knowing how it could have happened.

Now I will say that the coolest thing was that in the background, I could hear a "thump thump thump," which was somewhat distinctive even then. I now know it was the tom thing on "Lucy in the Sky With Diamonds", when the time changes. So I was able to unwittingly listen in to a Beatles' recording session. Whether they were tracking it, or overdubbing the toms, or monitoring it, I'll never know.

The final part of the story is that when I went to get the acetate, it was gone. I asked John if he had moved it. He said "No." I told him "I put it in your desk, inside of a...I think it was a book on airplanes." So he pulled the book out and there was nothing in it and he said "No, I honestly didn't know where you put it, and it's not here now." We took every book out, we searched the bookshelf; it was gone.

That's truly mysterious.

John said then and he said later that he did not know where it came from or where it went. I do still have my tape copy. I've listened to it recently. It's still on there. It doesn't start like on the record, it's clean. On the record, there are sound effects that fade into it and this mix is not from the album.

Can you tell me about the Albert King guitar case story? I know you were a big fan of Albert's.

I had a friend who had a vintage guitar shop in Memphis in the '80s, and I would go over there quite a bit. I went in this store one day. He wasn't there, but the shop was being watched by his guitar tech, the guy that did all the repair work. I saw sitting out on the floor this beat up, old raggedy case. I immediately recognized it as a case for a Gibson Flying V, a unique guitar, with quite a distinctive shape. I just said "What is that case?" And he said, "Oh, that's Albert King's old guitar case. His trailer that he had was in a flood; he brought his guitar in for me to clean it up and get it fixed. The worst thing of it though was the case, which got the biggest damage. So I just decided since it was Albert King and I had an extra Flying V case in good shape here, I just decided to give him that case. So this is his old case there."

So a light went right off in my head. "Oh, well this old no good, beat up case, can I get this one then, because I need one." He said, "Well the owner's not here. I don't' know if it's for sale, I don't know what to charge." I said, "Come on, it's in terrible shape, but I'll give you fifty dollars for it." So he thought "He, he, well, okay!" So he took the fifty dollars, and I took the case and ran.

I immediately put this case in the control room where I was working. Well, things went really well that day and I thought that maybe the case had something to do with it. Since then, I've always kept the case in the control room. And I've always felt that it gives what I'll call a "mojo," or a "strange magic" to the place. I've worked with a lot of guitarists, and they always love to see this thing. A couple of them have cut off tiny pieces of the felt from the inside to worship it more or less as a shrine, because Albert King is one of the top five guitarists of all time. If it came to the feel category, he would be number one. He was a very special man, a special player, a great, great artist: a real blues man through and through.

One night, at my Studio Six, I was working with an artist named Otis Clay; the co-producer had played in Albert's live band at one time and was quite friendly with him. Albert liked my place, and would come by fairly often. One night, my friend and I were up there working late and this horrible noise happened. My friend thought that a 747 had flown in on approach at the airport at Memphis, and had gone just a few feet over the building. I said, "No, they don't fly that low. I think it's an earthquake. It was a big earthquake, or a thunderstorm, or something like that.

Something along the lines of a natural disaster.

It was loud. It happened again, and it was shaking the building! I said, "Earthquake. See?" So my friend said, "No, no, no. It's a physical sound." So we went downstairs, and

Compass Point's Studio B, set up for vocal and acoustic guitar overdubs. *Photo by Kim Touzeau, courtesy of Hummingbird Media*

Custom "Lucas" Tele guitar. Rare autograph by blues legend Albert King on the back. *Photo by Kim Touzeau, courtesy of Hummingbird Media*

then it happened again; it turned out that it was Albert beating on the back door trying to get in. He ended up coming in and hanging around a while. Then I got an idea: "Mr. King! Two things I'd like you to do. First, I'd like you to autograph a guitar of mine. He started shaking and I didn't understand why. I got a guitar and a Sharpie. I told him, I've got some very special guitars autographed over the years, but I would be most honored if I could have your autograph. So he autographed it, but he shook the whole time. My friend told me later, "You fool, he doesn't fully read or write." So I felt just awful. I'm so glad I got him to sign it now though, because Albert King's autograph is apparently a rare thing and I didn't know that.

Once that was over, I said, "Mr. King, I'd like to show you something. Come over here." And I walked him over to in front of the speakers where I kept it, and said "This is your old guitar case that your Flying V, Lucy, lived for all those many years as you traveled around playing. You got a new case, and I got the old one. Now, it has become an icon to us. I work with so many guitarists, some very well known, and they all worship this case. It makes everything in my studio work well. It makes productions go well. Without it, we would probably all fall apart. It is just an icon to all of us in this music. Believe it or not, whether you know it or not, we all worship you. We worship what you are. I am so thankful to have this, doing what it does now." And he looked down at it, and it all went in one ear and came out the other. He kicked it, pushed it open a little, and said "Yep, with a little glue and some tape, we could fix this thing right up and I could use it again...."

Let's move on to Compass Point, where you've been for nearly two decades. Can you tell me what is so special about the live room there?

It's one of those freaks of nature. In the older days, when this was designed in the late seventies, room design was a little more of a mystery, not science; it was as much luck, mystery or voodoo. This room sounds magical, and is unlike any other room I've recorded in before, because of the way it's all wood at this end. As you walk a few feet, the sound completely changes [we walk to where ceiling material and height changes and where there is carpet]. I've never seen a room do that. It's obviously the lower ceiling, the deader surfaces. Whatever they did, it works.

Was a "live end/dead end" a typical mentality then?

It wasn't really typical then. Usually, you just sort of had a big room and you moved around baffles and gobos to change things. For years and years, at other places, I would try to get the drum sound on "Addicted to Love". Turns out it was this room! Or I'd try to get the *Back In Black* sound, which was recorded right here. This room just allows a lot of flexibility, and the amazing thing that I found is that you can have a pretty big group in here and still have very little bleed. The isolation is quite good.

That's a very unusual looking iso booth.

Well, that was built for Mick Jagger by Glyn Johns. It was used on "Emotional Rescue". It doesn't really sound so good inside it, though; it's just for isolation.

What is Chris Blackwell's involvement in the studio now?

He is still the owner of the real estate, and with us in the business, and he's very interested. See this ball? This is a cricket ball that always sits on the desk where I work.

It seems like you're very superstitious.

It's just...for instance, REM were here recently. The very first thing they do on any session is to get out their two mascot dinosaurs and put them on top of the left and the right speakers. They've done this on every album they've ever made, and that's the last thing that gets packed up at the end of every session when all the gear gets packed. And they have a lot of gear. When you are in a room literally every day, often seven days a week for a minimum of twelve hours, you just have to have a little levity.

Mick Jagger himself specified this vocal booth inside Compass Point Studio A. *Photo by Kim Touzeau, courtesy of Hummingbird Media*

Can you walk me through some of the history here?

Well, in 1977, Chris Blackwell had a small house here on this very site, where he lived. He decided this would be a great place for a studio. He chose the Bahamas versus Jamaica because there were logistical considerations, as far as getting in and out, and because there were a few social problems in Jamaica that made it not as nice as some places to get out in public. He felt like this was more of a "world" place. So he put his studio here and it was immediately very successful with his groups, and with outside groups. Brian Eno, Brian Ferry all worked here. Bob Marley was in here several times, in fact there is footage of him in here in a video for "No Woman No Cry" in the live room, I believe.

Was there a craving for people to escape the metro recording malaise during that time?

Creative people love to get away. As much as recording artists might like their friends, they don't want them dropping in all day. So they get into a little enclave, a little cell that goes to work. In '78, Chris added on and built the second studio, Studio B. If there is mixing done, this has traditionally been the mixing room. That is because it has a fully automated SSL board, and SSL boards are so mix friendly. Bob Clearmountain mixes on this very model, which is a 4000. The board in Studio A, on which I mixed Lenny Kravitz' 5, is a Neve V3, fully manual. Mixing manually for me is not a problem.

Aside from mixing, we've done a lot of tracking in Studio B. A lot of Talking Heads and Roxy Music was done in here. Roger Waters has come quite a bit and has been here recently working on his most recent solo album. He also brought in the *Dark Side of the Moon* surround mix for the final tweaking and approvals. It was amazingly fun to sit with Roger Waters listening to *Dark Side of the Moon* off the master tape. He's a very, very nice guy and a good friend of ours.

What happened at Compass Point in the '80s?

The '80s was really the first heyday here. Groups came from all over the world, like The Rolling Stones. Robert Palmer moved here, lived here for fifteen years, did all of his work here. Mutt Lange was quite a client and brought in several projects including AC/DC's *Back In Black*. I would guess that is probably the biggest selling and most famous rock and roll album of all time. Mutt has also been here very recently working on his wife Shania's stuff.

When did the "valley" occur when things slowed down?

There was a valley at the end of the '80s. Alex Sadkin, who was the producer on one of the Foreigner albums, and the Thompson Twins, which he recorded here, was resident, and oversaw the whole thing. He was the one at the time who tied together the world to our little island. Sadly, he was killed in a car wreck coming home from an outing they had after a session one night.

This place desperately needs a conduit from the outside world to foster interaction between us and the outside world. When Alex died, there was no one here doing that tying together and overseeing things in a proper business and musical sense. Sessions stopped coming, equipment degenerated and the studio actually got a "not so good" reputation. For example, there was a David Bowie session that had lots of technical problems, and there wasn't anybody here who could adequately fix it. The session ended up leaving. To me, that has always been the lowest point in the valley.

In those situations, it is important to have the technical expertise, but most important is your client relations. It's a trust thing. I can look at them as someone who has been there and done that, and relate to them on that level and say, "Hey, sorry this has happened. We'll do this and this in x amount of time and be back on line."

When we came here in late '92, first of all, we had to rebuild the studio technically, because it had gone down in many ways. Secondly, we had to rebuild the reputation of it. And thirdly, we had to go from there and make a new future.

Were you the one that made all the technical recommendations?

Yeah, it was me along with other technical experts that we brought in. From a client relations perspective, it was my wife Sherrie and I; she is a real people person who has done several kinds of businesses; she really knows how to put all those kind of things together, so the two of us make a really good team.

The all-wood live area of Compass Point's Studio A. *Photo by Kim Touzeau, courtesy of Hummingbird Media*

To enhance the facility technically, we tore apart the SSL and completely refurbished it. We tore up equipment that was here and brought in a lot of new equipment. I brought in a lot of my own gear and stationed it here. We made things simple and got it all functioning properly. We looked at it aesthetically and said, "This is not the type of place that needs an ultra modern, chrome and glass, blue steel, fancy spaceship look. This needs to look like an island boat, kind of funky, kind of vibey," so we put new carpets, new wall treatments, left all the wood, left some of the wackiness that's here.

The echo chamber was also here, right? How much do you use this versus using outboard reverb plates?

I use it on everything. There is just nothing like it as far as outboard devices are concerned. I cleared some old stored stuff out of there, put up the mics, and was just [gasp!] blown away when I heard it. I just couldn't believe it. So now I use it on everything, always.

You've worked for so many years on so many different things, what still gets you fired up?

To me it is always the song first, then the artist. Studios are great, and I love working in this studio, the sound of it and the things we have, that's very important. But if you bring a junk song and a bad artist into this, you have nothing. Don't even bother.

Can you describe what it was like mixing Otis Redding's "Sittin' (on the Dock of the Bay). You mixed it just after Otis Redding had passed away, right?

It was unbelievable. One of the worst days in the studio...you would think if you were at the board with the master tapes for "Dock of the Bay" up and you were putting it down to stereo, you'd think that would be incredibly fun and exciting. First of all, the producer, co-writer, and also highly skilled engineer, Steve Cropper, was mixing too. He was Otis' close friend, the co-writer of the very song. He was the person who was as responsible as anyone else for discovering Otis Redding. He was the most torn up by all of it. It was absolutely brutal.

On a lot of sessions, I can remember perfect details. For example, in my mind, I can immediately think of the Al Green songs, remember what was on certain faders, the thought process that we went through, on listening back. But on "Dock of the Bay", there's nothing but a haze to me because there was this overriding factor. Just a few days earlier, I mean three to five days – it wasn't long at all after Otis' death. It's just something I can't even describe, an awful day.

Opposite end of live area of Compass Point's Studio A, where drums were recorded for AC/DC's *Back in Black*. *Photo by Kim Touzeau, courtesy of Hummingbird Media*

Compass Point's Control Room A, with Neve console. *Photo by Kim Touzeau, courtesy of Hummingbird Media*

You are a collector of many rare artifacts. Do you have anything else here I haven't seen?

I've got Robert Johnson's guitar. [Terry pulls out a black hardshell case, opens it up to reveal a brown dobro style guitar, never touching the guitar]. It's one of the two guitars he played that is known. I'm going to put it in the Robert Johnson museum. It's a 1930s wooden National resonator that I got in Mississippi from an old, old guy, probably around '84-ish, something like that. This guy, who was in his nineties, said that he had gotten it on loan from his friend "Bob Spencer" in Greenwood, Mississippi, who played a lot of clubs around there. Robert Johnson was known back then as Robert Spencer. He had died before he could give it back to him, so he left it under his bed all those years. The museum thinks it may be authentic, so I'm going to give it to them on loan. You can't play it really though, it's really no good for fretting, just slide now.

That's okay, Terry. Even though I'm not superstitious, I don't think I'd want to play it anyway.

A 1930s National wood body resonator guitar. Believed to have once been owned and played by Robert Johnson. *Photo by Kim Touzeau, courtesy of Hummingbird Media*

Compass Point's echo chamber, roughly modeled on BBC specifications. *Photo by Kim Touzeau, courtesy of Hummingbird Media*

Sunset at Compass Point. *Photo by Terry Manning*

Fireproof Recording

Adam Lasus, Owner

Front view of Fireproof Recording. Studio is in top right of picture. *Photo by Kim Touzeau, courtesy of Hummingbird Media*

Adam Lasus is the owner of Fireproof Recording, a studio built within Brooklyn's oldest firehouse located nearby the shipping docks of this old port city. Adam is one of rock's indie-music scene's pioneers, albeit away from the stage and behind the controls. His career began in Philadelphia, where through an incredible amount of hard work and determination he built up Studio Red where he recorded groups like Madder Rose, Versus, Helium, and many others. While other independent recording scenes blossomed in places like Seattle, Portland, and Athens, Adam became a magnet in the unlikely city of Philadelphia, where he attracted some of the most influential bands in the New York tri-state area as they passed through Philly's seminal Khyber Pass club.

On speaking with Adam, it is immediately clear that he has never compromised his principles. He has managed to create a profitable recording business entirely on his own despite significant adversities and setbacks, recording only music that he feels is emotionally appealing and groundbreaking. He has never sold out and it is a safe bet that he would not have remained in the business if he had not been able to record the way he has wanted to.

The best way I can describe Fireproof Recording is by comparing it to a palette of colors that a painter might use. For an imaginative band or musician, Fireproof provides a huge variety of options and pigments, with its huge collection of highly unusual and vintage instruments. If a band has the drive and ambition to create something great, Adam can help them put together the right colors, helping create the image.

Adam Lasus on the roof of Fireproof with The New York Dock Company and Manhattan in the background. *Photo by Kim Touzeau, courtesy of Hummingbird Media*

The facility itself retains its heritage as a firehouse, combining generous open spaces and ambient light. The two pole shafts remain intact along with the original eighteen-foot-high tin ceilings. The room has a very special ambience and sound, especially when it comes to drums. Lasus' 1960s vintage Ludwig kit, when combined with the right foot, produces a kick drum sound not unlike a cannon.

Let's start with your current set up. Can you describe the firehouse?

It's Brooklyn's first firehouse, built in 1880. It's not an official historical landmark, because the fire department in New York goes back another hundred years. They put the firehouse here because it was near the docks. The docks were either always on fire, or people were burning down their warehouses to collect insurance. It's got lots of 1800s craftsman-style accents like the pressed tin ceiling and skylights that let in natural light to all the rooms. I think people are really into the fact that it has all this natural light, making the studio feel airy and open.

Can you describe what your part of Brooklyn is like for someone who hasn't been there?

Well, it's in the movie *On the Waterfront*, down by the docks with all these weird warehouses. In fact, I am pretty sure they filmed it in this area. The area became really decrepit in the '70s and '80s, then in the mid-'90s it started to have a comeback. Warehouses began to be used as fabricating shops for Broadway, for example.

It sounds like you got in at a good time.

I did. There's a revitalization going on around here and all these coffee shops, diners, and French restaurants are popping up. It's much safer then it was in the '80s and early '90s. The proximity to Manhattan is excellent: you can take a cab from Manhattan and be here in ten minutes.

What kind of view do you have?

You can see the East River and Wall Street from my roof. I have access to the top where the fire towers were, and I can see a bunch of cranes for the container ships. I used to be able to see the Trade Center right from my control room. I was at home when 9/11 happened, and when I came here the next day there were pieces of paper with identifiable writing on it. It was really frightening and I was freaked out. There were fragments of floppy disks, pieces of paper, and family photographs. It was heartbreaking, because they just flew right over.

That's really sad. 9/11 impacted us all in so many ways. Can you take me back a little and tell me about how you got into recording?

In high school, just like almost everyone else who is involved in this business, I was in a band and was the designated guy that had to learn how to use the 4-track. At the time, I learned a lot about bands and about working a 4-track by watching my cousin's band, Miracle Legion, in Connecticut. I went out and bought a Porta One and some Shure SM58's when I was fifteen.

So this ignited your interest in a basic sense.

Yeah. Even when I was in high school I can remember going to bands' rehearsal spaces with my 4-track and various weird gear that I had collected, helping bands do demos. I was way more into recording than anything else, so I decided not to go to college and instead tried to forge some kind of rock and roll existence following high school. My dad was cool because while I was still living at home, he let me take a couple rooms that we had on the third floor next to my bedroom and let me turn it into a little studio. I saved up and bought some basic equipment, and ultimately got my career started as a producer/engineer.

So your dad gets a lot of credit right out of the gate.

Yeah, no question, he was great. Then my own band got signed to a label that was part of Studio 4 in Philadelphia, and I was able to hear what a world-class studio sounded like, with a Neve console and Studer recorder. This made me want to push my own gear harder at my 8-track home studio. The fact that my first and second studios operated out of my house was a great thing for me; I could easily set the tone for a fun and vibey session. From the beginning, I always charged a day rate and still do so clients don't have to stress out about a track taking too long or going another hour to get something else down on tape.

Where do things go after the bedroom scene?

Well, I eventually started working out of my apartment near South Street in Philly. I called it Studio Red. It was a small basement studio but had an amazing drum sound, with rock walls and a concrete floor. Bands were coming in from Boston and New York by word of mouth, and the stuff I was doing sounded like a big studio, but at a nominal rate of $250 per day. One November however, I had a massive flood. A water main broke and filled the entire basement with four feet of water. Luckily it was clean water. I almost electrocuted myself trying to save tapes and move gear to higher ground.

Did you lose a lot of gear?

I lost a lot of instruments and drums. The water was there for two or three days and eventually my gear just drained. I brought it all to this tech guy that I used in Philly, and he said "The water was so clean, we're just going to clean things up and turn it back on." And almost every piece worked. Every once in a while I have a scratchy pop that I hear and it reminds me of the November flood.

Following this setback, I ended up getting a larger space in Philadelphia, on 3rd and Cherry. I called it Studio Red also. It had some remnants of the '70s Studio that had been there and it ended up being really nice. Kind of like the "Fort Apache" of Philadelphia. It was a predominant indie/alternative place to record, and became a really exciting place for me to work.

What recording formats were you on at this point?

I was using 1" 16 track format, therefore was kind of constricted because bands that had 2" tapes couldn't come to me, and I couldn't track drums and give people 2". But it was the era where ADATs started to pop up, and people didn't really care what format it was in, as long as it sounded good. And I'd really mastered squeezing a lot of sound out of that Soundcraft console and 1" deck [laughs]! It was frustrating because I did want bigger gear, but we couldn't quite afford the jump.

One thing that distinguishes you is that you were very selective about the kinds of things you wanted to record.

I lucked out in that I was really close to Khyber Pass in Philadelphia, so I was constantly going to see bands and be-

A few of the 40+ guitars available to the artists at Fireproof. *Photo by Kim Touzeau, courtesy of Hummingbird Media*

came confident enough to say "Hey, you guys are great. I did the new Helium and Versus records and I'm just around the corner if you want to check out my studio." I probably had two or three or four bands a week coming to look at the studio who were out of town and from all over the country. It helped broaden my whole spectrum and made me feel that I could branch out from Philadelphia.

You had a good reputation in Philly. Why would you want to "branch out"?

Well, the studio started to become more and more like a "commercial facility," which I started liking less and less. My relaxed, fun vibe was getting harder to keep up. Plus, I was beginning to feel overworked and overwhelmed at times by the pressure of co-running a business that supported many people. At the same time, I was becoming increasingly drawn to New York City.

Was there a scene in New York that you felt particularly drawn to?

Well, I had many friends in New York City, so I took a break and went to record in some studios there with a band called the Godrays. I became excited by the whole scene and could see myself possibly freelancing; I wasn't sure. In a bizarre way, this was when Studio Red was at its highest commercial peak.

Maxed out?

And I killed it. I was like, you know what? I'm not having a good time, it has gotten to the point where I would go to a local bar, and bands that I didn't want to record would harass me. They'd be like "You're too good to record us, huh?" After a couple of beers, I'd be like, "If you guys practiced more and wrote some catchier tunes maybe I would do it." Even though I was being brutally honest, this was perhaps not my best political move.

It sounds like you were experiencing growing pains and just needed to get out of Philly for a change.

I think so. So I moved to New York with all my gear and put it in a friend's loft in the summer of '96.

Racks of compressors, eq's, preamps, and effects in the control room. *Photo by Kim Touzeau, courtesy of Hummingbird Media*

A big risk?

Totally. It was tremendously frightening because I only had enough money to get an apartment. I had all my stuff in storage with the intention of doing freelance stuff, but quickly realized I wouldn't be able to make ends meet this way; especially in '96 when the shit hit the fan in the industry and things were really going bad. The big studios were just starting to fold then, a trend that has now become even more rampant than ever. I was feeling like, "Maybe this isn't the best time to be doing this."

I would show these studios my discography with Juliana Hatfield, Madder Rose, and all these indie bands that people in my circle really revered. But they were like, "Well, you can make coffee." And I thought, "I'm not going to start that far down on the ladder this time." [Laughs.] So I was living in this neighborhood, Cobble Hill, and I stumbled upon an ad on the main street in a realtor's window, saying "Firehouse for rent."

Fireproof logo. *Photo by Kim Touzeau, courtesy of Hummingbird Media*

Were you aggressively looking at this point, or were you just poking though papers?

Well, the going rate for a commercial space in Manhattan was $10,000 per month, and I couldn't swing that. I was just sort of wandering around, trying to figure out what to do. Once I saw the ad, I was intrigued. It's an old firehouse that has two main huge doors on the front for the trucks and horses, and then two kinds of living quarters above the main areas. I ended up renting one quadrant of the firehouse, about 2,600 square feet. It's directly above where the first set of engines and ladders were.

What kind of condition was the space in?

It was a little beat up and needed some paint, but it had this whole cool old vibe of firehouse and wood floors. It had an

Brooklyn Bridge; get one free with every session booked at Fireproof. *Photo by Kim Touzeau, courtesy of Hummingbird Media*

Photograph of Fireproof exterior circa 1870 with horses pulling the fire wagon. *Photo courtesy of Fireproof Recording*

original pressed tin ceiling from the 1800s, and was one giant room. At the end of this giant room was an office with lots of windows, perfect for a control room. When I saw it, it was only $1,000 bucks. I found every cent I had, because I had to lay out a single big chunk to secure it. I thought "I've gotta have this place or the creative part of my brain will go soft."

So you jumped right on it.

The combination of having all my gear in somebody's spot, being desperate to have my own place, and realizing that I was almost starting to lose my own identity made me jump on it. Then a slightly nightmarish situation occurred.

I had signed a lease that said I could make noise 24-7. About two weeks into doing some drums to test the room, my neighbor came in and said, "It's awfully loud in here...what are you doing?" He saw all my gear and said, "What is all this stuff?" I said, "Well, I have a recording studio." He says, "Well, I live next door. You can't have a recording studio here." And I was like, "I have a lease." He said, "I've known the landlord for twenty years, and you can't do this. My wife gets up at 7:30 in the morning."

Is this the beginning of the soundproofing phase?

I panicked and I said "I just had enough money to get in and get the place. Can you give me a couple of months to soundproof it?" They were kind of cool, and said, "Well if we can set up some kind of curfew, whatever." So I kept saving money, but still didn't have enough. I finally got a call from the landlord saying, "Hey, it's July. You have thirty days to soundproof, otherwise you'll have to go because the neighbors are complaining and it's really bad."

So this was a lot of pressure. You must have felt your world coming down.

It was insane, so I called my dad right away. He's a sculptor/general contractor, and had actually designed two other studios for people in their apartments. He helped me

The live room at Fireproof. *Photo by Kim Touzeau, courtesy of Hummingbird Media*

This Stephen Keane mural was given to owner Adam Lasus by Mary Lorson of Madder Rose. *Photo by Kim Touzeau, courtesy of Hummingbird Media*

make an iso room and also tuned the room to the exact frequency required to develop the low end properly. You can hear the note [pounds wall to the sound of a resonant, low frequency thud]. That's the note needed to keep the low end from building up and causing standing waves. It's a bass trap that goes back about three feet, and the low end waves actually go in there and get stuck. They don't come out.

Last year, a new neighbor moved in, and they don't care about the noise. The drums are back out in the big room and now I have this great iso room for guitars and vocals [laughs]! It has all worked out great, especially the control room.

Can you describe your control room?

The control room is all natural light; I have giant windows, and it's bigger than most control rooms in New York, since real estate is such a hard thing to get there. It's really nice having windows and knowing what time it is outside. Unfortunately, sometimes I see the sun coming back up in the morning [laughs], but for the most part it's just great to see. I can open up the windows and get some real air. In both of my old studios, I was like a "cave dweller" for the most part.

Can you describe what the main room looks like now that you've settled in?

Well, I have this huge Stephen Keane mural hung on one of the walls, given to me by my friend Mary Lorson of Madder Rose. He's done several things, including covers for Pavement and The Apples in Stereo. He's the "indie rock artist", and I do a lot of indie rock bands in here, so the mural fits particularly well.

It's really comfortable in here.

Yeah, and it's deliberate. Every time I went to another studio, it felt like a hospital. It was like, "Where do I put my drink down?" "Am I allowed to put my feet up on something?" I tried to create a home studio vibe combined with the gear and space of a bigger pro studio.

What's amazing to me is that you've had some very significant challenges and hurdles, yet you've remained just as passionate and driven as you ever were. A lot of other people would have said "enough already".

Well, it was tough. The first year here, in addition to having that soundproofing fix, business wasn't really great. At Studio Red, I built it up to be eight or nine hundred a day facility with my producer fees. When I started here, I was lucky

The control room at Firehouse features a Neotek Elan console. *Photo by Kim Touzeau, courtesy of Hummingbird Media*

to get two or three a day. The industry had just bombed out and it was a bad time for indie labels and bands. I am so glad indie music has made a big comeback.

I guess it's all a big cycle that comes and goes. Hopefully it comes more than it goes.

Exactly. You have to kind of wait it out. There are definitely days when I'm running the studio all alone, thinking "I'm out of my mind doing this." And like many other people in this business, I'm definitely a workaholic. I work twelve, thirteen hours a day because it's just me.

You're really putting a lot of yourself into it.

It's really important to me that at the end of every day, people leave here psyched about what they did; it's not my problem if bands have a bad day, but it sort of is. I don't want things to go badly. I don't want someone to leave not having sung the vocal tracks that feel right. I work hard so that everyone has a good time and leaves with a good vibe. Fortunately, that's what's sort of kept me going and kept people coming back.

I just turned thirty-six and I feel that I'm doing better work than I've ever done in my whole career. It's funny; I go back and listen to records I did on my little Soundcraft thing and a 1" deck and I think, "What was I even doing recording on that stuff? What was wrong with me?" At the same time, I realize that nothing was wrong with me. That was the gear that I had, and it was all about capturing a vibe and getting records made so people can listen to them.

It sounds like with Fireproof, you now have everything you need to make the sounds you're after.

I have a great set up that works for my clients. I have a really good old Ludwig kit. I don't need to spend more than fifteen or twenty minutes on the drum sound. I know this room, I know the kit, I know which mics sound best. That's a huge relief to the band, where your actually creating music within two or three hours instead of "It's 9:00 pm and you're still working on the kick drum." I also have many vintage guitars, amps, and pedals that are a big part of the sounds I get.

What are some of the more unusual pieces of gear you own?

Fireproof is like a playground for musicians. Have you ever seen the Optigan? The toy company Mattel made this in the '70s to compete with the Hammonds. You'd buy all these cheesy discs and they all have different sounds on them. You take these twelve inch, clear discs, like records, but optical. It has a sample that goes around and around, giving you all these crazy rhythms and things. The whole way you control tempo is that you speed the motor up, so as you change key, you change the tempo. The best thing is that you can put it upside down, and everything plays backwards. When band members become restless, I set them up with the Optigan for hours of entertainment.

How would you describe Fireproof's "sound"?

There's always been this low-fi/hi-fi thing coming out of my studio. I tend to attract people who are into different sonic concepts because I don't want to make records that are too straightforward or that sound like every other record. I try to imagine myself a member of the band, to hear the record how they would want it to sound. I think there is a discernable sonic imprint I hear when listening to records I have done.

Are the bands that are coming in being financed by themselves, or from indie labels? Where are your clients currently coming from?

It'll be the bands, the management or small labels, which you're now seeing more of. I haven't had work from a major label in quite some time, and I kind of enjoy it in a weird way: no nervous industry folks around saying they don't hear a single! It would be nice to have the super big budgets, but there is more artistic freedom all around when people are putting out their own records or are on indie labels.

Also, I tend to get a lot of bands coming to me just to mix with stuff that they have tracked on computer; they know they need a real console like my Neotek Elan so we'll run the tracks through compressors and dial in some vintage analog EQ and I'll mix to my Studer A-80 deck, which is a key part of my sound. All those Fleetwood Mac, Clash, and Zeppelin records were mixed down to half inch Studers.

Who have been your favorite artists to work with?

I really enjoyed working with PJ Harvey, who was super focused and very hands-on. She knew exactly what sounds she wanted and that made it fun and easy to keep things rolling. I also love working with Chris Harford, who got signed to Elektra and brought me up to Bearsville to work on the *Beheaded* record. Chris is very spontaneous and always strives to get the vibe on the first take much like Dylan or Neil Young.

Does it feel like a good time now, in terms of the industry and the interest level in your work?

I guess the emergence of the Internet and the revolt against all the giant record companies has ultimately been a benefit to me. People are now putting out records by themselves and there's definitely a huge influx of new bands just getting into it.

I always wonder how someone like you, working such long days, is able to find the time to keep up with everything else that's going on out there in terms of bands, trends, and everything else.

Adam holding a disc for an Optigan, one of the more unusual instruments in his studio. *Photo by Kim Touzeau, courtesy of Hummingbird Media*

In a crazy way, I owe a lot of it to the iPod. There's always a member in the band that says, "Hey, can I play you a couple things on my iPod?" And it opens up this whole discussion and educates me on things I've never heard of. Also, with the advent of *Tape Op* magazine and its related conventions and web board I feel like I am part of a community of bands, engineers, and producers.

Are you still a musician? Do you write any of your own music?

Yeah. I've been writing music for film and television. Most recently I did about fifteen instrumental songs with some friends of mine for the TV show "Queer Eye for the Straight Guy". They were looking for fun fast indie rock or new wave stuff. It all ends up in scenes while they're shopping or they're getting their hair done. It has been great to get on the other side of the glass. I hit record, run into the cutting room, grab my bass and rock out with my friends.

What is the process for all of these songs? You're not going to 2" are you?

Well often I go right into the computer for that stuff but always use the 2" 24 track for albums. Since it's just going against dialog, they don't always want it so hi-fi sounding or too warm. I actually gave them the rough mixes, and then I gave them the final mixes. They said "the final mixes are way too big." Now they want us to make more straight ahead sounding stuff, because some of our tunes were sounding too indie and too cool. They wanted some cheesy '80s stuff like Huey Lewis and the News and I had to say "I can't! You'll have to get it somewhere else!" [Laughs.]

Do you see yourself doing any more work like this?

Yes, absolutely. I've also done music for HBO, IFC, and Sundance and would love to do more.

This originally served as a fire tower from which firemen would be on the lookout for fires in Red Hook, Brooklyn. *Photo by Kim Touzeau, courtesy of Hummingbird Media*

The iso booth, with direct view into the control room, was designed by Adam's father. *Photo by Kim Touzeau, courtesy of Hummingbird Media*

Helioscentric Studios
Heidi Miller, Owner;
Chris Difford, Artist

Helioscentric is housed in an old barn on a farm near Rye, England. *Photo courtesy of Helioscentric Studios*

Helioscentric Studio is located on the south coast of England, nearby a town called Rye. The property itself is secluded on a working farm at the edge of a forest, accessible by a two-mile long private road: you wouldn't know it was there unless you knew which road to take. The town of Rye itself is a tourist attraction, an ancient walled city that has suffered many invasions by the French since its original settlement by the Romans in the twelfth century.

The history of the Helios recording console is nearly as illustrious. Dick Swettenham was a maintenance engineer at the famed Olympic Recording Studio in London during the early seventies when his employer was considering purchasing an expensive new recording console. Swettenham raised his hand and said, "If you pay for the parts, I can build a console that sounds exquisite, better than anything you can buy." He did; in fact it sounded so good, that he was approached by Island Records to build seven of them for their own studios. Swettenham left Olympic and started his own company, Helios. Many artists in the '70s ultimately used Helios consoles in their own studios, including The Rolling Stones, 10cc, and Eric Clapton.

The genesis of Helioscentric Studios itself goes back to 1996, when Chris Difford of Squeeze located a rare, original Helios recording console for sale while at Alvin Lee's home. Not one to pass up a good opportunity, he called his friend Elvis Costello, who purchased the board and acquired a set of other Helios modules, all of which were combined to make a 32 channel Helios desk. It was subsequently repaired and rebuilt, and ultimately installed into Heidi Miller's barn in Rye, located on a secluded farm only five miles from the coast.

Helioscentric was originally conceived as a studio that would serve the needs of Squeeze, Chris Difford being one of the group's principal writers. It was also going to be used as an in-house recording vehicle for Elvis Costello's Demon Records. Once it was built, however, Helioscentric's reputation as a sonic hideaway quickly spread beyond the quaint farm in Rye in which it was situated.

Soon, Heidi Miller, who lived on the farm with her family, dogs, and horses, unwittingly became the owner of one of the most sought after funky music studios in England. She quickly adapted to her new lifestyle as a business owner, playing host to fantastic groups like Keane who soar above the ever present mediocrity in music today. In fact, they recorded their masterpiece *Hopes and Fears* entirely at Helioscentric. For Heidi, owning a studio is a very personal affair and her ultimate goal is to make her artists feel like they are part of the family.

Detail photo of the studio's original Helios console, which was completely rebuilt to original specifications. *Photo courtesy of Helioscentric Studios*

Helioscentric's live room, where Keane recorded its *Hopes and Fears* album. *Photo courtesy of Helioscentric Studios*

Iso booth at Helioscentric. *Photo courtesy of Helioscentric Studios*

Heidi, first, can you tell me how Helioscentric evolved and how you became involved?

It originally started off as a glorified home studio. I have the house and the barn here, and we've converted it. We've made it into a studio. Originally, it was just because the Helios desk came up, which was in a terrible state. We bought some more bits of the Helios desk, but they came in all these boxes that had been in somebody's shed for years. It was just going to be really for Squeeze to make an album, and also for Elvis to make an album, and then it was to be recouped.

This was eight years or so ago?

Yeah. The idea was that if you recouped, you saved on that and your friends and family could use it. At the time, Elvis [Costello] had Demon records, so Demon artists could use it. It was a funky place, and it wasn't going to be a business that was too intrusive to my home life, because I had kids and all the rest here. It was just going to be this fun idea.

So of course it all got rewired, it didn't all work properly, and it was very unreliable. Then somebody else came along and cut all the wires and said that the engineering was crap and started it all again. It just became a bottomless pit.

Adding to the difficulty was the fact that there are only about seven or eight of these Helios desks in the world and presumably not many technicians that know it?

Yes. I'm not even sure there's that many left. I think there's only two left in Europe. There are a couple in the States, a couple in Japan maybe? I don't know.

And what was your level of interest in owning a studio in general when all of this transpired? You mentioned you already had a family life and so on. Did you know much about recording studios?

I wanted it to be an indoor swimming pool [laughs]! Well, in my original background, 300 years ago, I was a makeup artist. I did hair and make up, wardrobe and fashion, and I went to the States a lot. I also went on tour with bands a lot, hence meeting Chris. I think I did three American Squeeze tours before we got together. As for my interest in studios, from the technical side at least, it's about two percent?

But now this has become a full fledged business.

Yes. I'm in partnership with Elvis Costello, and it has become my business. Actually, I'm really pleased to be a studio owner now.

What I find incredible is how low Helioscentric has flown on the commercial studio radar so to speak, despite having recorded so many wonderful artists such as Keane and Supergrass.

Well, places like Rockfield will match my price, and they can probably even do it cheaper than I can, but I really struggle to make it work for these guys. And the reason producers want to come here is because I'm here, and I am mom. I look after them and they get something very different here than from any other studio. I've got kids running around, I've got dogs running around, I've got horses running around, it's just...people become part of the family. So when these guys are away from home, they get invited into our life. You have to fit in, otherwise it doesn't work.

It sounds like a really warm, kind of more intimate experience.

It's great. People come back and if I like the band, they get invited for supper in the house. The house is a fourteenth century house, and it's fun. It's a bit shabby chic I would probably say. There are lots of people and dogs. Everyone feels really comfy and hangs out; that's how I run the studio. So really, since Chris and I split about three years ago, I had to make a living. I had the studio there, so that was it, really.

Can you describe what Rye is like and the environs of the studio? Is there anything special about the region?

Rye is a lovely old medieval town that sits up on a hill; it's walled. We're actually just across the channel. Rye is right on the coast and its thirty miles to France. For me, it's quicker to go to Paris than it is to go to London.

The mural in Helioscentric's iso booth features an abundance of books, not unlike the studio itself. *Photo courtesy of Helioscentric Studios*

Helioscentric's control room, with plenty of light and plenty of vibe. *Photo courtesy of Helioscentric Studios*

Really?

Yeah, on the high speed link, through the channel tunnel. And we've been invaded by the French forever and ever. It's a very pretty little town, very quaint. Americans love its cobbled streets. I'm actually on a working farm, a mile off the main road. So you come down a very long driveway, through woods, and it's an old farmhouse and this old barn. It's a smallish farm, 600 or 650 acres [**author's note: smallish?**] and it has wheat, potatoes, and rape.

Can you walk me through when the conversion of the barn took place after you purchased the Helios desk?

Well, Chris found the desk, which was Alvin Lee's. It's got this history of being left with ex-wives [laughs]! Which is fine, you know, if it keeps the business going, it's great fun. I had a very small baby at the time, and I really thought it was a mad thing to do, but I thought "Maybe I'll just go with the flow here." I decorated it, but really left the boys to do the technical side.

So there were people coming in and out, fitting the acoustics and all that?

Well, the acoustics are very basic. Like, there aren't any!

Is your studio particularly suited for a certain genre of music? Is the booking still done through word of mouth?

This oil and canvas rendering of the studio hangs inside the control room. *Photo courtesy of Helioscentric Studios*

Definitely. We don't even have a website anymore, because the company that was actually running it for us went bust. Things just come through by word of mouth. I do really try to choose my acts that come down here, because as I've said before, it is a family environment. I choose my producers and also my bands very carefully. Now that I've got a teenage daughter and little ones, I just have to have the right sort of people here.

The studio features rare instruments, including Steve Naïve's grand piano from The Attractions. *Photo courtesy of Helioscentric Studios*

You need to make sure the personalities fit right.

And I would rather it be empty, because people spill out of the studio. We've got loads of natural daylight; there are windows and doors everywhere. Generally, I have to hear the bands because, especially in the summer, everyone opens doors and windows and spills out into the lawn, so they become part of my life. And since I'm out in the sticks and I don't see anyone, they're my entertainment [laughs]! They come down here to make an album, I'm being paid for it and I'm being entertained for five or six weeks. That's how it works.

I'm very careful of who I have down here, because of the hours that they want to work, I generally like proper bands that have proper songs. Most of the people that want to work with analog tape and a Helios desk want that sort of thing as well.

The few pictures that I've seen of the facility look gorgeous. Maybe you could walk me through some of the décor and give me a visual tour of what it looks like?

Sure. Well, we kept the outside looking just like a barn because of planning permissions. It's still got the old metal windows that were originally there, a big green sliding door and a stable type door.

So you've preserved the old look and feel of the barn.

From the outside, it still looks exactly like a barn, but it has been converted. We didn't want people wandering down and thinking there's a recording studio down here, especially if we've got someone famous here. That's the last thing you want. So we really wanted to preserve our privacy and that was part of it.

Was there a hayloft?

No, it's a single story barn. The control room actually has normal level ceilings in it. You walk straight in and there's a gallery of red walls. We've got big red velvet drapes, mad old antique mirrors, and the fantastic old Helios desk in there, which is beautiful and classic. Then you go through into the live room, which is all strip pine all the way up into the roof, with all the old beams. In there we've got Steve Naïve's original grand piano in from the Attractions, Elvis' original group, which is really lovely.

You can have a whole band play in there for middle money; we're not the Abbey Road type money at all, it's very cheap! You can get a whole band, they can all play together, and it sounds fab. There's an old Hammond B3, a harpsichord, and I've got all sorts of other little keyboards that have been collected and left. Then I've got a funny little booth down one end that has all red velvet drapes. Finally, there's a mural all over the wall that's all about books. It's quite a nice little thing; people write names on the book spines, whatever they want to call them. The whole place is covered in books; I think there are about 4,000 of them.

The iso booth, with its selection of vintage Fender, Mesa Boogie, and Marshall amps. *Photo courtesy of Helioscentric Studios*

There are built in shelves that go top to bottom?

Yeah. There are books everywhere, and that is our acoustic treatment. We also salvaged old doors and pieces like that. There's also a little kitchen area, a little TV, a little old dresser. There's just more and more crap like little old radios, and the first TVs. I've got an old Beatles tea set up on the dresser.

Is it ever done, or are you always thinking about a new way to decorate it? Is it where you want it to be?

It just has evolved, really. I have to clear stuff out. Every band that comes down finds me something, like a Xylophone. Then you end up with too much stuff. I did actually have to clean out not that long ago because it was getting to be a bit much.

In addition to its 32 input Helios console, the studio features other Helios mixers that can be used for preamps and further signal processing. *Photo courtesy of Helioscentric Studios*

What are some of the more special sessions that have occurred there over the years?

Well, there's so many. Supergrass was fantastic. They did their *Life on Other Planets* album here. They are great because their work ethic is so poor but their fun factor is superb; they were so naughty and we had so much fun. I'd wake up in the middle of the night and they're pissed on the kids' trampoline. One night they bought hundreds and hundreds of fireworks. They were very naughty. And the kids had so much fun with them.

They had a top ten hit single called "Grace", which was written all about my oldest daughter because they were inspired by her. For her, that was a really special moment seeing them on Top of the Pops playing a song which was all about us. The lyrics to that song capture the whole vibe of the studio; just listen to them and you'll realize what it's all about. We went off driving down the farm in a four wheel drive; I've got a horse and carriage as well and I picked them up and we just hung out.

Supergrass wrote and recorded its top single "Grace" for Heidi Miller's daughter. Pictured is a coin bank presumably inscribed with "Save Your Money." *Photo courtesy of Helioscentric Studios*

Entryway to control room. *Photo courtesy of Helioscentric Studios*

Chris mentioned he was working on a new jazz album. Are there any other particular genres that you have recently attracted to Helioscentric?

Well, strings sound really fantastic here. People have come down and done strings. I've never done a classical album down here but I can see that it would work. Keane are back in next month. Their *Hopes and Fears* was a very, very special album.

Yes. It sounds fantastic and is being played all over in the states at the moment.

Andy Greene was the producer on that, and it was almost his first album. He said, "I really hated you Heidi, because you kept saying 'Well, what else have you done?'[laughs]." The boys from Keane actually walked down the driveway in the rain one day and I had just taken one of my dogs to the vet and she'd just been put down. I felt so miserable, and these guys just walked right down, having no idea obviously how far it was. I thought, "Oh, they're my band that are coming down," so I just waved them.

They finally came into the studio and I made them a cup of tea. The heat wasn't on, and it had been a mess because I hadn't cleared up from the last session and there was something very special about the whole thing. It sounds a bit mad, but even Andy Greene said something special happened there. He was actually very complimentary to me the other day, he said, "That session wouldn't have happened without you. You made everyone so comfortable and they [Keane] were really nervous; it was their first record and the label was really pushing them."

It sounds like it felt very natural and unguarded.

Keane are very lovely, lovely men. They're very shy, very reserved. Andy and Tim, the main songwriter, really worked very well together; they were very creative together. They would bring the best out in each other, which was fantastic. It was just a really great session and I told them I'd actually forgo my studio fee and have a point on their album." And they laughed and said "Yeah, yeah, yeah." And I said, "No, seriously, I would."

That's sweet.

Yes. Four million units later, I really wish I did [laughs]!

How exciting was it to get your first number one record? I know you had a few top tens, right?

I have. Keane's *Hopes and Fears* as an album has done so well. I mean it's really great for me, because not being with Chris and having the kids, one of my kids turned around and said, "Um, Mom, I'm really proud of you." That was special.

Obviously, running a studio, you're only going to earn x amount, because there's only so many studio days you can do, and you can only have a fee of so much. So I have a limited income, but I live in one of the most beautiful parts of the country. My kids are really happy, the property's great, and I'm doing it on my own.

The fact that you are running the studio and raising a family simultaneously is incredible to me.

I joke and say "My kids are my entertainment", but my kids are meeting really lovely people. I'm never going to make a fortune out of it but I'm living very comfortably. Sometimes it's really hard work, but it is good fun.

Do you ever have time to do anything else, or is it always full on with the studio and the family?

I don't have much time. I've got horses, and the kids are my downtime. They're very sporty kids. They swim at a national level. It never stops here and there's always something going on.

Where would you like things to go in the next few years for the studio's evolution? Is it kind of self-evolving?

I think it is. My kids are a priority. As you say, it's very hard to juggle a family and a full time business. I can only have so many days in the studio, therefore I would rather have really decent bands and creative sessions. I want people to have a lovely time here, rather than experience all the angst that often happens in studios; all the egos. I generally don't have any of that because I don't allow it. Even the kids don't tolerate it. When someone starts throwing their weight around, demanding this and that, the kids go "Nah! Not here!" [laughs].

It just doesn't fly.

It's not the sort of place where you're going to be able to say, "Oh, tonight I want sushi, or tonight I want this," because you're really out in the sticks and can't get that sort of stuff.

Chris Difford

Chris, when did you first get the bug to record?

I guess the recording bug for me, if you're talking about the studio, came when I first moved to the country and realized that I had access to a barn that could be utilized and made into a studio. And I just put some imagination into it and thought, well what would be really nice is if I could record at home and I wouldn't have to go anywhere else; because before that, I've never really been that interested in recording.

So when you were with Squeeze all those years, while you were touring extensively and working hard on the road, you never took an interest in recording from a technical and engineering perspective?

No, that was more something that Glenn enjoyed. Glenn really enjoyed being in the studio and I would get kind of bored with it, to be absolutely honest. I couldn't think of anything more boring than trying to figure out how a studio works. And to be absolutely honest, I still feel that way [laughs]. You know, I'm good at the ideas, and I get an engineer to work with, because they're good at what they do! I can't do all of it.

Kitchen area at Helioscentric. Note the book collection, memorabilia, and artifacts.
Photo courtesy of Helioscentric Studios

How active are you these days writing and playing? Obviously you're a very gifted lyricist and I'd be interested to know of your recent endeavors.

I'm writing lyrics all the time. I'm just working on a new album as we speak and I'm very happy with that; it sort of going in the jazz neighborhood, which is something that I've never done before. So the studio has been great for that, because I can get all the musicians in there and it's a great environment to work in because of its size. I don't know if you've ever seen James Taylor's video about him making an album in a studio near where he lives...

Martha's Vineyard, I think?

Yeah. I mean that's where I got the inspiration for my studio, really. I thought, wow, that's a great idea to be recording a record in an atmosphere that's very poetic.

Can you tell me how it sort of evolved? What was going through your mind as you put the idea together?

Well, I was recording a record in Alvin Lee's studio and one day his wife came in and said that they were splitting up and that she was selling everything. And she said, "Do you want to buy the desk?" and it was an old Helios desk; which is pretty rare, not many of them around. So I put my hand in the air and said, "I'll buy it." I didn't have any money, so I contacted Elvis Costello, who is a friend of mine, and he bought it. But he didn't have anywhere to put it.

Tell me a little bit about the barn. I imagine it had to be retrofitted with heat and hot water. What were some of the considerations you had to face?

Oh, it was a bullock shed originally, so we had to lay a floor, because it was a dirt floor, and we had to put heating and water in to just try and make it a building that people could work in, and an environment that would be friendly. Then once we built the room we had an acoustic research team sort of consider where the desk would be. I said "This is rubbish, we don't need an acoustic treatment of the room," so I got rid of them and I just put the desk where it felt like it was the right place.

Now, I've never seen the barn. Could you give me your best description of what it looks like and how big the rooms are?

Well, the control room is large enough to be able to fit the Helios desk, four tape machines and probably about ten people. And then the playing room is easily big enough for a band to play in, with room to spare. It's got two grand pianos, antique keyboards, and a kitchen area where people hang out and watch television and eat their dinner. There's a writing room, called The Pink Room, which is in the process of being rebuilt to be a state of the art programming room. Everywhere you go there is a tie-line so you can record anywhere, really.

So it's all interconnected?

Yeah.

Tight view of Helios console, looking toward the live room. *Photo courtesy of Helioscentric Studios*

I'm sure that you have acquired some interesting gear over the years, including the Helios desk which must have an illustrious history in itself. Can you walk me through some of the more interesting pieces you have on hand?

Well, we've got a 38 channel Helios desk and then we've got a Studer 24-track, an Ampex 16-track, and an Ampex 24-track. We have Pro Tools as well; that's linked so you can transfer from one to the other if you wish.

On top of that, we have lots of outboard gear; a lot of Helios compression units and the usual sort of suspects, compressors, limiters, reverbs. Then we have two Hammond C3s, an L100, actually we've got four Hammonds. We've a 1960s thing with a drum machine in it, which is pretty cute. Then we have two grand pianos, one antique and one modern. We have two Harmoniums; one from Canada and one from Europe. We've also got a great collection of amplifiers, foot pedals, and microphones.

How high are the ceilings in the barn? I'm just trying to get a mental image.

They're like a chapel in a church.

In terms of the acoustic properties, was it overly reflective when you first set it up? What kind of acoustic challenges did you face to make the room sound good?

Not many; we were really lucky. It all fit together really well. We do have stage curtains that you can pull around, but one of the things that I found was the best way to minimize sound problems is to buy loads of books and put shelves up and put books everywhere. The whole studio has about maybe three or four thousand books. And they're just lined along the walls, and that's all for the sound. But it also gives you a great flavor for recording; it gives you a good feeling.

You mentioned that your new album is along the lines of jazz. I'm wondering if Helioscentric lends itself to any particular genre?

No, I mean it's open to everything. We've had everything in there from The Pet Shop Boys to Brian Ferry and we've just had two number one albums recorded there, a band called Keane and another one called Athelete who are number one this week. We've had a real eclectic mixture.

Do you ever get involved in any of the sessions?

It's not for me to get involved. I don't get involved unless people ask me to come over. Like next week, some people have asked me to come over and write some lyrics so I'll come and listen and see where I can apply myself, but I don't make it a point of being around at all.

Can you characterize the staff you've gotten together to keep things running? What types of people do you have on board?

Well, we have a Frenchman called Pom who is our technical guy and fixes the whole thing. We also use a guy called Phill Brown, an engineer whose history goes back to Led Zeppelin, the Small Faces, Traffic, Joni Mitchell, and recently both Dido albums. I mean he's just a good pair of solid ears, you know?

Could we talk about some of your recording projects with Squeeze? What kinds of methodologies did Squeeze use to record?

Well, Squeeze only recorded in Helioscentric once, and that was for the last album. Squeeze recorded everywhere, really. America, Belgium, everywhere; wherever we could lay our hat.

Your recordings with Squeeze sound as if they are very immediate; live, with very few overdubs.

We didn't really have any special techniques. We just recorded whenever we weren't on the road. We didn't have much time to make records, because we always had to go back on tour again. Our manager kept us busy, you know? So one minute we were on the road, the next minute we were writing, and the next minute we were recording, and then we went back on the road again. It was a pretty whirlwind time. And I think that's a really good thing for a young band. You don't want to be hanging around in studios too long because you can lose your focus on why you're there in the first place, you know?

Squeeze was very popular and you guys toured all over the world. That must have been exhausting.

Yeah, I'm still exhausted [laughs]. I still need to take deep breaths sometimes and realize how much work we did. And that's great! It was a really fun time. I can't tell you. I really miss it, you know? I miss the energy of it.

How does the songwriting process work for you typically, and how is it working for this particular record?

Well, I just do the lyrics. That's what I do, and right now I'm working with a trumpet player called Guy Barker. He's writing all the music, and we're just using a jazz quartet. I've never done anything like this, so it's kind of unique for me. It sounds great, I love it.

Are you a jazz fan? What sort of music do you typically listen to?

I listen to everything. I'm not overly scrupulous and I'm like big on everything. Nothing's ruled in, and nothing's ruled out as they say, apart from heavy metal.

Was there ever a point when you really just wanted to keep this place to yourself as a personal home studio, or did you always kind of have your eye on going commercial?

Umm, I've never wanted a studio just for my own purposes, I'd get bored stiff. It's always been for friends and other musicians to enjoy, really. It's become commercial by its own accord, really. Not by any design.

Is this studio really a full time deal for you? How much time do you have for yourself?

It doesn't take any time at all really. It's great fun.

Front entrance of studio (alongside Studio Dog). *Photo courtesy of Helioscentric Studios*

Imaginary Road
Will Ackerman, Artist, Owner

Side/rear exterior of Imaginary Road Studios at night. *Photo by John Cooper, courtesy of Imaginary Road*

William Ackerman is mostly known as a gifted musical artist and founder of Windham Hill Records, a truly original music label that began in the '70s and defied definition. He is a modern day renaissance man, educated at Stanford and having pursued (and succeeded at) many wide ranging interests in his career. He is an accomplished builder/general contractor (he built every structure on his property and has been featured in *This Old House* magazine), musician, record company founder (founder of two record labels: Windham Hill and Imaginary Road), writer, producer, diver, surfer, the list goes on and on. On meeting Will, one is immediately struck by his artistic sense, passion, and intellect – which is razor sharp. His studio, Imaginary Road, was built as a vehicle for him to realize his artistic vision as a producer.

His property in Vermont is stunning. He owns approximately 800 acres in Windham Hill County, Vermont. As you will read in the interview, Windham Hill is not only the namesake of the company(s) he founded. For Mr. Ackerman, there is a great deal of emotional equity in the name itself and the region. He also has a deep connection to the land he has acquired and to his neighbors as well.

Will Ackerman, a man who befits his surroundings in Windham County, Vermont. *Photo by Jeff Touzeau, courtesy of Hummingbird Media*

Will's journey in becoming an artist and producer is a tale in itself, one met with many unexpected coincidences and serendipitous moments. He has taken things full circle; doing general contracting work out of a pick up truck, to becoming a wealthy recording executive leading what he refers to as a "poodle existence" in Mill Valley, California, to finally walking away from the whole scene, ultimately preferring the peacefulness and serenity of the Vermont mountains. As an artist, he has created contemplative, emotional pieces such as "The Bricklayer's Beautiful Daughter" and countless others that have withstood the test of time.

The label he created, Windham Hill Records, is nothing short of legendary. The early success of that label is mostly due to Mr. Ackerman's relentless pursuit of original and emotionally engaging music. Will maintains that a series of serendipitous moments acted as a catalyst for the label's success, but there is no doubt that a primary driver was his ability to take risks and act on his acute instinct of what felt right, despite industry types attempting to convince him otherwise.

It is widely agreed that Windham Hill created a genre unto itself, one that its contemporary competitors failed to identify and match and one that music critics lamely and desperately came to define as "New Age". Since Will's departure from the company, the earlier part of the catalog has been elevated to mythical status, with the likes of George Winston, Alex deGrassi, Michael Hedges, Liz Story, Mark Isham, Shadowfax, and Will himself having created music that is so emotionally rich with content even today.

As much as Will appears to be "in his element", he is always rushing off to do something new. He has been an avid international surfer since he was a teenager, employing a guide to take him to the most exotic and challenging locations around the world. He wants to write a book (indeed, his gift for writing has been made evident in his liner notes throughout the years, along with his poetry and contributions to various magazines) and commits himself to building one "substantial" wood project per year – these "substantial" wood projects are often on the scale of a house or a barn. In addition to these "hobbies", he continues to produce when the right artist comes along.

What was your first pressing at Windham Hill?

I started with a little vanity pressing of my first record, *The Search for the Turtle's Navel*. The pressing order was only 300. I remember thinking that I'd probably have 200 of these in my closet for the rest of my life. I had a graphic designer friend who designed the cover and I had another friend who was in the printing business who printed the paper, which we then glued onto generic plain white covers.

What year was this?

It was all in '75. I remember, the weirdest thing happened, Jeff. As a contractor, I was called in to do some work for Chris Stratchwitz, the guy who created Arhoolie Records, a brilliant blues and ethnic label. Somehow or other Chris got my name despite the fact that he was in the East Bay, and I was in the Palo Alto area. He asked me to come in and do some remodeling of an industrial space that he had. I ended up building his retail store, which was called Down Home Music. But behind that in this industrial space was a brand new company called Rhythm Research Record Distributing, headed by a guy named Tom Diamont and at the back of the building was a new guitar label called Kicking Mule Records.

What was your profession at this point?

I was a general contractor. My company was called Windham Hill Builders. As a matter of fact, my business card, as late as 1980, read Windham Hill Records/Builders/Music BMI. So here I am being a contractor in the middle of the independent record business about a month after I bring out my little private release record. So I gave my record to Tom Diamont and he said "Great...I'm looking for stuff to distribute." So suddenly I've got a distributor in the Bay area. I've got Chris Strachwitz offering me a deal from Arhoolie, I've got Ed Denson offering me a deal from Kicking Mule Records, all in a week!

With you as the artist.

Yeah. It was my first record. Imagine that as a general contractor I step into the middle of the independent record business, right next to Ed Denson, who created Takoma Records, the label that I am trying to emulate. Without knowing Ed personally, I'd already made the first catalog number for the Windham Hill label, C1001, in tribute to the first number on Takoma Records, which was guitarist John Fahey's first record.

And what exactly was that genre that you first had your eye on?

Well, it didn't really have a name. Do you know Leo Kottke?

Yes.

Well, Leo was all about rhythm and big twelve-string stuff, whereas John Fahey was an ethno musicologist and had been brought up on the blues. He did instrumental impressions of the blues stuff he'd always loved. Of all of the Takoma artists though, Robbie Basho was probably the greatest influence on me. So I'd done this album of guitar solos, *The Search for the Turtle's Navel*, and one thing leads to another. It was a genre in evolution and comfortably without a name at that time.

Coincidentally, my next door neighbor growing up was a guy named Michael Kilmartin. He was actually the first guy to put a guitar in my hand, a starburst Gibson electric, and taught me the basic notes for "What I Say" by Ray Charles. It was the first thing I played on guitar and I was about twelve. I'd also been a big folk fan and was into the Kingston Trio, who were very famous at the time. I used to sneak out and go to all their rehearsals; they would play in the basement of the old Stanford Student Union, which was the size of my living room or something. So you've got a kid whose always loved folk music and was nuts about Rock n Roll, too.

So Michael Kilmartin puts a guitar in my hand when I'm twelve. Now I'm twenty-five, and see him in the street in Palo Alto. He says, "What are you doing?" I said, "Well, thanks for teaching me the guitar. I just finished my first record." He said, "Well, give it to me. I'm doing radio promotion for a new record label that no one has ever heard of yet called Fantasy Records and we've got a band called Creedence Clearwater Revival that we're starting to work with." I swear I'm not making this stuff up. So here I've walked into the independent record business, I've gotten two offers which I don't take because I figure I've got Tom Diamont to distribute my record and I can probably get more, I run into Michael Kilmartin, my old next door neighbor, who is now the promotional head of Fantasy Records!

Michael takes ten of my records, goes to WCAS in Cambridge, KTWN in Minneapolis, KCRW in Santa Monica, KINK in Portland, KZAM in Seattle, KCFR in Denver, and KFAT in Gilroy, California, among others, when progressive FM was still happening. In those days, you could actually still get some fairly powerful FM play. The whole point of progressive FM was that the music director kind of didn't do anything. The mandate was "bring in the most obscure damn records you can find, and turn people on to new music." It was a beautiful, eclectic era. I'm getting radio airplay and there was a lot of momentum behind this tiny little record of mine. And it just so happens that my cousin, who was my apprentice on the build-

Mr. Ackerman pictured in his shop. In addition to being a gifted musician, he is also a woodworker. *Photo by Jeff Touzeau, courtesy of Hummingbird Media*

ing crew, was a guy named Alex deGrassi. So I say, "Alex, do you want to do a record?" And he said "No."

One of my favorite guitarists of all time. Was he a great guitarist at this point?

Oh, yeah. He was always four times better than me. I mean, I'm sitting here playing my ballads, and he's writing an opus like "Turning, Turning Back".

The way Alex started playing with me was hilarious. The first paying gig I had in my life was at the Seattle Opera House for 3,700 people, sponsored by KZAM radio, which was going completely nuts on my record. So I walk out onstage, I've got one guitar. I've got to do all these tunings, I'm snapping strings, telling jokes, finally, I'm running out of music and they're still clapping and going crazy. So I take a little piece of paper, stick it in between the strings and retune, start doing "Mrs. Brown You've Got a Lovely Daughter", and everybody breaks up. I say "Listen man, I am out and I don't have any more music. My cousin is down here, right in the front row, he plays better than anybody. Get him up here." So everybody starts chanting "Alex! Alex! Alex!" and DeGrassi bolts out the emergency exit, setting off the alarm. The next thing I know, he comes in with his guitar. I help him onstage, he plays a set and everybody goes ape shit. Finally he says, "Yeah, I think I'll do that record now!" So dig it. It's crazy that all this stuff is happening.

Were you ever nervous being onstage at that point?

I was scared shitless, but loving every minute of it. It's the drug they say it is.

So everything is coming together in its own way with fate nudging things along.

The point is it wasn't like any of this was conceived. There wasn't any master plan. There was never going to be a second Will Ackerman record. There was only going to be this one little vanity pressing. I get the airplay in Seattle, Portland, Cambridge, and Denver and there's distribution now because there are stores that want it.

For every store that takes it, there's a distributor right behind saying, "Hey, what is this record? It's selling like crazy!" so next thing you know, I've got nine independent distributors around the country all in a matter of months. And my cousin is Alex de Grassi. So I guess we're a record label, and I guess we're kind of a guitar label.

We're kind of folk, but it's not folk because Alex de Grassi studied Ralph Towner and I'm into open tunings and all this Indian stuff. Next we sign David Qualey, a guitarist from Germany and we sign my old mentor, the guy who meant more to me as a guitarist than anyone, Robbie Basho. He was number five in the catalog. *The Search for the Turtle's Navel* was number one in the catalog, Linda Waterfall's record was number two in the catalog, a wonderful vocal effort that sadly disappeared. Then my *It Takes a Year* was number three in the catalog. Four was de Grassi's *Turning, Turning Back*. Five was Robbie Basho, my third record was number six. A blues group, Kiddafrika, was number seven. It's interesting that the vocal projects didn't make a dent, but the instrumental releases were so easily successful.

Then I did something different. I did an album of Eric Satié piano solos by an artist named Bill Quist after looking for someone who could do this. Eric Satie was always the most important thing to me musically in the world. We had some success with it; later on it went gold in Japan. Nine was de Grassi's *Slow Circle*, ten was another Basho recording, eleven was David Qualey, and twelve was George Winston's "Autumn", released in 1980. And I remember bringing "Autumn" to my distributors and having them say "Well, that Bill Quist thing didn't really happen, you ought to just stay as a guitar label, or it will confuse people." And I remember, Alex and I were touring Germany and we had the demo tape from George Winston, and I kept playing it, and I thought it was amazing and that the distributors were just plain wrong.

Was he kind of doing with piano what you had been doing with guitar in a way?

Well, some writers actually said that Winston was actually the first document folk piano that they'd ever heard, and there's probably some truth to that. There's sort of a basic folk element to his composition, and people just weren't used to hearing it on the piano. If you translate those pieces to guitar, you'd have something that people recognize as folk. Once we'd recorded *Autumn*, the doors just blew off. We'd had regional press, but suddenly we had a four star review in *Rolling Stone* by Chuck Young, and four stars were as high as they went in those days. Suddenly, the exposure was national, and things just went absolutely nuts.

So then do you have your business hat on or your musician hat? Do you still want to be an artist? How are you managing the growth of what's happening?

Well, forget all that, I'm still a general contractor! This is like a hobby on the side!

One of the many interesting pieces of stonework on Ackerman's property. *Photo by Jeff Touzeau, courtesy of Hummingbird Media*

So this wasn't even your real profession yet?

It wasn't even a day gig. It became so more and more, though. I found myself neglecting jobs and getting in trouble for not turning up when rain fell and destroyed the ceiling of a building I was working on.

Pretty damn good excuse, though.

Yeah, yeah. Again, the point is that all this was unplanned, unscripted, skin of your teeth, just read the signs and go with what's working. That created momentum beyond what I was doing by myself.

It's interesting how the vision kind of developed because glancing at your catalog, it seemed to be immaculately planned and executed.

We weren't deliberately being responsive to "the marketplace". Nonetheless, if you have an enthusiastic response from a radio station or people in general, you're likely to try to achieve that again. If you look at the early history of Windham Hill, it's pretty much all solo instrumentation. It floats somewhere on the fringes of folk, but it's not that either.

It's safe to say that you carved out your own genre.

I think that we did that as much as anyone ever has. I think the Windham Hill thing struck people as utterly different. I remember walking into the Tower Records in San Francisco on Columbus Avenue. I came in and the manager had made a Windham Hill bin. I said, "What's this?" And he said "People just walk in off the street and say 'What's next on Windham Hill?' We used his idea and made bin dividers, sent them out to all the stores, and it was great." The perception was that

Windham Hill was doing something very, very different, doing it in a time when Disco was ruling the airwaves. We were about melody and contemplation, where everyone else was about electronic drums and dance. I think that we looked very brave. I think, however, that we were more naïve than brave. We looked like David to the Goliath of the industry.

This was a very strong brand that you created. Not just the sounds, but the visual elements of the presentation. When the disco era ended, people didn't know up from down and there were a lot of alternating currents in popular music. Punk, Disco, Rock, the mainstream really lacked a direction, right?

Well, you have to look at the demographic of everything. You had this group of people who had created the record industry as it was at that time. It was the baby boomers who through the sixties and seventies listened to The Beatles, the British Invasion, the Byrds, and everything else. It just went insane, and it was my generation that did that. We listened to music more intently. It was more of a cultural phenomenon than it had been previously for any generation. The industry has believed their own hype and skewed the business toward an ever-younger audience, leaving behind the group of people that virtually created the industry itself. Stupid.

Also, wasn't some of the "free form" philosophy of FM radio being eroded by the early '80s? Maybe people sensed this sort of freedom in your music since the traditional music industry was turning into more of a machine at this point.

Windham Hill was a genuine alternative and it appealed to the vibe of my generation. Regarding brand identification, this didn't happen entirely deliberately. It happened out of frustration because I got so sick of people asking me "What do you call this?"

I actually designed an ad which I ran modestly in some music papers. It consisted of the words classical, rock, folk, and jazz all crossed out. Then it said "Windham Hill". It wasn't meant to be pretentious and it wasn't really designed as a trademark identification thing. It was really done out of frustration. Nonetheless, it became an incredibly eloquent statement of who we were. We were unique in large part unto ourselves, nobody was doing what we were doing. Every few months, we'd create a new insert going into the records talking about who we were, encouraging communication back.

You were developing a community.

Exactly. These people were incredibly loyal buyers. If they owned one, they owned thirteen. They were buying them as gifts. It was a snowball created by our fans, not by expensive advertising or marketing that we didn't have the money for anyway.

You mentioned the word contemplative, which is really an appropriate word to describe Windham Hill.

There was a writer, I think it was in the *LA Times* or *New York Times*, who described Windham Hill as an antidote to the urban madness. We picked that up and ran with that too.

When did you finally give up the contracting?

I think that it disappears off the card in '82, which is the year that we signed the distribution deal with A&M. You know, I went into meetings with pretty much every major label: everyone wanted a piece of this. Everyone was like "Come on down to LA and talk to us." Then I got a call from a guy named Gil Friesen who said, "I want to come up to San Francisco and talk to you." I said okay.

So the president of A&M records comes up, and he says, "I represent Herb Albert. He created the Tijuana brass himself, started a record label, and if anyone's going to understand your experience, it's Herb and Jerry Moss. That's Albert and Moss, or A&M. And me, I'm the president of the thing. I think we can have incredible success here and overseas." So I'm waiting for the plan. He finally says "Whatever you're doing, just keep doing it. You understand it better than we do and we're not going to tell you a damn thing." These are people you can work with.

Music to your ears.

I said, "Okay, let me come down and meet with Herb and Jerry." They were great. We signed an amazing deal. A lot of people thought I was giving away the store. They funded everything and we split the profits 50/50. There was a lot of incentive for them. We were doing $30 million a year and it was just unbelievable. The thing with A&M and Gil, it was just brilliant. They were absolutely wonderful to me.

When do you move to Vermont, and what ever becomes of the Windham Hill operations? Describe the transition between running this label and setting up shop in Vermont?

Well, let me first say that at Windham Hill, I owned it, I was head of A&R, I was the only guy and made all the artistic decisions. I produced everything on Windham Hill. I designed the first fourteen covers.

Again, I think those covers were such a strong expression of the Windham Hill brand, because there was such a remarkable visual identity that always accompanied the music. I think about *The Dark Side of the Moon* by Pink Floyd, and that's a clear example of how artwork and music really seem to gel together in a natural expression. For Windham Hill, the artwork and the music always seemed to come together, making for a stronger, more holistic expression all around.

I think it felt like art.

At this point, you had a lot of balls in the air: producer, artist, business owner, the list goes on. What about your health?

I had a couple of girlfriends through that period of time, and they would just leave me because there was simply no time off or vacation. One girl finally dragged me off to Hawaii, and I just went stir crazy. I was just on the phone the whole time, and she dumped me about a week later.

Rear of Imaginary Road Studios at night. *Photo by John Cooper, courtesy of Imaginary Road*

What ultimately happened to the record label?

Let's go to 1984. I wake up one morning and I feel really, really lousy. And I stay feeling really lousy and I go to every hospital in America trying to find out what was wrong. I went to Rice, Johns Hopkins, Stanford, I went everywhere. Everybody said, "Mr. Ackerman, you're in perfect health." And finally, I was introduced to this doctor in California who said, "Will, you're clinically depressed." I said, "What do you mean I'm clinically depressed? I'm selling a billion albums a year, we're playing Carnegie Hall, the Hollywood Bowl, you're crazy. I've got everything I've ever wanted." And he said "It's time you start digging in and look at what's going on." I kind of resisted it and found my way around it.

Probably some burn out, too?

Oh, yeah. I was going to be this small time general contractor building residential stuff, drinking jug wine out of the back of a pickup truck for my whole life. Here I was leading what I later called "the poodle existence." I'm driving my Mercedes SEC, living in a perfect house, around thirty years old; a long way away from what I thought I was going to be doing.

I grew up as a kid who would spend his entire summer up in the Sierra, Nevada above 8,000 feet building trail for the forest service. That's what I always loved. So here I am not going to the mountains, barely getting to the beach, not getting any time off. I had been taken into a world where I was driving fancy cars and eating at fancy restaurants.

My blood pressure was through the roof. My doctor said, "You're going to be dead in six months. We're going to put you on heart medication." I had seen my dad go through that, and I said, "Yeah, great. That's what I want, impotence and drool. I'm not doing it." "Well, you're going to die." So I say to him: "I'll tell you what: I'm going to go to Vermont for two months."

What year is this?

'82. I say "I'm bailing. I'm leaving here." And I went to Vermont. I had so little strength in those days, I would crawl out of bed. Eventually I met a guy named Dan Snow, now my next door neighbor. He had won one of my records from WMUA radio station down in Amherst, Massachusetts, in 1976, writes me a little letter with directions to his house and says "Come visit", and I finally do. I drive up in my father's Chevrolet with New Hampshire plates and he comes out and he says, "Hey, Will, come on in." He somehow knows it's me despite never having seen me before, and there was no photo of me on the LP; he never has told me what that was all about.

He and I became great friends and are still very much to this day. I say to him "I've got to buy some land in Vermont." And he says, "Okay, we'll go around the county." We looked at land everywhere, but nothing really got to me. After all of this running around, Dan said that his dad was willing to sell the land next to his, so I became Dan's neighbor.

The natural beauty surrounding Ackerman's estate includes Vermont's second tallest pine and elaborate stonework. *Photo by Jeff Touzeau, courtesy of Hummingbird Media*

Why did you want to buy land in Vermont?

Well, remember that the label name is Windham Hill and I now live in Windham County, Vermont. That's a long story too, involving my mother's suicide, my father's remarriage, and my finding a home in a way.

So why were you originally drawn to Windham Hill and what was the namesake of the company?

As a kid, my mother commits suicide, the family goes all to hell, the first home I find is at a place called Windham Hill Farm, which is a country inn about a half an hour from where I live now. It's still a beautiful inn and it's called Windham Hill Inn now as opposed to farm. It was owned by Hugh and Mary Folsom. Hugh was one of the most fascinating men who ever existed. I was the dishwasher, I also painted the place, I split wood, you know, it was a home for me. When I was at that kitchen table after everyone was served out in the dining room, it was home to me and those of us who worked there; we wrote poetry, music, and plays together. All very '60s.

So you're a teenager at this point?

Early twenties, but I started going there when I was sixteen. That red and white tablecloth in the kitchen at Windham Hill was home to me, and Hugh and Mary were my surrogate parents. It was incredibly important to me. The first thing I name is Windham Hill Builders, and then I name my record label. I call Hugh at some point and ask him if it's okay that I name my record label Windham Hill.

Side view of Imaginary Road office building. *Photo by Jeff Touzeau, courtesy of Hummingbird Media*

Front view of Imaginary Road Studios. *Photo by Jeff Touzeau, courtesy of Hummingbird Media*

There is so much emotional equity attached to that name. It's obviously more than a geographic location or a county.

Oh, yeah. It's very, very deep: arguably what saved my life at one point. The West River Road, Route 30, which is a mile and a half down the road from Imaginary Road Studios today, was my lifeline. When I hit Route 30 out of Brattleboro, I was going home and my heart would soar.

So I bought a little twelve acre piece from Dan's dad, then ended up buying another three or four parcels from his dad, and kept buying half the county here. Then I build this little tiny cabin called "The Dream Garage" and my '72 green Ford truck from my contracting days sits in there, which I still love despite the fact that I'm simultaneously leading the poodle existence in California, and I put a little apartment in the upstairs.

Natural light permeates Imaginary Road; this is a view of the second floor, with French doors leading to balcony. *Photo by Jeff Touzeau, courtesy of Hummingbird Media*

It's got no electricity, it's got no plumbing, but I love it. So here I am in 1984 in a clinical depression, exhausted beyond belief, getting up late every day. I get up in the fall and I've literally got energy to rake leaves for five minutes and then I'm done. But then it's six minutes, and then it's seven minutes, and then it's ten. Then it's taking a little bit of a walk and then it's moving some rocks. Then it's like, okay, this is what I need to stay healthy.

So you're getting your energy back and things are looking up.

I'm feeling better and I go back and resign as CEO. This nomenclature used to be a joke: you be the President, I'll be the Vice President. However, when it's a corporation of tens of millions of dollars, it not a joke anymore. I've had it with all of this; I get a nice simple car and quit with this ostentatious crap.

So the poodle existence gradually goes out the window.

Yeah. So I start doing some volunteer projects in building, life changes, and its all for the good. Fast forward to 1990 or so. The label has various divisions. We've got eighty people working for us, we've got offices in foreign countries, and it's just crazy. We've got Magenta records, we've got Open Air records, and we've got all these things in development like creating a wine label for Japan.

I remember when a batch of new releases were about to come out: I'm looking at these and thinking "I've never even heard half of these records." Sure, there were five A&R guys that I really trusted, and we're moving along nicely, but I realize all this size and momentum wasn't what I had in mind.

That's when I started thinking, late '90, you know, I just can't do this anymore. And I had one attorney who said to me, "You know, Will, one of the smartest things you could do is just close the doors. Let the money come in. You'd walk away with a bare minimum of $60 million dollars." And boy, you talk about a movie scenario where you have the devil on one shoulder and an angel on the other; that sounded pretty good. But I couldn't do that to all those artists. I was like, "No, we've got to find a buyer for this." So BMG came along and offered a really substantial chunk of change, so I said "We'll take the deal." And I sold it in May 1992.

So you were out.

Yeah. I decided that I would take the publishing with me, which was one of the greatest decisions I ever made. The publishing catalog was making me well over $2 million a year for years and years and years.

So did you get back into the record business at any point?

I had a three year non-compete. They wanted a seven year non-compete and I wouldn't sign it. I created a spoken word label called Gang of Seven and I had fun with that. It was sort of inspired by Garrison Keeler's "Lake Woebegone" monologues. It was not about money, it was about having fun.

How were you drawn to the spoken word genre?

Well, as a kid, I always loved that Hal Holbrook, "An Evening with Mark Twain". Of course there was also Spaulding Gray's "Swimming to Cambodia". So one of the first guys I signed was Spaulding Gray and we did "Monster in a Box", and a couple of other programs by Tom Bodett, the Motel Six guy who is also a brilliant writer and radio personality, and Nora Dunn from "Saturday Night Live".

Was that a difficult thing for you to learn, the spoken word genre? It sounds like you picked right up on it.

Since my father was an English professor, I was already steeped in literature one way or another. I had to get used to book distribution, but it was more or less the same thing. So I had that for three years, then jumped right back into music.

I started a label called Imaginary Road with Polygram in 1995 on the day that the non-compete ended, which kind of brings us to Imaginary Road studios. Basically, it was a little room, incredibly high quality, for doing my guitar recordings and spoken word.

It sounds like you honed in on what you loved to do but that in so doing you had to cut a lot of other appendages in your life.

Ironically, no. I actually regained them. I think in some respects, I'm more active in a lot of other things these days. I do one building project a year. Last year it was a beautiful cherry and oak frame for Tom Bodett, a three story barn with this cherry frame that was just insanely beautiful. My engineer and closest friend on Earth Corin Nelsen, who won the Grammy with me this year, designed it. It's more like furniture than it is a frame. You know, blind mortices in cherry and oak.

So you've really kept your building chops all these years.

Yeah. There's seven structures here, every one in which I have built with trees felled and milled on the property. I was on the cover of *This Old House* magazine two years ago, April, for a barn we built across from the studio. I think we had about $1,700 in materials for this huge structure.

Because it was all milled by yourself.

I mean, 8 x 14 x 36 hemlock beams? Go to the lumberyard and ask for one of those sometime. And we mill 'em. We find the trees, we knock them down, and we mill them. That's what we do here.

You're just amazing. I can't believe this.

I have a wood shop where Corin and I do all the furniture. I'm writing a book, I'm surfing more than ever. I'm a complete wacko-ludicrous surfer. I try to spend at least eight weeks a year surfing. I hired a guy to take me around to help me find all the cool places. I've been surfing since I was nine.

Mr. Ackerman's live room was purpose built to be an exceptional environment for acoustic instruments.
Photo by John Cooper, courtesy of Imaginary Road

Will, have you ever tried building a guitar?

No. I have way too much admiration for that craft. I've encountered people who work in wood and think "Oh, I'll go out and build a guitar." Sure you can build a guitar, but it's not going to sound good. There's too much magic in doing it right. Just up the road from me in Newfane, Vermont, is the shop of Michael Millard and Andy Mueller of Froggy Bottom Guitars. It's just sheer coincidence that what I think is the finest guitar on Earth happens to be made in my backyard. When you're faced with the genius it takes to make an instrument like a Froggy Bottom, you realize that its about a lot more than clean woodwork.

Do you still take a lot of great joy in playing the guitar? In other words, is it relaxing for you to do, or must it be a full-on, serious endeavor each time you pick it up?

I would say now that everything on earth is more enjoyable for me than it ever was. I enjoy performance more than ever. But I've never been somebody who practices. I've never done a scale in my life.

When did it become clear that Imaginary Road would be used for producing music projects, and what considerations were given to the room's design in light of your own acoustic background.

The room was designed for acoustic instrumentation, close mic'ing, and small ensemble. We've managed with the upstairs room to move into some isolation and have a good space for drums when we need it.

What role did light play in the room's design?

A lot. I simply hated coming out of lightless studios in urban environments and squinting like a mole. I promised myself I'd make a room where I, and hopefully others, would feel as if they could work on music and still be a part of the cycle of day and night. I didn't want to be robbed of this. I don't think it's healthy for mind or body.

How does the room lend itself to enhancing performance? Do you like to record during a particular season?

I just think people feel more present. I've heard arguments that the dark box studio eliminates distractions, but I find that most of the people I work with draw energy from being in Vermont in all seasons. Beyond the light, we have mountain bikes, kayaks, hiking, and cross country skiing trails. West River is just below us for swimming. I encourage a couple of walks a day and find that people are more productive when they can pull their heads out of microscopically intense, high quality music making environment we have here.

The live room set up to record acoustic guitar in stereo. *Photo by Jeff Touzeau, courtesy of Hummingbird Media*

Ackerman and Corin Nelsen built all the control room's racks and furniture. *Photo by Jeff Touzeau, courtesy of Hummingbird Media*

So it helps to bring perspective back. Can we talk about some technical aspects of the studio? Why did you choose Jim Hemmingway preamps?

I use Hemmingway preamps because they kick the shit out of anything else I've ever heard. Every piece of equipment in the chain has a color to it, and the Hemmingway imparts a warmth to the signal chain that I find attractive. While I recognize that analog provides a warmer baseline in general, Pro Tools has redefined the way I approach production structurally in some cases. That said, the master for which we won the Grammy this year is an absolutely state of the art digital recording but we chose to run it through some Studer heads before mastering for still greater warmth.

What about your own playing? How has your recording technique evolved over the last two decades? Take me through a typical session with you.

Very little has changed. I evolved a process over years and years and it still works for me very nicely. Corin Nelsen is my engineer and partner in this and it's a seamless machine at this point. I work in sections of songs, utilizing long note decays as a place to shift from one set of tracks to another, rather than making a hard edit between these sections. The newer notes seem to emerge from the decay of the former. I've spent years using double tracking almost to the point where this is a trademark for me. The bridge of "The Bricklayer's Beautiful Daughter" is a perfect example, where I simply play the part again.

Interestingly, I find that real precision can be counterproductive. For me, it's the subtle variations in the performance that make it come alive sonically. We may move a note or two around in Pro Tools to pull in the really errant one, but generally the human imprecision can be performance enhancing.

What have you learned about recording your specific technique?

Well, to begin with, my style of playing is far less "gymnastic" than a lot of other guitarists. I don't have the precision of my cousin Alex de Grassi or the staggering innovation of Michael Hedges. I try to render a melody with as much expression as possible, which involves exploiting a range of basic dynamics to their fullest potential: volume, tempo, and use of the contrasting effects of proximity to the bridge or sound hole are pretty much my stock in trade. A song of mine may go from the faintest whisper to some seriously loud passages, often driving Corin and Bob Ludwig [mastering engineer] crazy. Corin and I have an expression for the infinitely delicate sections which we refer to as "circumcising the ant." In these, we do need sometimes to resort to edits.

Do you use fingerpicks?

Yes, I still use metal fingerpicks, but am envious of David Cullen, who turns up here with these incredible fingernails to play with. With all the work I do in construction, tree felling, wood working, and gardening among other things, the idea of maintaining good nails for playing is out of the question.

What are the most difficult instruments to record for you?

Well, I've recorded many different instruments in different rooms using different mics, and feel I know my way around them to the point where I could be almost formulaic. I now try to push the edges a bit so I don't fall asleep. The only trick is listening to the damned instrument, really, not assuming anything, but usually finding that the assumed positions are indeed the best. Luckily there are always surprises that keep you on your toes.

The current mic set up I have consists of the 256s, U67s, 414s, and KM 84s, all on the solo guitar. I would never print a mic that didn't have a real function. Even though I have a small room, I'm able to achieve some amazing space without simply relying on reverbs.

Do you prefer studio recording or live performance?

A combination of the two. I can't tell you how many times I've heard a demo tape of a piece which was energetic and emotionally rich, only to have the final product be antiseptic and lifeless. I will take an emotional performance over a flawless one any day. I love working with people who can achieve both. I admit to being pretty demanding of clean signal and controlled sonic environment, but I never want what I produce to compromise what I think is the essence of good music: emotional communication.

The control room at Imaginary Road. *Photo by John Cooper, courtesy of Imaginary Road*

Maggie's Farm

Matt Balitsaris, Owner

Exterior of Maggie's Farm Studios, built in a turn of the century stone barn. *Photo by Jeff Touzeau, courtesy of Hummingbird Media*

Maggie's Farm is a century old stone barn owned by Matt Balitsaris of Palmetto Records, the highly reputable jazz label. The studio is in Pipersville, Pennsylvania, very close to the Delaware River, the banks of which are steeped in history from colonial settlers and the Revolutionary War. There are also many state and local parks in the immediate vicinity, making for a beautiful setting that is off limits for outside commercial activity. To get to Maggie's Farm, located in Bucks County, you must first drive through many small towns built entirely of stone, not unlike what you might see in the rural English countryside. The studio itself is located on Balitsaris' beautiful ten acre lot, off a dirt road across the street from a Christmas tree farm.

When I met Matt, I was anxious to learn about the facility itself: the history, the acoustics, and the process of how he adapted it into a sonic retreat where artists from his label, Palmetto Records, could create music. After he described the structure of the barn and the history he knew of it, I went on to ask him how he went about converting it. I was immediately struck with the degree of respect he had for the structure itself, which was built with beautiful stone and hand-hewn beams. The key thing in the back of his mind the whole time was that he didn't want to permanently alter the character of the barn itself, especially for any future property owners. Instead of gutting it out and building it from the inside to suit his needs, he chose to adapt to the existing structure, ultimately finding that it suited his style of music perfectly.

One thing I found particularly interesting as I spoke to Matt was how he described the unique fashion in which jazz is recorded: the immediacy and the camaraderie that is so prevalent among players. He impressed upon me the importance of capturing the performance on tape, a principle that seems so rudimentary, but has somehow become more elusive in our era of spoon fed pop, Pro Tools, and overdubs. Maggie's Farm plays host to the world's most innovative jazz musicians on a regular basis, and capturing the chemistry of a performance is not only important artistically, but logistically, since many of these musicians are living and touring all over the world and will likely be on a different continent tomorrow.

Maggie's Farm and Palmetto Records are interdependent. As Matt indicates, neither could exist without the other. In fact, Maggie's Farm helped Palmetto Records spring to life and vice versa. Matt himself has become increasingly savvy as both a record company owner and an engineer as the following paragraphs will testify.

Can you give me a 50,000 foot view Buck's County, Pennsylvania, and describe the region for someone who has never been there?

Bucks County is really a fascinating place. It's roughly half way between Philadelphia and New York, a little closer to Philly. We're located about two miles from the Delaware River. There are towns within a few miles of here that you can drive through and not see a building that's been built in the last 200 years. The Colonial architecture was mostly built of fieldstone, with 18" thick walls; they just don't fall down. It has the flavor in many ways of parts of Europe where you see these lovely old stone abodes. This area was actually settled by William Penn, when he came up from Philadelphia and bought a bunch of land from the Indians. Historically, this area has been kind of a refuge for artists. A lot of visual artists, writers, including S.J. Perlman and Dorothy Parker, and theatre people have lived here over the years.

How many acres are you on?

This property here is ten acres. There's a Christmas tree farm across the street from our house. We're also half a mile from a huge sort of a series of contiguous parks. There's a state park, a county park, and a town park running along this canyon. There's a stream running through that has sort of prevented further development in our area, which even gives us the feeling further of being a rural oasis.

You record primarily jazz at Maggie's Farm. Can you walk me through how you first became exposed to this genre?

I played guitar in a lot of soul bands while in school in East Tennessee and North Carolina in the late seventies: when Jimi Hendrix had had an influence; the Isley Brothers were making music with very intense electric guitar; and Earth, Wind, and Fire was really just happening. In many cases, the horn sections in those bands were jazz players, or aspiring jazz players. That was sort of where I was first exposed to what that music was about and in kind of in an ancillary way, got to hear jazz for the first time.

You mention Hendrix and the Isley Brothers, but what were some of the key jazz influences that defined your own style?

Well, I kind of worked backwards. I was being exposed to Pat Metheney, John McLaughlin, Ralph Towner, and John Abercrombie. In fact, I studied with Abercrombie when I moved back to New York for a while. And a lot of the playing that I did at this point was improvisational with an acoustic twelve-string. It was jazz, but it wasn't straight ahead mainstream jazz. Also, as a performer in New York City, I played with some Brazilian musicians and became very interested in world music.

Were you making a living entirely on your music at this point?

Yeah. We were playing a ridiculous number of gigs. I still have my date book from those years, and the two of us would play sometimes two or three little cafes and restaurants in the village a day. Two sets one place, three sets another, and two sets at another. By doing that, we built a huge repertoire of this original material, which was really complicated and interesting. We did three records that were on three different labels. It actually became more of a jazz/new age/world music ensemble that went on for several years. Part of the problem was that we were doing this interesting music, but we didn't have any idea what it was! [Laughs.]

There was a big appetite in the village for that type of material during that time, wasn't there?

Yeah, there was. The whole Windham Hill thing was just starting, sparking an interest in acoustic music that hadn't been

Owner and founder of Maggie's Farm Studios and Palmetto Records, Matt Balitsaris.
Photo by Jeff Touzeau, courtesy of Hummingbird Media

there before. Although what we were doing didn't really fit in with their stuff, it was akin in a lot of ways. We were finger picking, but playing in different meters from one another, and sometimes different chord changes; really sort of stacking these harmonic and rhythmic things in unusual ways. It was also the time when the minimalist classical movement was thriving with people like Philip Glass and Steve Wright.

Can you tell me how your interest in performance ultimately evolved into music production?

Well, it was percolating simultaneously to my playing. Once I found myself in studios fairly often, I had an increasing desire to be able to express to an engineer exactly what I wanted in terms of my sound. It forced me to learn what the gadgetry was, what all of these devices did, and why it was that when I went into a studio I never came out sounding like myself [laughs]! It was kind of like a self-defense measure initially. Somewhere along towards the end of the '80s, I found myself in a situation where I realized I liked to make records for other people as a producer.

What were the key things that helped your talent bloom around production? What could you bring to the table?

By the time I built my studio here, I had been involved in studios in pretty much every way possible: I had been a side man, a band leader, a self-produced musician, an assistant engineer, an engineer. I could sit in a control room and understand what musicians are experiencing: what life is like inside the headphones, and what the players' needs are. I knew what you need coming back as a musician and what makes you comfortable and able to play.

What about your jazz label, Palmetto Records. Was starting a record company a natural evolution out of your increased production work?

Yes. In the late '80s or early '90s, there was a studio in New York, East Hill Studios, which I had the opportunity to access during its downtime. That's when I started producing and ultimately the Palmetto label grew out of that.

That's when you began looking at groups with an idea of developing them, or taking them under your wing?

Initially, it started out with a couple records that I had made, then I realized I had others I had worked on with other people that hadn't really been releases. It just sort of took on a life of its own and a couple of things happened simultaneously. First, it became clear that East Hill wasn't going to survive, one of the reasons was that they had so much downtime! [Laughs.] Second, at that time my wife and I had a

Exterior of barn, tape/equipment storage area. *Photo by Jeff Touzeau, courtesy of Hummingbird Media*

wonderful 200 year old stone barn in Pennsylvania that was kind of falling apart. Ironically, we had just done some repairs to it, because some of our friends wanted to get married in there. So I was spending a little time out there and....

Exterior from driveway. The statue is called "Leo", by Balitsaris' friend and neighbor, Steve Snyder. *Photo by Jeff Touzeau, courtesy of Hummingbird Media*

You mean they wanted to get married in a barn??

Yeah. They met at our house; as it happened, they didn't get married here, but we fixed the barn up anyway [laughs]. So I started going out there to practice, because I had this giant practice room all of a sudden. I also began to realize at the time that while I was living in New York and commuting to Pennsylvania, my wife had actually started living in Pennsylvania [laughs]. So it seemed like it was time for me to make a change. I also came to the realization that I'd started this label and that I didn't have a clue what I was doing. Amateur hour was over and I needed to get some people who really knew how to run a label.

The result of that was that I found a great guy, Pat Rustici, to run the label in New York City and I moved out here in the hope that people would actually come here to work. And that actually caused the label to happen and the studio to survive, because it wouldn't have gone much longer if I had continued to run it! [Laughs.]

Balitsaris aside his barn's beautifully weathered stone exterior. *Photo by Jeff Touzeau, courtesy of Hummingbird Media*

Clearly, your strategy seems to be working and the label is thriving. One of Jazz' most prominent publications, *Downbeat*, has given Palmetto high marks and you just won Jazz Journalists Award for Label of the Year.

Downbeat is sort of the standard. There are three sort of major publications: *Downbeat*, *Jazz Times* and *JazzIs*. All in all, we do sort of refer to it as the jazz ghetto, because it's so difficult for jazz to get covered in the mainstream press, like *Newsweek* or *Time*. They'll do one thing a year, and it usually has something to do with one of the bigger labels. We're mostly reduced to those major publications as our outlets and occasionally *The New York Times*.

Running a studio and a label must have seemed like an enormous task, despite having someone capable to run the label. How did you manage your own time?

Well, by then, I was really curtailing my own playing and my own performing. By the mid-nineties, I was still playing a lot, but I was so torn in so many different directions, that I felt it wasn't the best use of my time.

Do you remember what your wife said when you told her that you wanted to turn the barn into a recording studio?

Actually, she thought it was a cool idea! I wasn't entirely convinced that I could, but it seemed like it was worth a shot.

The studio's 1908 Steinway B Grand Piano, seen from the control room.
Photo by Jeff Touzeau, courtesy of Hummingbird Media

I think the beauty of it was that the musicians want to work here, and since people have gotten to know the place there is sort of symbiosis between the label and the other work that comes to the studio.

When musicians come out is it typically for several days?

It varies. Most of the tracking sessions will be two days, and we'll put people up at a bed and breakfast. Pat Rustici used to have a restaurant, so he comes out and cooks big meals and the artists are treated to the spectacle of the president and vice president of the record company doing dishes. Typically, one of our projects will involve a couple of days of tracking and a couple of days of overdubs and editing. A lot of editing goes into jazz, because you're mostly playing live, which often make punching impractical. Then we mix.

One of the great things in my life was the decision to focus on jazz. For one thing, I really like the immediacy of it. I don't like going in and doing rhythm guitar parts for three days and then fixing bass tracks for a day and a half. That's so antithetical to what music is to me.

By playing everything live simultaneously, you're also producing a lot of natural harmonics and overtones.

When people play together, there's not as much mixing to do. You only need automation when you have four or five layers of vocals and overdubbed parts that were played after the fact. During our two day sessions I function more like a player because I've got to be prepared. Everything has to be done right in that moment because you don't get another chance. The guys that come here for two days won't be on the same continent next month if you screw it up. You're not going to get them back [laughs].

When they do come out to Maggie's Farm for this purpose, is there a special kind of "community" vibe?

Yes, very much so. And that is also one of the beauties of jazz and the jazz scene. It's such a small community and I find jazz musicians the most normal musicians I know in terms of ego. It isn't about the money. It really is a very disciplined and dedicated bunch of people.

Most of the people who are in jazz know all the other people who are in it [laughs]. It really is a community, so you might get a group of guys who really only see each other a few times a year, but they're so happy to be here. That's a lot of what our sessions are about; creating an environment that feels as much like a simple playing situation as possible so they can get in and play as they would any other day.

So you make them relaxed and try to create a natural sort of vibe where they can just express themselves?

Yeah. It's about getting in, getting set up, and getting comfortable as quickly as you can, so everybody's not standing around. You can't take three hours to get drum sounds, or all day. We've got two days to make this record. You need to be playing within two to two and a half hours. We'll typically record three to four hours of stuff, enough to get a CD out of, then there's that much editing that then goes into the making of the record.

How hands on are you in terms of the engineering?

I'm pretty much doing the engineering most of the time. On some projects I'll use another engineer if the music is really complex or if I have to follow a music score very closely. Initially, I was bringing engineers out for everything when I built this place. It came to a point where I had to learn the stuff. The engineers that would work out here, like David Baker, James Farber, and especially Michael McDonald, were all more than happy to tell me how things worked and what they did. These guys learned to record in pure analog environments and have a very good understanding of the physics and the mechanisms of recording.

The classic principles of sound, acoustics, mic selection and positioning don't change, right?

Exactly. And that's the stuff I'm still learning. I had to assimilate and learn a lot of stuff before being able to function out here.

Can you kind of walk through what was going through your mind when you first wanted to convert the place?

Well, yeah. In my heart, in a generation from now, if someone didn't want a recording studio out there, I wanted them to be able to convert it to the very barn that it had been before.

Did it have stalls broken out on the inside?

It was basically like a big open space and the loft area. The floor was divided into three even sections divided by a structure of beams and joists that holds up the ceiling, essentially. It was made out of this rough hewn wood that is quite beautiful and was quite functional when it was a barn. I realized early on that I couldn't take that stuff out without having to really change things structurally. As a result of that, that division into thirds was going to have to roughly stay the same. So I took one third of the space and created the control room and the booth, and left the other two thirds just as the big open live room.

So these natural divisions ultimately would define what the studio space was to become?

Yeah. The only drawback was that I was unable to get the sight lines I wanted from the booth into the live room. You can see from the booth into the live room, but you cannot see the whole live room. You see, I built the control room and the booth, but didn't finish the live room for almost two years. I just couldn't afford to do it all. The control room and the booth, which is fairly large, have accommodated as many as four musicians. It's a little cozy [laughs], but they've been in there before. Also, at that time I was still doing a lot of singer/songwriters, so it was more than adequate for that purpose.

When we finally got the live room together, it was becoming clear that jazz was both what I was happiest doing and what the label was having the most success with. The label was doing lots of different kinds of music but didn't have the marketing money to accommodate such a wide range of styles. If we focused on jazz, we knew we could have an impact; for example, if we put out a jazz record, then put out a singer songwriter album a month later, we couldn't advertise in the same publications. Also, we would have to hire different radio promotion people. It was like having two different companies when we could barely afford to have one. Since we were having success with the jazz products that we were doing, it just made sense to focus on that and let the other stuff go. When you put out a singer songwriter product or some kind of pop record, you're suddenly competing with budgets that are way out of our reach. In jazz, even competing with labels like Blue Note, the playing field is level enough that we have a shot.

If you have a good enough performance, you can go right up against it.

Yeah. We can't buy as big ads, and we can't buy as many of them, but if you're accepted by the critics and by the radio people, you can penetrate.

When did you finally begin to engineer your own projects out here?

Within a week or two, I realized that I couldn't just let this place sit empty with no artists. I would have to be engineering. You know, after a while, there's sort of an arc where you get to know something and you might as well start making your own mistakes.

That's a sign of confidence, I think.

I was also totally blessed by the coincidence of finding a wonderful technician, Jim Hildenberger, of Analog Brothers Custom Amplification out here, whose main business is renovating and maintaining guitar amplifiers for touring bands and stuff. Since I've known him, he has built me from scratch a

The barn is a "bank barn", with an A-frame interior that Balitsaris has kept completely intact. *Photo by Jeff Touzeau, courtesy of Hummingbird Media*

Entrance to the iso booth at Maggie's Farm. *Photo by Jeff Touzeau, courtesy of Hummingbird Media*

customized LA-2A from UREI parts, he's racked up a couple of custom Telefunken V72s for me with controls that I specified, he owns and maintains the organ that I keep here, and he's fifteen minutes away. He will also sometimes assist me engineering, particularly during organ sessions or sessions that are going to involve a lot of people and a lot of complications.

It was a total coincidence I found him. I had a local rock band here and they had him as their guitar tech. I noticed there was this guy constantly taking these amplifiers apart while they were doing other tracks! I was like, "Man, who is this guy?"

You've got a great eye for talent!

Yeah. And in building this studio, about 100 miracles happened.

Do you actually record local bands?

Most people that come here come from New York or Philly.

Has anyone ever struck a chord with you and you wanted to bring them on your label?

It's one of the very awkward things that people do. They think that maybe if they book a session here, it will lead to a deal. I have to be pretty candid about that upfront, I don't think it's ever worked that way.

Piano, looking toward the control room. *Photo by Jeff Touzeau, courtesy of Hummingbird Media*

Did you use an acoustician to bring your live room up to a professional spec?

We used Fran Manzella, who I knew from Skyline. I also knew him from East Hill and we had so many common friends that it was a really natural thing to have him out here. I'm so glad I did. Last night I had a woman came in here who was doing some vocal overdubs, and the minute she walked in, she loved the place. She said "This is so wonderful."

I had so many bad experiences while I was playing as a side man that I resolved early on that I would have a professional design the place. I would have it wired by somebody who knew what they were doing. Even if I had two identical sessions back to back, I would strike everything and put it all away, and set it up all over again. I didn't want to wind up with the dreaded tangle of cables and crap on the floor.

You have really high ceilings, at least twenty-one feet high. Did you treat the room in any particular way in light of this?

Well, actually, when we first finished the room, I didn't put any treatment on the ceiling. I really wanted to see what it was like to work in a totally live room. It was like being in the cathedral of St. John the Divine or something. Then, at Fran's suggestion, I started making these panels and put a few up every week or two. He told me, "You won't notice any difference until you're ninety percent of the way there."

Did you make them yourself?

Yeah. They're just little sheets of insulation with fabric wrapped around them. And you know, I got it to a place where it's still fairly live, but it's workable. It's a very nice sound that feels good to me as a player and seems to feel good to other people. Then the process becomes, depending upon what the ensemble is, damping the room down additionally by using gobos and packing blankets. It's also placing the musicians in a relationship with one another so that their mics are bleeding into one another in a complementary rather than a detrimental kind of way, which often means putting them very close together.

The grand piano awash in the bountiful natural light at Maggie's Farm. *Photo by Jeff Touzeau, courtesy of Hummingbird Media*

This was one of those great counterintuitive leaps for me, that leakage is more ugly the greater the distance involved. If I put everybody close together where it's the equivalent of mic'ing a drum kit, then you still have the presence on everything, you know? On one session recently I put the bass in the booth and put the drums and the percussion in the room with the piano and cut the horns kind of facing each other. We then put gobos behind everybody with blankets on them. We put padding behind everyone so we wouldn't get the reflections off the walls.

So you make a sub-environment.

Exactly. And it really worked quite well. Any time you've got drums in the same room as the piano, it's a problem, mostly for the piano player [laughs]. It's very old school stuff, and it's the kind of thing that many people just don't have to deal with because they either have the luxury of having multiple booths, or they're not even recording that many instruments at once. I'd say on that session, that I had at least fifteen mics open on the room at once. They're going to talk to one another, you just have to make sure it doesn't sound really bad when they do.

You have a really good mic collection including Coles, RCA.

Yes, and those are all recent additions, probably in the last year and a half. I had started with what seemed to me a good, but very functional arsenal. I think I got the two '87s, the two 414s, 57s, 421s, just the stuff that you know that you're going to have to have.

And then built up the luxury additions?

Yeah. The C12 was the first thing that I bought that was really just more than "adequate". The Coles were reasonably inexpensive. The same thing with the 44. Michael McDonald had a collection of them and wanted to sell one of them off. Now I can acquire a mic when I can afford it.

You feel like your current equipment is in a good state, and you have all the tools you need to complete any kind of session.

Yeah, there's always something you kind of wish you had. And now there are a few things I wish I could sell off and get one really good thing, but you never know. It's good to have extras of everything.

Would you agree that Maggie's Farm has been a great vehicle for your work overall?

Totally; this studio couldn't have existed fifteen or twenty years ago. This sort of place has flourished as the technology has allowed it to, to do things on a smaller scale and less expensively. It's a cool thing to document that. For me, as someone who wasn't a technician or that technically accomplished, the ADAT was the thing that sort of liberated me from having to go into the big studios and spend a huge hourly fee just to throw some tracks down.

Balitsaris' on-site digital voodoo technician, hailing from Tanzania, keeps unwanted interference at bay. *Photo by Jeff Touzeau, courtesy of Hummingbird Media*

Studio Miraval
Patrice Quef, Producer/Engineer

A helicopter's perspective of the grounds at Miraval. *Photo courtesy of Miraval Studios*

Studio Miraval is situated on a winery in Provence, near Nice in the south of France. The grounds, which were in close proximity to Via Aurelia, one of the five roads radiating from ancient Rome, date back to the twelfth century and once encompassed over 9,000 acres. Through the years, Miraval seems to have had many lives. It was once a monastery and was also once inhabited by Roman soldiers. In the nineteenth century, the cellars of its circa 1300 farmhouse were used to age the red wine varieties that were made and aged at Miraval.

Miraval Studios was conceived in the mid-seventies, when then owner Jacques Loussier, a famous French composer and pianist who lived on the estate, asked his good friend Patrice Quef to set up a project studio for him at Miraval. Quef, who was already an accomplished engineer based out of Phonogram Studios in Paris, was intrigued in the idea, but wouldn't do it if the project was simply to be a vehicle for Loussier's own recordings. In order for the studio to become commercially viable, Quef felt that it needed to rival the best studios that Paris had to offer.

Loussier agreed, and Studio Miraval was born. As history has shown, Quef and Loussier were pioneers of the destination studio in France; in the mid-seventies, a high-end studio more than six km outside of Paris simply didn't exist. In order to succeed, Quef knew that Miraval would need to provide artists with a good reason to leave the security of the metropolis. A breathtaking vineyard environment with state of the art sonic facilities would be more than enough to create the draw.

After taking substantial financial risks that included converting an enormous sheep barn into a live room and purchasing the first SSL in France, Miraval set out to put itself on the map. Success came shortly after when Pink Floyd made arrangements to do overdubs for it's multi-platinum classic recording, *The Wall*. Quef's careful preparation and professionalism had paid off, since the session went off spectacularly (he is a credited engineer on the album, no small achievement). Soon after word got out, the phone was ringing off the hook and Miraval was the destination studio, becoming a temporary home to the likes of Elton John, Sting, Yes, The Cranberries, Sade, and The Cure.

How did you get into the professional audio and engineering business?

I started engineering in Paris in a studio that is now called Studio des Dames. It was a Phonogram studio.

Was this a highly professional set up with an SSL type desk?

No, it was a Phonogram desk, before SSL existed. It was a fantastic desk, made by Philips in Germany. It had compressors and noise gates on every channel. The only problem was that Philips only produced it for their company to use, not for clients.

Were you recording international artists or mainly French artists at this point?

Mainly French artists.

And at this point, also, there was no such thing as "residential studios" in France, correct?

That's correct. All the studios were concentrated around Paris, or just outside Paris. There was one famous called Studio de Rue Ville, which closed thirty years ago, maybe more. It was the first big studio outside of Paris. It was six km outside Paris. They would get international clients on the scale of Elton John.

When you were an engineer in Paris, what genres were you working in primarily? Were you working in pop, jazz, what?

Well, we worked on many different clients. Primarily, we worked on Phonogram artists, but we had clients from many other record companies as well because of its advantageous location in Paris and because it was a really good studio. All the companies would bring their artists to this studio.

Can you describe to me how you discovered Miraval and what prompted your interest in acquiring it?

I discovered Miraval thirty-five years ago because at this time Jacques Loussier was the owner of the place. I began working with him on some film scores in Paris, and on his own albums. Soon we became close friends and he invited me to Miraval on holiday when I had time. When I saw Miraval for the first time it was a shock to me because it was so fantastic, unusual, and so big. The grounds were enormous. There was not only the main house, but also a lot of outbuildings you would typically find on a farm, because they made wine there.

Patrice Quef, owner of Miraval Studios and credited engineer on Pink Floyd's *The Wall*. *Photo courtesy of Miraval Studios*

Do you remember the first time you saw it?

Oh yes. I was so surprised by the beauty. I lived in Paris for thirty-five years, and hadn't seen the south of France, except Brittany, where I was originally from.

At what point did you think "Wow...this would be a great place to get artists out here to record."

I think that must have been around 1975 or '76. Because Jacques was living there, he didn't want to have to keep coming to Paris every time he did an album or did some music. Since we were close, he asked me if I wanted to set up something in Miraval. I said "Sure", it was one of my dreams at the time. So I thought about what kind of equipment to bring out there. We had to be careful in our choice of equipment, since this was a private venture. There was no guarantee we'd be able to get any outside clients. Remember, at this time nobody was recording outside of Paris.

So it was around 1975, and your primary goal was to record Jacques own music.

So once I agreed to set up a studio there, I said "Okay, this will be good to record your stuff, but we also need to record other things, since I cannot survive on your work alone." I said, "If we do a studio, we have to do it professionally. Not like some composer might have at home. He said, "Okay, oui, oui." We got the equipment we needed and tried to bring people out to record. We got a new desk and a 24-track analog deck.

Now Patrice, your main background was engineering. Did you need to bring in a team of acousticians or maintenance folks to help you set up the studio?

Well, the walls were firm, concrete. I think we succeeded in making it sound good on our own, because I knew enough about what we had to do to get the big room into shape. At this time, the studio acoustics were completely dead; no echo, no nothing. And the control room was just partially dead, with no acoustic treatment like we think of today. At this point, we only had a desk, recorder, and acoustic monitor. We used the wine cellars as an echo chamber, because we didn't have echo plates or equipment to facilitate reverb [laughs].

Now that we're in 2004, can you tell me how the room set up has changed or evolved over the years? Are the rooms still in the same relative positions?

Yes. We destroyed the first control room in 1982, because we needed a control room with real acoustics. We had to move forward in order to stay with the market. The control room needed to be bigger, since we often had British clients who were very demanding. They wouldn't have continued using our existing room if we hadn't changed it.

And you got your SSL desk at this point?

Yes. We were the first French studio to buy an SSL desk. It was in 1982. We chose the SSL because when I first heard it doing a session in the UK, in Ridge Farm (Surrey), I was very impressed with the sound quality and functionality. You had automation and so much more flexibility.

At what point did it become evident that artists would become very interested in being isolated among the beauty and serenity of Miraval for their projects? When did you realize that there was a real market for what you were doing?

Well, we always had the intention of being commercially successful, but it takes a long time for a studio's reputation to develop and grow. The first client was Jacques Loussier, and we worked with people from Marseilles initially, mainly artists from the South of France. Then we were lucky. We had Pink Floyd come to record *The Wall*.

How did that happen, how did they find you?

I don't know how they found me, but they were working at a studio called Super Bear, one hour to the north of here.

View of Miraval's live room, from the back door. *Photo courtesy of Miraval Studios*

Super Bear shut down around twenty-five years ago. The Pink Floyd were working in this studio, and after several weeks they left.

Did having a session this big put a lot of pressure on you? Clearly this must have been a very demanding client, at least technically.

Yes. It was a lot of pressure. It was so important for the studio and its reputation once they left Miraval. We tried our best to make everyone happy.

So you made all the arrangements to make it go smoothly.

Yes, and I engineered on that project also.

Can you describe how having them may have influenced your technical set up?

When they came in, the studio was still only 24 tracks, but they seemed happy because it was sufficient for the work they had to do. At this time, they were synchronizing 16 and 24-track decks, and they were one of the first to try this. They began this album in the South of England, then Super Bear, then here, then New York. You know, they recorded it everywhere.

So you worked on overdubs at Miraval for *The Wall*?

Yes. We worked on vocals, bass guitar, some keyboards, and that was about it. They stayed five or six weeks, and they worked very slowly.

Was this a positive experience for you overall?

Yes. It was very good. Especially after what I heard, I loved it. I was able to hear this album before everybody. This album is still selling now, and it's a masterpiece.

How was Pink Floyd to work with? Were they friendly people?

Yes, I engineered right alongside them. I was surprised, because I knew the engineer at Super Bear and he said they can be very, very hard. I didn't know what would happen, but in fact, it was very relaxed, very professional. We had a very good time, and no problem at all.

It must be wonderful to have involvement in such an important album.

It was significant for us. Because when people heard that Pink Floyd was at our studio, it put us right on the map. We started to become a famous studio.

And your phone was ringing after the Floyd left?

Yes. Then we started to get many international artists and big stars. Not only French, but German, Spanish, Dutch, Swiss, Belgian. Most of them were French and English, though.

Miraval's control room, with its SSL console. *Photo courtesy of Miraval Studios*

What did you do with the money you got from your success with Pink Floyd and all the commercial interest that followed?

Well, the problem when you own a studio is that the money you earn, you must reinvest in equipment. Not to get ahead, but to stay in the game. The latest equipment is absolutely necessary to have, and you never seem to get ahead. So a lot of our income is spent investing in new equipment. We try to follow the technical path as closely as possible.

Did you expand the structure of any of the rooms?

When we decided to put the new control room in, we made it significantly larger. The '80s was a time when many of our clients were using synthesizers. At this time, control rooms were often used more than the studios because you could play these instruments right in the control room. They were machines, not acoustic instruments that needed to be mic'ed up. So we decided to put in a control room where we could have all this equipment, with people. The room we had before was too small and was a problem.

Can you give me a personal view of where you are in France, what your surroundings and grounds look like? Describe the geography and the grounds.

Miraval was inhabited in the twelfth century. It was a used as farm lands but was also inhabited by soldiers. The main house is from the seventh century with a chapel in front. The rest of the buildings are part of the farm, except for the building that we use for the studio. The studio was originally where the sheep were kept. It is a very big building eighty meters long, by twenty-five meters wide.

Like a big barn?

Exactly. And we just use a small part of the building; we didn't need to use all of it. The building consists of two floors, the studio being on the first floor.

Are there still animals on the farm?

Not any more. We used to have horses, sheep, and pigs, but no more: only equipment and good wine. We have thirty-five acres of vineyards. The vineyard is owned by an American company that is a famous winemaker. They do red, rosé, and white and have been very successful; they receive medals every year for their wine. Jacques sold this place back in 1992.

Did you ever get involved in the winemaking operations?

I often take part in the tasting, but not the winemaking. You have to know what you do in the wine business.

How many years have they been making wine at Miraval?

Well, I don't know how many years, but Jacques bought this place about forty years ago. Eighty, one hundred years, maybe more. I don't know really.

This statue of an angel is found in Miraval's chapel square. *Photo courtesy of Miraval Studios*

Are there many other vineyards in the area?

Yes, there are many in the South of France. We are part of the Provence region, and it's all vineyards. The quality of this wine is very good. The competition in this area is so hard that the wine has to be high quality.

How far are you from Nice?

We are about 160 kilometers from Nice, and about 70 kilometers from San Tropez, and 70 kilometers north of Toulon, which is a big military harbor on the Mediterranean sea.

Can you give me a little detail of the grounds and residences?

Well, in the twelfth century, Miraval was 9,000 acres. Over the years, owners would just sell off parcels until what you have here in the modern ages. We have three different towers. In the main tower, which is adjacent to the studio, we have a living room where clients can relax and dine. Then above, there are full bedrooms with bathrooms. Then we

View of Miraval Studios section of the estate from main road. *Photo courtesy of Miraval Studios*

have a red house, which is a house with living rooms, bathrooms, and bedrooms. The third place is called New House because it was just renovated by the new American owners. This is another great place for artists to stay, where they can watch T.V., listen to music, or whatever. It's very big, very green, with nothing around.

Clients can go hiking here; they can walk for miles and miles without seeing anyone. Also, there is a 2.5 km private road leading up to Miraval.

Who keeps the place going? Are there groundskeepers?

Yes, there are about ten people who keep the vineyards going. They are all employees of the vineyard.

What is next for Miraval?

Well, we are at the end, I think. I am over sixty years old, and I have to retire myself. I think we are looking to sell. It's finished.

Do you think any buyer would want to continue a studio?

No, because if it's not me, the current owner wouldn't want anyone else managing the studio.

That's really sad.

Yeah, but that's life!

Where do you plan on retiring to?

I would like to stay in the South of France, even though I am originally from the North. It's sunny and beautiful here.

What has made you most happy during your times at Miraval?

Well, we have had a nice experience with clients over the years. Most of them we get along with very well. They like to record in a quiet, green place such as this. I have never worked with clients who cannot be pleased. Clients and artists who came to Miraval, we had a common point. We go for the quality of life.

So you never missed Paris?

No, no. I was so happy to leave Paris. I never missed it even after a few years. Now I never go to Paris unless I am really obliged to go.

What type of music do you like to listen to, and what is the most rewarding for you to record?

Well, at the time, I enjoyed listening to The Cure, Elton John, Pink Floyd, but I listen to more classical music now. We recorded part of The Cure's *Kiss Me, Kiss Me, Kiss Me* here.

Really? What was it like to record The Cure?

It was very interesting because the way they worked was not the usual way. At the end, it was magic: the composition of all the guitars, everything. Robert Smith was very creative. He knew exactly where he wanted to go. At the beginning I was surprised, because nothing was necessarily in tune, nothing really in tempo. But at the end, when they mixed it all together, it was The Cure, the way they were. It was very, very interesting, and he's a very intelligent guy. He knew a lot of French poetry, more than most French people sometimes. I was surprised; he was quoting Descartes and many other French poets.

This road leads to the main country house on the Miraval grounds. *Photo courtesy of Miraval Studios*

What music has been the most rewarding for you to record?

Well, have you ever heard of the dancer Roland Petit? He is a French dancer who has his own company in Marseille. This is wonderful classical music. We had over eighty-five musicians in the studio and it was amazing.

What is your perspective on how the music industry has changed over the years?

Well, for one thing, everyone is recording their music on their own computers. You can do many things that you cannot do on a tape recorder. You have plug-ins, many things to help.

Did any of your sons take an interest in taking over the studio?

No, all my sons have different jobs. They like music, but they are not involved in recording music at all.

Pond at Miraval. *Photo courtesy of Miraval Studios*

Real World Studios
Owen Leech, Studio Manager

The famous Big Room at Real World, with custom wraparound SSL console. *Photo by Kim Touzeau, courtesy of Hummingbird Media*

Real World Studios was built in 1987 by one of the world's most creative and accomplished recording artists, Peter Gabriel. Following the release of his immensely successful So album, Gabriel had the financial means to create a studio complex that provided a technically unsurpassed, artistically challenging environment for musicians from all over the world. He hand picked a team consisting of the most innovative acousticians and engineering minds and turned the traditional methodology of building a recording studio on its head.

Peter's previous studio, where he recorded and mixed So, was situated in a barn on a farm in the environs surrounding the ancient Roman city of Bath. He was once again drawn to this region due to its all-consuming beauty, pervasive history, and surrounding prehistoric mystery: Stonehenge, ancient temples, and burial mounds are all within short driving distance. Real World, a modern technical and aesthetic marvel of its own, seems to fit in with its surroundings perfectly.

The Real World complex is built on thirteen acres, filled with diverse vegetation and topographical features, including lots of water and many streams. The main building is approximately 200 years old and previously served as a water mill, a flour mill, a girls' school, and a semolina factory. Currently, the old mill and its adjacent buildings function as an extended campus for Peter's business operations, all of which are interconnected in some way. Businesses on the grounds include Real World Studios, Real World Records, Peter's publishing outfit WOMAD, and a video studio.

The main studio at Real World, the famous Big Room, is partially submerged underwater. In fact, first thing you notice on entering any room in the facility is that it is awash with air, water, and light, three basic elements necessary for human sustenance. In the Big Room, enormous plate glass windows look out to a magnificent pastoral pond, complete with resident geese and a waterfall. The Stone Room features a glass floor, under which a stream is readily apparent. Huge ceramic pipes circulate fresh air throughout the facility, fulfilling Peter's wish to make it feel like "someone left a door open in another part of the building."

The performance and technical areas in Real World represent the ultimate in flexibility and community between performer, engineer, and producer. The Big Room, The Workroom, and Writing Room are all integrated recording/mixing environments in which the aforementioned parties all perform together as one. After speaking with professionals at Real World, I understand this approach raises the level of expectations for all concerned, making for a synergistic result.

Since its opening, Real World has proven its capability to acclimatize to the needs of a diverse contingent of artists and clients. Whether during its Summer Weeks, in which 300 artists pushed the technical limits of the facility's eleven studios (and then some; cables were patched into a local mine) or during a twelve hour live BBC broadcast that required precise timing cues across multiple locations, Real World provides a symbiotic platform on which clients build their creativity.

Owen Leech was originally a general contractor responsible for the construction of the second phase of Real World. After building a relationship with Peter and the studio's management, he was asked to come on as Studio Manager. Since then, Owen has been partly responsible for bringing in interesting, unique artists from all over the world, keeping all the facilities up to specification, and helping the studio remain successful in a difficult market. Owen feels immensely privileged to be a contributing member of the Real World team.

Can you tell me about what is special or mystical about the region of England where Real World is located? I've heard about ancient burial grounds, UFO sightings.

Owen Leech, studio manager at Real World, was originally acquainted with the Real World team as a contractor. *Photo by Kim Touzeau, courtesy of Hummingbird Media*

Well, it's a very beautiful region, for a start. As far as the UFOs are concerned, there are these things called crop circles which are nearby the Marlborough Downs. Whether they're all a hoax or not, who knows. There are also ancient stones sites like Avebury Stone Circle, which is a very notable one, and Stonehenge is not very far either. There are a lot of ancient of burial sites around these locations. Then there is Glastonbury, down to the southwest, which isn't very far either. So there are all these sacred burial sites that we're surrounded by. Then of course there's Bath, which was originally inhabited by the Romans. The region is steeped in history.

You are an hour away from London?

Yeah, we're about an hour and ten minutes.

Was the complex originally a mill?

It was originally built in about 1820 as a flour mill, then they added a big silo for storing flour. There's a whole line of

The production room at Real World. *Reproduced with kind permission from Real World Studios Ltd. http://realworldstudios.co.uk. Photographer: York Tillyer. © Real World Holdings Ltd., Real World Studios Ltd.*

mills long this river, which is called the Bybrook; it eventually runs into the river Avon, which then goes through Bath. If you go up the Bybrook from where it joins the Avon, which is about four miles down the road from here toward Bath, you come across lots of old stone mill buildings, of which this is the second one. If you walk up the river, you come across one mill after the other.

Some of the buildings on the grounds at Real World go pretty far back, right? Producer's Cottage, for example, is one of the older structures?

Yeah, it was probably built at the end of the 1700s. There was a much older building where the current house is, an old mill owner's house which joined the mill building. I think that was torn down at the end of the nineteenth century though.

What are some of the other lives the grounds and the buildings have been through before it all became Real World?

It was owned by a company called Spafax prior to us and it was used basically as offices and storage. It was quite an institutionalized complex when Peter bought it in 1986, I think.

And in 1986, he had just a home studio and a barn?

Yeah, he rented a barn at a place called Ashcombe, which is about six miles away just on the north end of Bath in a little valley. That's where he made So on an SSL desk, which he subsequently brought here and put in a studio upstairs. We sold that desk about ten years ago.

So the real birth of Real World came about after the success of So? That's what catapulted it if you will?

That's right.

Can you walk me through some of the larger concepts that Peter had in mind when it was designed? Was the intention to make an interconnected, fluid recording environment clear from the start?

I think that grew rather organically. I don't think it was intended at that point. I think it all developed, partly out of the studios, partly out of WOMAD. The record company kind of grew out of WOMAD, and so on and so on. And then the multimedia gradually grew out of the stuff that Peter was doing.

When it was designed, what were some of the key concepts in the brief?

Well, I wasn't here at that stage, I came just slightly after the brief. But the use of natural materials throughout was the main thing; natural materials were to be used as much as possible. So you find a lot of natural stone, a lot of the original

Real World resembles a "creative village", marrying traditional and modern styles of architecture.
Photo by Kim Touzeau, courtesy of Hummingbird Media

View of the Big Room exterior. Air, water, and light are fundamental elements throughout the facility and its grounds. *Reproduced with kind permission from Real World Studios Ltd. http://realworldstudios.co.uk. Photographer: York Tillyer. © Real World Holdings Ltd., Real World Studios Ltd.*

wood; things like clay air conditioning ducts. The idea behind the clay air conditioning ducts is that you are pushing air through a natural material rather than through a rattly, echoey steel chamber.

And the water and light were key too, right?

Yeah. It was fundamental to provide as much daylight as possible in all rooms.

How did you get into studio management and did you have any real musical interests coming into this field?

I only had domestic musical interests, if you see what I mean. I got into this business by way of being a builder. I ended up building part of the site at Real World, then staying on and developing the site. I fell into the studio job in 1991.

What was your role in building the site?

Well, I was running the building company that was employed to build part of the studio, so I was running the job. And at the end of that job, they asked me to stay on, because there were various other bits of development work to do on the site. So I stayed on, employed by Real World. In fact, the reason I stayed on was because I was coming up to forty and I always spent life in ten year cycles. I felt my building cycle was coming to an end, and there was a chance to do something else! [Laughs.] And low and behold, there was.

What can you recall about the building phase itself, depending on what your level of involvement was?

Well, I didn't do the main studio. When I started there, phase two, which included the big room, was just beginning. I think that phase included work on the wooden room, which had just opened. I think that the first people in were Tears for Fears. So I started initially converting the house, then building the writing room and other bits and pieces including the rehearsal room.

Can you describe how the transition phase felt for you, going from a builder to studio manager? What was going on in your head and was it exciting?

It was interesting, but it was similar in that it was management. We had a technical manager and we had engineers in the studio, so I was already coordinating that first hand. The experts were already in there, if you like. I was coordinating, getting the bookings, and moving it all forward.

Did all this occur before Real World had really taken off?

No, by this time it had taken off. The studio had been probably going four years, so that was all running. WOMAD had been running for years and years, and Real World Records had begun to grow at that point. Real World Records became our largest client at Real World Studios by a long way, really. That of course, has dramatically changed over the years.

Can you recall some of the more personally rewarding moments you've had during your tenure there? Did any bright moments stand out?

Well, the BBC did an overnight broadcast from three of the studios; that was a lot of fun. It consisted of eight hour stints of setting up things in one room, moving to another, and back to that one. It was continuous, all going out on a stereo feed into the wooden room at the front of the studio.

The Summer Weeks were the other high point, I guess. During the Summer Weeks, we would host over 300 international artists, producers, and engineers throughout the facility and have about eleven studios running simultaneously. There was stuff going on everywhere; studios running in every little cupboard in the place. We haven't anything on that scale since about 1996, but we've done some scaled down ones since. For example, we did a Writing Week for Polygram France in which they brought over about twenty writers, and we had four studios going at once.

These kinds of projects must be very challenging from a management aspect, and the whole facility probably has to function with the accuracy and dependability of a Swiss watch.

You've got to get it right, because you've only got one chance at it. The problem with being a studio manager is that there are so many people to please and the customer is always right! [Laughs.]

What about just being around such a creative environment personally? Do you feel privileged to be around a region that is so aesthetically beautiful from a geographical point of view?

I feel incredibly privileged. I lived in the Falkland Islands for quite a while as a traveling teacher for about six years, which

The interior of "The Stone Room", which can be accessed on two levels. *Photo by Kim Touzeau, courtesy of Hummingbird Media*

This statue is in the Big Room, directly in front of the room's plate glass windows overlooking the pond. *Photo by Kim Touzeau, courtesy of Hummingbird Media*

was in the real wilderness. Then I moved back to London for about fifteen years, and I really wanted to get out of the city. We had two small children, so when we moved here where you can see the seasons change, it was just really fantastic. Then getting a job at Real World, which is ten minutes from where I live, was remarkably lucky.

Bath and its surrounding region is one of the most beautiful areas I've seen in the UK.

It is one of the most beautiful areas, and it's perfect. It's near enough to London to be able to use London, and the studios are near enough to attract people down from London. So we get the best of both worlds, really. Plus, there's nearby wilderness. There are Brecon Beacons and Dartmoor, so within an hour you can be on a wild hill. It's great.

How far from the coast?

We can go south to the coast in about an hour and a half, or west in about two hours.

Can you think of some of the key facets that make Real World such a big draw for artists, aside from the pastoral setting and the state of the art equipment?

I think that the big room is one of the things that people are drawn to. Also the setting and recording environment is not so corporate, we are different. It's a very user friendly place and the staff is composed of all special people. I think people feel very at home there and they generally want to come back.

Can you tell me about how Real World was designed as an interconnected organism if you will, and how this idea evolved?

Well, the idea was that you could record anything from anywhere. It was just to create an incredible, flexible recording environment. We put tie lines all over the place, even into the house. For instance, we used them during that BBC broadcast when we had a party going on at the house. You could just patch right through to the studio from anywhere in the house. So that was the concept. If you found a little space and liked it, we'd create a patch on the wall and you'd be able to use it. I think that kind of vision to start with really paid off.

So the facility was built completely interconnected with itself, but it was also connected with its outside environment in a more aesthetic sense, with the water and the setting.

Yes, I have a story about the water. During one of the recording weeks, a recording artist, Michael Brook, was working outside just by the writing room where the waterfall is...he wanted the water turned off! He said it was making far too much noise and he seriously expected us to turn it off [laughs], which we refused to do.

At that time, also, we recorded inside a lot of underground mines which are all around the area. We used one of those in a recording, which was quite fun.

What kind of mines are in the area?

Well, the whole city of Bath is built with this pale yellow stone and there were all these mines, which they no longer use. There was a big one just up the hill from Box. So we got

Rear diffusion and ceiling treatment of the Big Room. A riser at the rear of the room can accommodate a multi-piece ensemble. *Photo by Kim Touzeau, courtesy of Hummingbird Media*

the guy who owned it to let us go in there and use it. During this particular Recording Week, we'd go up there with different artists. You get an extraordinary dead kind of sound in there.

What kinds of facilities does Real World compete with? Or are you competing more with the home recording thing?

Well, we're competing with all the big studios, on an international scale. Allaire is perhaps similar, in a way. Randall Wallace, the owner of Allaire, came over and looked at Real World while he was in the process of building his facility. It's a similar concept, actually. He started with a much bigger site and building though. I mean the Great Hall looks huge. I think there's a similar concept with the desk, where you can do everything in a single room.

Yes. It's a stunning, great sounding room.

There's also Rockfield and some other places of varying sizes and prices. Overall, things seem to be getting less expensive, which obviously has a net effect on the market. I guess the main London ones we compete with are Air, Abbey Road, Town House, Olympic, and some others. As for us, we are currently thinking of replacing the desk in the big room with a new custom SSL, the same shape.

What is your ideal client at this point? You've been around Real World for many years now and you probably have a good idea as to what fits and what doesn't fit. What type of artist or group really uses Real World to its full advantage?

I think bands do. The whole garage/Pro Tools thing is limited in a way and there will always be the need for a studio like ours.

Is there seasonality to Real World? Does business seem to ebb and flow?

Not really. I guess if anything, maybe August is a quieter period because bands are doing festivals and everyone is on holiday. It goes in cycles, but there seems to be no particular reason or explanation for it. It might be quiet, but then the phone is ringing off the hook.

Right now we've got an American jazz band in from Sony New York for two weeks doing an album. I think the first album they did in four days, which was a few years ago. This one they recorded the whole thing live and mixed it. We've also got a band in from Manchester called Performance who is doing their first album for Polydor over here. Then we have the lead singer for a band called Powerderfinger from Australia, who is doing a solo project.

So you're really getting clients in on a truly international scale.

Well, especially now it is an unusual thing to get an American session in, partly because of the weakness of the dollar. It's a killer.

A running stream is viewable through the partial-glass floor in the Stone Room. *Photo by Kim Touzeau, courtesy of Hummingbird Media*

Tchad Blake, who moved over here, loves the big room. He calls the big room the best room he's ever mixed in. And he also married one of our engineers, which helped. He brings in a lot of work for us.

Is Peter bringing any projects in these days? To what degree does he use the facility currently?

Well, he's working all the time and he's currently working on a new album, which amazingly, will be completed by early next year. In May, I think. He's also involved in a couple of other projects, like he always is.

When Real World was originally developed, wasn't one of the intentions to create a full on video production facility? How has that been going, and do you do much video these days?

There were plans to build a big video studio, a huge studio, on the lawn. It was supposed to be enormous, even larger than the Big Room, with these huge ceilings. But it never got built. We currently do all our own in house videos. We occasionally do videos for people outside as well.

One would think that your philosophy on drawing people in from London for audio would also be relevant for those wanting to shoot video outside of London, in the pastoral countryside.

We do TV documentaries and things, and there is always the possibility of doing more. We have interesting spaces to do these kinds of things so we can always move in that direction.

The exterior of the Big Room, seen across from the pond. *Reproduced with kind permission from Real World Studios Ltd. http://realworldstudios.co.uk. Photographer: York Tillyer. © Real World Holdings Ltd., Real World Studios Ltd.*

Can you talk briefly about the strengths of the big room from a performance perspective? There is the obvious aspect of the producer/engineer/artist working in the same room, but what are some of the other strengths of the room?

Well, I think a lot of it is the abundance of natural light and the fresh air. There are huge plate glass windows in front, and natural air circulating all the time. You can work in there with the door open, and it's not a hindrance. Peter's vision from the start evolved from his working in cavernous, dark, underground studios with no light. So one of his primary concerns was to build a place with a lot of light and one in which fresh air doesn't come out of a hole in the wall to be recycled round and round. The space is very amenable to the whole thing. Plus, the way the rear of the room is raised, you can have small audiences in there. We've thought of doing more intimate performances in here that could be broadcast on the web, that sort of thing.

What were some of the acoustic challenges dealing with the Big Room? Does it have an acoustic flavor?

I would describe it as very even. I don't really know how to describe its acoustic flavor. The acoustician was Neil Grant. The task was to prevent sound from going around and around the room, endlessly. Some people get unnerved when they see it, then they love it.

What was the transition to the big room like for Peter, who formerly worked out of a small barn on his property with his SSL?

Well, in fact, he doesn't often work in the big room. He's got two other rooms, which are much smaller. Peter's got the writing room, which we're actually in the process of transitioning into a more portable studio in which we can relocate the equipment following a recent fire we had on the grounds. This type of portable set up would be advantageous for Peter. For example, he is working in Sardinia this summer, so he could take his set up there, and then bring it back when he returns.

You have an interesting vantage point from an operational perspective. What does it take to keep the whole machine running?

Lots of money [laughs]! It just takes money. I think the good studio years were probably the early to late nineties. It's not easy. Talk to any studio manager. You need to keep up with all the latest technologies.

RealWorld's door plate on entrance. *Photo by Kim Touzeau, courtesy of Hummingbird Media*

The exterior shell of the Big Room. Though built only recently, the structure's appearance is classic and workmanlike.
Photo by Kim Touzeau, courtesy of Hummingbird Media

How many staff members are there at Real World, and what different functions?

Well, in the studio, we have two technical maintenance guys full time. We used to have three, but we've trimmed that down to two. We have three engineers, and then Peter has an assistant engineer. Then we have various domestic staff, including the chef, who keep the house running. On the whole, there are about eighty people, when you include WOMAD, the studio, the art and design, etc.

Some of the structures on the grounds date back to the late 1700s. *Photo by Kim Touzeau, courtesy of Hummingbird Media*

How many acres do you guys have?

Thirteen.

Is there a trend that you are seeing between mixing and tracking? Are you getting mostly one or the other?

Well, traditionally, people would use Real World for tracking and then they would often go back to London to mix. That's partly because producers quite like to get rid of the artist for the mixing period. So naturally, you wouldn't go to a residential facility to do that. Having said that, we do many complete album projects where people record and mix. I don't think there's any change there, really. I think that what's really changed is the size of the market; the people who are willing to pay more to go and use the Big Room.

Can you describe Peter's day to day involvement in the studio operations?

Well, he's very interested in who is in the studio, because he will eat in the house with them and talk to them. Quite often, he will go off and get them to play on his record.

He's presumably helped recruit some of the artists that he feels aligned with to come to Real World and record, right?

He's done that, yeah. He's always very interested in what's going on.

The Writing Room at night, Peter Gabriel's personal studio and composing environment on the grounds. *Reproduced with kind permission from Real World Studios Ltd. http://realworldstudios.co.uk. Photographer: York Tillyer. © Real World Holdings Ltd., Real World Studios Ltd.*

Exterior view of the workroom (top). *Photo by Kim Touzeau, courtesy of Hummingbird Media*

When I visited Real World and saw his personal recording space, it was very clear to me that he's also deep into the technology aspect. I saw loads of gear which presumably he evaluates and demos on a regular basis. Is this the case?

I think to a very large degree he is interested in what technology can do and all the latest changes and developments.

Is Tchad Blake there now? Do you often have "producers in residence" for extended periods of time? That is an interesting concept, especially for a place like Real World.

Ideally, Tchad would like to have the Big Room to himself and have all his projects go there [laughs]! But that just doesn't work out. He's just been working with Tracy Chapman in San Francisco for the last two months, and he was working with Bonnie Raitt before Christmas. He lives close to Box and he has two young children, so he likes to work close to home. And as I said, he loves the Big Room. But sometimes, unfortunately, you have to go away.

Big Room exterior at night. *Reproduced with kind permission from Real World Studios Ltd. http://realworldstudios.co.uk. Photographer: York Tillyer. © Real World Holdings Ltd., Real World Studios Ltd.*

Red Barn Studios

Al Jardine, Artist/Owner

Exterior of Red Barn Studios. The grounds were originally part of many cattle ranches owned by The Pfeiffers, a regionally influential and wealthy family from Germany. *Photo by Kim Touzeau, courtesy of Hummingbird Media*

Al Jardine is a founding member of arguably the most important musical group ever to emerge out of the United States: The Beach Boys. While they need no introduction here, suffice it to say that they had an unrivaled string of number one hits and even gave The Beatles a run for their money. Their album *Pet Sounds* is widely regarded as one of the most classic recordings ever made, standing right up against The Beatles' *Sergeant Peppers Lonely Hearts Club Band* and Pink Floyd's *The Dark Side of the Moon* in timeless quality.

Their legacy, which has become ingrained to American and Californian culture, is a lifelong achievement that Jardine remembers with great fondness, despite having worked on a relentless schedule during the group's heyday in the sixties. His decision to create Red Barn Studios was partly an effort to escape the confines of the L.A. recording scene, to which he was literally imprisoned, spending twelve hours a day for weeks inside the concrete walls of Western United Studio on Sunset Boulevard.

Al built Red Barn Studios from an existing structure on his eighty acre ranch in Big Sur, California, thirty-one years ago. Big Sur is located directly off of Scenic Highway One, which provides a breathtaking if challenging drive, about 150 miles south of San Francisco. Big Sur's coastline is staggering in its beauty, with rugged terrain and diverse vegetation. During the turn of the twentieth century, the area of Big Sur was largely supported by the Redwood lumbering industry, requiring transport by ship that was often treacherous due to the rocky and unforgiving coastline (despite the addition of a lighthouse in 1889).

Jardine's ranch was originally owned by the Pfieffers, a German family who raised livestock in the area. It is situated directly adjacent to Pfeiffer Beach, renowned for its breathtaking beauty and ornate rock outcroppings. As is the case with many other places in this book, it is not difficult to imagine how close proximity to such natural breathtaking beauty could inspire and enhance one's recording experience.

When Jardine built the studio, he didn't cut any corners and maintained a very high standard working with acoustician George Augspurger. Jardine has recorded many of his own pieces in the studio over the years, but says that the environment works particularly well for Jazz. Noted trumpet player Roy Hargrove recorded his critically acclaimed *Roy Hargrove With Strings* album here, a project which Jardine felt quite privileged to host.

Al Jardine, original Beach Boy and owner of Red Barn Studios. *Photo by Kim Touzeau, courtesy of Hummingbird Media*

How did your project studio start out? Why did you build a recording space?

Well, it really emanates from a desire to be in a less hectic environment. We are a product of the Los Angeles-based, or Southern California traffic, and essentially, I was doing the great escape as we all did. Carl Wilson went to Denver, Colorado, to Caribou, another great destination studio, which unfortunately burned down in its entirety. Jim Guercio, who owned it and never rebuilt, was an inspiration to both Carl and myself. His studio was responsible for producing all of the Chicago albums, the early ones, through 22, whatever the number was! He also recorded a lot of country folks, a lot of cross-the-board folks. I thought I would love to have something in that order along those lines. Jimmy was very helpful in getting me established here; I mean, I was already here physically, but he encouraged me to build a world class studio.

And you decided to stay in California.

Yes. Carl was the only one at that time who escaped to that area of the world. Mike Love now resides in Lake Tahoe and Brian is the only one who really stayed home. He is a product of Southern California, and he seems to enjoy it there. The rest of us just felt a little too claustrophobic. Most of us spend our lives on the road anyway, but the real issue was that as soon as we got home, we'd have to go into the studio. We had very little time for any kind of quality existence. So this was my statement. I wanted to go for quality rather than quantity, so I established this big base in Big Sur, California, thirty-one years ago this summer.

Could you tell me about Big Sur?

It has a transcendent beauty in that it eclipses everything that you could imagine. I guess if I could give you a parallel description, it would be the Hawaiian Islands on the mainland of the United States. It has that kind of beauty, and its not just subtle. We have some serious mountain ranges, some seascapes, some great beaches. A lot of artistic folks, people in the arts, photographers, and painters live here.

What about the grounds on which Red Barn Studios is specifically situated?

We're on about eighty acres, with trails and things. This estate was originally settled by a family from Germany called the Pfeiffers, and they ran livestock here. In fact, a lot of the families down the coast had cattle ranches. Once a year they'd drive their cattle to town, they'd come right through here to our place, pick up the cattle, and keep going. And this was kind of a breeding area for livestock. When those days died out, a real estate developer came up here and started cutting up all the land around and selling off parcels. I got the last remaining big parcel, which was where the homestead was, and the facilities for the ranch. It's about forty minutes from town; not too hard to get to and it's a beautiful drive. That's my favorite part. I never get tired of the drive, because you have that beautiful ocean vista, whichever way you're going. It never gets boring.

Al's fire helmet. *Photo by Kim Touzeau, courtesy of Hummingbird Media*

Following this period of cattle ranches, did Big Sur become known more as an exclusive vacation spot?

Do you know who used to vacation here every year? Bobby Darin. He used to trailer back there behind the barn. I was in that end stall doing some tinkering, and he came up behind me and I said, "Who is this coming in?" He was bald, he was kind of puffy, and he had his son with him. It was about a month before he died. He was driving to LA at that time and told me that he always used to summer here. I didn't know he was dying at the time, but he brought his trailer in and parked it behind the barn. The former owner allowed him to stay, you know, because he was Bobby Darin [laughs]. Everyone knew who Bobby Darin was, at least in the early sixties. The long and short of it is, he said something very poignant. It was a self-recrimination, "Why didn't I ever buy a place like this? My whole life I spent in the city, in L.A. I've always been, you know, doing the city thing. And I never spent any time and bought a place like this and spent more time with my kids." So I said "Well, you can still do it!" Now I see what he was getting at. Again, he didn't look like Bobby Darin then, because he was going through chemo.

He clearly must have seen it as a retreat. Al, when you found this estate originally, were you looking at it as a potential recording environment, or fundamentally as a residence?

It was primarily a residence, but I always had it in the back of my mind to put the barn back in order. It was pretty much falling down and ready to go to the scrap heap. There was a leaky roof and all my stuff got rained on. I literally had to build a building inside of a building. It was just an exterior, really.

And you probably had a little home recording set up all along, right?

Oh yeah. I had a little four-track studio in one end of the barn. It was an old cattle barn that the original settlers here erected for their livestock. So, again, when we started working with Jim Guercio at Caribou, he got us recording in that beautiful environment in Colorado, and I thought Big Sur is just as beautiful and could be just as productive.

Can you tell me what makes the interior of Red Barn special?

What I liked about this space in the barn here was the thirty foot ceilings, the space, and the light. I built the control room so there's a lot of light coming in, rather than the dark, closed in feeling of a regular recording studio where you stay up all night and don't want to see the sun come up. You don't care. Your life flashes before your eyes after about thirty years, and you realize that you do care. I would really love to see the sunrise and the sunset. And I don't like living the life of a vampire. So I put windows in the back so I could see out. There are a couple studios in Canada that have that same thing. I was inspired by a couple beautiful visionary type things up there....some studio on a lake somewhere.

I guess windows aren't popular among many acousticians, but a lot of people really like the feel of being able to see out, bringing the environment in.

As long as you can manage the reflective surfaces; anyone can treat any room with anything. And you can treat it. Just figure out where the problem areas are. If there's too much bass in one end, just trap it with something. Or if there's too much reflection, absorb it. In rock n roll, it's definitely more about atmosphere.

Having this place be part of your residence must be great; obviously it makes the work/life thing easy, right? And it must be a good retreat to write as well....

Yes. Recently I've been using it mostly for live sessions. We're just dropping a couple of stereo mics over the stage and the band can come in and just cut live and feel the ambience of the room rather than going to the 24-68, whatever tracks they have now. A live performance band can really sound the way they sound, and I can capture that on my old ATR 2-track.

You've had some remarkable recording experiences, especially the vocal sessions you did as an original member of the Beach Boys. Were these vocals with the Beach Boys mostly done live? Was it just you, Brian, Mike, and Carl around a couple of mics?

Oh yeah. We'd sing as a group. We'd do the backgrounds. Sometimes we'd just do a trio or a quartet. Actually the trio would sing the backgrounds, then Mike Love, who has absolutely no patience for mistakes because he was born perfect, would be upset and pout so we let him go. He could leave the room. We'd get our parts done, then he would come back and within a few hours, he could get all his parts done by himself. He would overdub because he didn't have the patience to wait for the rest of us; when

This kind of breathtaking ocean view is typical in the Big Sur region. *Photo by Jeff Touzeau, courtesy of Hummingbird Media*

you're singing a triad or more, there's invariably going to be someone who is flat or sharp, and sometimes you have to retake it. Afterwards, you'd put the lead on.

Al, what was typically your part in these triads and multiple harmonies?

I was the second tenor. Brian was always the high part and Carl was below me. He was kind of a tenor too. We were all tenors, really. Mike was a Baritone, and Brian was a falsetto on top of that. He would overdub the falsettos on top of our triad.

He'd double-track them?

Oh yeah. He always double tracked. God yeah.

And would you double-track your triads?

As soon as we discovered how good something sounds double-tracked, we never went back.

So you double tracked your triads, too?

We always doubled everything. Then we triple-tracked after that. When Jimmy Guercio got involved, he and Carl had a production on one song and he insisted on triple-tracking everything. That got really hairy, because it took so long. How much is too much? Or how much is enough? A song called "Good", "Good Time", or "Good Feeling". A song co-written with Carl and Brian, and Jimmy was the producer. Good vocal sound. That triple-tracking can really get fat.

I would imagine that you guys probably nailed these triads many times in the first take, right? Did you really have to work hard or were there a lot of really good first takes when you did these harmonies?

No, we had to sing a lot, particularly when our voices were cold. We didn't warm up or anything, I mean we weren't professional singers. We just started singing around the piano. We'd go to the microphone and invariably someone would flat; Brian was real, real particular about that. He didn't want anyone flatting or sharping. Sharping was better than flatting, but it's a tendency of the human voice to flat a little bit. So we would invariably, at least during the first six or seven albums, work very hard at getting it right. Then after *Pet Sounds*, *Pet Sounds* was the pinnacle. That one we worked on from six months to a year.

Was it ever competitive in terms of getting vocal parts within the Beach Boys? Did you have to fight or speak up to do a lead vocal? Or were the parts sort of dished out?

Yeah, Brian usually assigned us. He always had somebody in mind while he was composing, except for "Sloop John B". We all tried out for that.

The main stage/live room at Red Barn. Jardine often hangs a pair of ambient mics to capture whatever is coming from the stage.
Photo by Kim Touzeau, courtesy of Hummingbird Media

Did you play guitar before you joined the Beach Boys? Or were the instruments kind of assigned to each of you?

Well, I played bass originally. Carl picked up a guitar, Mike Love picked up fiddlesticks, Dennis had to play drums. Actually, Brian played drums on our first record. He played a snare beat. We just made do with what we had. I had a folk music background, so I was able to get through surf tunes. That was easy.

Did you have any idea how much The Beach Boys music would affect American and Californian culture when all this was happening? I mean, when people think of California, its synonymous with The Beach Boys. Did you realize the influence you were having?

No. We were stuck in Hollywood in little cement boxes and never saw the light of day. It was brutal to be honest with you.

Did you have fun, or was it just a dizzy whirlwind for you looking back?

It was the hardest work I've ever done, and I've done a lot of different kinds of work. Being on a ranch like this is hard work, but it's nothing compared to being confined in a studio twelve hours a day, and the next day going off on tour for thirty days, then coming back going into the studio. It's more like being in confinement, almost like being in High School. Did you ever get that feeling that you couldn't wait to get out?

You were controlled by other people?

Yeah, you were controlled by other circumstances rather than controlling it. Outside things started to control us; these A&R people started having expectations about what they wanted. And Brian of course was one of the first ones to say "Fuck you. We're going to work in our own studio." Thank God; we were at least able to get out of being under the tutelage of the Senior Vice President of Marketing, or whoever it was. We were able to pick and choose the studios we wanted. Nonetheless, Brian was so prolific and had so much creativity that we were just breathless just trying to keep up with him. It was like a marathon for like four, five years straight.

Al Jardine poses beside his grand piano as he works out a key for a recent recording project. *Photo by Kim Touzeau, courtesy of Hummingbird Media*

The "saloon" at Red Barn, where people can take a break from recording sessions and be served by none other than an original Beach Boy. *Photo by Kim Touzeau, courtesy of Hummingbird Media.*

It sounds exhausting.

Plus, the expectations at the time: the record companies wanted you to tour, and the agencies. Everyone takes a piece of your earnings, so you're always being encouraged to work, which is good. Now it's cool, because we can work whenever we want to work, if we're not suing each other. As you may or may not know, Mike Love has this little license towards the corporation and I'm not allowed to call myself a Beach Boy on the road. I can discuss my history with the band and all of our wonderful years together, but I'm no longer able to capitalize on it in a certain way. And I love the songs. I miss singing, I miss performing, and I can't wait to get back on the road.

Now that you're beyond all the busy, busy times with the Beach Boys, I'm sure it was a relief in a way to have more time to yourself, and more time to perform or record. Did you find that life was a lot less stressful when those Beach Boys years toned down?

Those first five years were just a grind. It was really great from '75 on, to about '90. Those were wonderful years because we were more in control of our destiny.

That's when you were working at Red Barn, too.

Yes, beginning from the early seventies. In fact The Beach Boys did an album up here called *Keeping the Summer Alive* before there was a control room. We just used the main atrium and the studio itself as a vocal chamber. We set a mic up completely outdoors and we did a beautiful a cappella. It sounds kind of like "Our Prayer", it has that same vibe to it. I think it's called "America" and it's on one of our lesser known works. Bruce Johnston actually wrote and arranged that; we set a microphone up on the back steps, right out in the middle of the woods in the back of the barn there, and got a great natural sound.

Didn't you take some Christmas tapes from some other studio and finesse them at Red Barn or something?

Oh yeah! Capital wanted to do an *Ultimate Christmas* album and I ended up just cleaning up these tracks with the original engineer from our Surf's Up days, Steve Vesper. He came out of retirement and helped me finish up; it was a lot of fun. It was like working at Brian's house in Bel Air in the seventies when we did the *Smiley Smile* project.

Each Beach Boy really had his own home studio at one time or another. Actually I think Mike Love has his own now too. I don't know what he could possibly do with it, since he doesn't play any instruments, but maybe he produces things. We were going to do "Kokomo" here at Red Barn, but the studio wasn't done in time, so we had to do it down in Santa Monica at this little studio called 4th Street Studio.

One of the many outbuildings found amongst Jardine's lush green estate. *Photo by Kim Touzeau, courtesy of Hummingbird Media*

A Wurlitzer jukebox stands beside the window looking into the control room. To the left are Jardine's nostalgic collection of Beach Boy tour posters from around the world. *Photo by Kim Touzeau, courtesy of Hummingbird Media*

So at some point, you decided you didn't just want a project studio. You wanted a state of the art facility.

Well, the Beach Boys wanted to continue recording as the way we had been, on analog, because we never really graduated successfully to the digital format. We always sounded better on tape, so I put in an analog studio. Then Bruce Johnston came up with a bright idea of us having something called Pro Tools, entirely without tape. And I'm going, "What you mean, without tape?" It turned out that we spent half our time on the phone with Digidesign, because we were the very first group ever to record a whole album on Pro Tools.

Is that right? That's good nostalgia.

Except it was a shitty experience since the engineer didn't know what the hell he was doing and we kept having to stop and start. It was just a different technology. I love Pro Tools, by the way, and I'm not knocking it. As a mixing and editing medium, it's beautiful.

But not for tracking, right?

Well, no. We didn't get any bass response. It was just kind of like a gutless sounding production. We were pioneering the thing, and quite frankly it wasn't very fair to them or to us. We did sell a few albums, but it didn't have the production.

No comparison with the Ampex ATR anyway.

No way, no way. But it has come a long way. I mean this is back in 1989. "Kokomo" was not done on Pro Tools. It was a little analog recording. But there you go; it sold millions of records, right? Suddenly we have this massive frickin' project on Pro Tools, I think the engineer just wasn't ready for all the nuances. But now, you can get a little outfit for your studio, and man, it's awesome. It's so fast and so clean.

I would imagine you are somebody who has some pretty strong opinions on the vocal chain. What preamps and mics do you use on your vocals?

You know what? I'm not that technical. There are people who are, but I'm not that sophisticated about that part there, I guess I should be.

Well, they say that the most important part of the signal chain is the instrument or the source, and if that's the case, you're starting from a pretty high common denominator.

I've got a Trident TSM in my studio. They say it's got good preamps in it, but then they all talk about getting Neve is it? I don't know, there's so many kinds. Like you say, the main instrument is your voice. Those things can enhance, but they're

Red Barn's Trident TSM console came from Gold Star. *Photo by Kim Touzeau, courtesy of Hummingbird Media*

not going to change anything that dramatically. Truthfully, I think it's the rooms, the mics, the preamps of course, and the echo chambers. The Capital chambers and the Gold Star chambers, I think there's nothing like them.

These chambers clearly made an impact on your sound?

Shit yes! Are you kidding? Listen to Frank Sinatra and all the big stuff that came out of Capital. Most of ours were done at a place called Western United on Sunset Boulevard. It was the seminal early years for us.

Which is now Ocean Way, right?

Yes. That then moved next door to United, but it's not in the same building we were in. Now we're using these plates and it's just not the same. I'd like to build a real chamber. I'd like to build several. I've got the room for it.

So the plate and digital reverbs really don't cut it for you.

Well, they're cutting it for the kind of music that people are doing these days. I would like to have a real chamber. We converted Brian's chauffeur's quarters in his Bel Air mansion. There was a little room down there underneath the studio, and Steve Desper had it converted into a chamber; it sounded great. As long as you get enough distance between the microphone and the little speaker in there, it's great. That's how you get your different slap sounds, by positioning the microphone at different positions within the room. It's kind of fascinating, really. I really enjoyed that: a real, live chamber. That's kind of where it's at. Capital still has the best rooms.

What about mics? Do certain microphones give you the best sound?

Neumann's of course, they're the best. But there's this other one I like on myself. 413? No, no 414. 413 is a Dodge, a Dodge engine [sings] 413's really diggin' in! You know, the new German mics are still the best.

Can you take me through the rooms at Red Barn and describe the features of each room?

You walk into an entry room on the ground floor, the kitchen. There's kind of a chandelier there, and a bar in the back and a place to prepare food. And then the main room is through a couple of large sliding doors into a roughly 25' x 25' main recording room.

How are the ceilings? Post and beam?

Yeah. We preserved all the hand-hewn beams, which are in evidence. It still has that character; when you walk into that studio it feels like 1970 all over again. And there's acoustic treatment on the ceilings, which are about 30' at their highest point. The control room is then through a door to the right. It's a trapezoidal room designed by George Augspurger. It was a live end dead end originally, and I suppose it could still be considered that, but it's not really. It has that trapezoidal shape to it, though. Desper put a nice bass trap in at the front. We used to get a little overload in the back as the ceiling comes down, but again, we figured that out and put in a bass trap. It's got a lot of glass and you can see all over the room. Good visuals.

Is there glass in the big room?

Oh yeah. There's some beautiful glass, and a stage where we're doing the live performances on one end. To the rear is an isolation booth for drums or for a jazz ensemble. Roy Hargrove, this young Jazz phenom, cut a string section there, and with the bass, you would isolate some members. When they tracked the basics, they would put the bass player in the isolation room, and the drummer in the big room, with baffles of course. It was just great.

Do you often sit in on sessions and take an active interest?

On that one I did. We had the Big Sur Jazz festival here, and I wanted to catch how they work. I wanted to mix with the musicians and see how they work together.

That's great that you get so involved.

Well, it was a great honor, because these guys are such great players. It's a particular medium. These guys are so polite, laid back, you know, no drugs, you'd think there would be, but now everybody is so mature. And these jazz guys don't make the big bucks, you know. Not the millions that a rock star has, who can come in and have everything that he wants: tear the place apart and bill the record company. These guys are real gentlemen. It was a real learning experience for me. I realized how great this studio is.

When did you kind of realize that you wanted to share this special place with other people commercially, rather than reserving it strictly for your own use?

I don't know, it just kind of evolved, really. A studio engineer from San Francisco actually gave me the green light and said "It's time to build a studio", because he loved Big Sur, still does. He likes to come down and visit. He basically brought the

The barn's loft has a pool table and comfortable seating for clients in between takes. *Photo by Kim Touzeau, courtesy of Hummingbird Media*

construction folks that did the actual wiring. Doc Schaffer is his name, out of San Francisco. Those guys are good, I'll tell you. Never had any cataclysmic problems, it's always been very, very smooth.

I bet that was kind of fun to watch that construction go down.

I was on the road most of the time, actually. I didn't get to see too much of it, but I bet they had a lot of fun [laughs]!

So you came back and it was completed.

Yeah, we had to get ourselves a mixing console, and we ended up buying this Trident TSM out of Gold Star just after they tore the place down. The owner took this console home with him. It was brand new, or had very few hours on it. He just covered it, and put it in his living room. So I grabbed it. There are a lot of those TSMs in the area.

Sounds like that one was meant to be in Red Barn.

Pretty complicated barn, I tell you. It's got a lot of modifications. We are state of the art 1970, so the technical stuff wouldn't be that impressive to an audiophile these days. It gets interesting. It works. Again, we're just an old-fashioned analog studio.

Do you have people on hand to help you?

Yeah, yeah. I can't do it myself. I just am not wired up that way. I thought I could run it all by myself [laughs] but I was so surprised. I couldn't believe it. I even had an instruction tape made up for it. I had a guy come in and film everything, then I lost the goddamn tape or something. The next week or two, I was completely lost again. 'Till this day, I still can't find the darn tape. I always seem to forget everything I learn.

I guess that makes you more like an artist, right side of brain kind of guy.

I don't know. I used to think I could handle it. I can handle the smaller consoles, but I just need that objectivity. It's just not good to do it all yourself.

What else have you been doing in your spare time?

Well, I just finished a children's book here, called *The Adventures of the Sloop John B*. On my website, we're offering like a hundred or so to my fan club and I'll sign them and everything.

Is this an audio book, or a real book?

It's a real children's book [laughs] with a little CD. So I reproduced my version of "The Sloop John B." in the studio, and I found I could not punch in fast enough, because the punches were too tight. I'd end up erasing something before I'd get there or rushing the pattern because I was so tight to the punch. I don't know if you've ever had that experience, but punching in is an art form to itself. Punching in and playing is

Bixby Bridge, a engineering marvel, was built in 1932 and crosses a canyon in Big Sur.
Photo by Jeff Touzeau, courtesy of Hummingbird Media

These descendants of the Pfeiffer's original livestock enjoy picturesque surroundings and a most agreeable climate.
Photo by Jeff Touzeau, courtesy of Hummingbird Media

The rocky coastline of Pfeiffer Beach offers Red Barn clients the best of regional scenery. *Photo by Jeff Touzeau, courtesy of Hummingbird Media*

An original Wurlitzer jukebox graces Red Barn's live room. *Photo by Kim Touzeau, courtesy of Hummingbird Media*

a real art form. So I went though this whole damn thing and realized I had to have an engineer down here. I called him in here and he did all the punches for me because you can't do it all yourself. I played all the instruments on it, but I couldn't do the punches.

So why did you write a children's book?

Well, someone asked me if I would, and I thought, "Well, I could write one about the Sloop John B. and these pirates chasing this little ship and the child rescuing his grandfather." And they loved it. It was just a conversation I was having, and they really liked it.

It sounds really neat.

And it came out really good! I was really happy with it. And, I did have a grandchild.

Congratulations!

She's a little girl, and I autographed my first book to her.

Well, that's good timing and that's a good thing for a granddad to do! Do you have any other recent projects you've been working on that you want to talk about?

I haven't done a whole lot lately, to be honest with you. A couple of local things, some of my neighbors are musicians and they've worked here, the Big Sur Natives. It was quite good, called *Barefoot*; more of a drumming experience. There are some songs and there's some singing, now that I think about it.

You're not listed in any studio directories, either, right?

No. I should be, though.

But that's a pretty big chasm to jump across, to become a full on commercial studio.

Yeah, then you'd have to keep an engineer on full time. I guess I like it this way. It's a beautiful place, we're about a tenth of a mile from the beach, the artists can get some fresh air, walk around, and there are some fantastic restaurants around here. There are wonderful people and a variety of cuisines.

So what are your plans for the future? What's next for you?

Thank you for asking. I'm creating the Endless Summer Band, and it's in its formation as we speak. It's fundamentally the same thing I've been doing all my life, but in a new way so as to be a little bit more beneficial to me; more generic, perhaps. To describe the music, it's basically going to be the Beach Boys catalog. I have to have some name though that doesn't say the Beach Boys.

That's such a great choice. I remember when my brother turned me on to *The Endless Summer* album when I was little. That album captures the whole feel of summer and The Beach Boys.

We thought that was right. And the Bruce Brown films that spawned the genre of the wonderful surf movies that we grew up with, I mean these surf movies were our first live engagements. We would play during intermission in between the films. That's how we became aware of that medium.

Where were they playing these films?

Southern California, mainly. People actually came in and paid to see a surf movie. It's really interesting if you think about it. I don't know if we even got paid. I just recall being asked to play in between shows. It's funny; I don't remember being paid for that.

Were these films a catalyst or did they inspire you to pursue surf music even further?

We were influenced by the environment we were in, just like anybody else; like the Beatles were influenced by their Liverpudlian neighborhoods. They saw life from a different point of view than we did, and we were more of a harmony group. We found the Dick Dale family of guitar playing, which was a distinct West Coast sound.

Were you a fan of the really early surf bands?

Oh, I loved Dick Dale. We would play some of those songs on stage, for example "The Midnight Sun" was one, and "Pipeline", it was great.

I noticed your new set list includes more obscure Beach Boy tunes.

We were trying to differentiate ourselves from the other band. It seemed to be the best way to do it. But lately we haven't had enough shows to expand our repertoire. I don't really have the resources to keep everybody sharp and rehearsed and learning new material all the time until I can get a string of dates together.

What do you do in your free time? Do you kick around with the guitar, do you write?

My wife, Marianne, just bought me a new guitar. It is a Country Gentleman, a Chet Atkins guitar. Believe it or not, it's the surf model. I couldn't believe it. When I saw this thing, I nearly fainted. It actually has a wang bar with a damper on it. In surf music, you kind of dampen the strings and make it sound kind of poppy, and it pops a little bit. It's a beautiful sounding guitar, and a beautiful color, I might add. I go down and try to pretend I'm Dick Dale or something, to keep myself sharp, but I don't have enough work yet to get inspired. If I started to get some bookings, I'd really go down there and get sharp.

You typically played Fenders all these years.

Yes, we always played Fenders, of course!

Southern view of Big Sur, taken from a cliff beside California's famous Route 1. *Photo by Jeff Touzeau, courtesy of Hummingbird Media*

Rockfield Studios
Kingsley Ward, Co-Owner

Rockfield is the original destination studio, set on what was once the old Rolls estate in Wales. *Photo courtesy of Rockfield Studios*

First, a few facts: Rockfield Studios is the first residential studio in the world, and arguably the most famous. The first hit to come out of Rockfield was Nick Lowe's "I Hear You Knocking"; it is where Queen wrote and recorded it's masterpiece "Bohemian Rhapsody", and where countless other acts have soaked magic vibes into its walls: Black Sabbath, Nick Lowe, Rush, Echo and the Bunnymen, and far too many others to list. Suffice it to say that Rockfield literally wrote the book, and the world is still trying to catch up.

Rockfield itself is situated on a hundred-acre farm, seven miles away from Monmouth in Wales. From 1870 to 1920, the estate was owned by Lord Llangattock, whose son, Charles Stuart Rolls, would go on to create the most famous automobile manufacturer in England. The Rolls family built several enormous stables entirely of stone to house the massive shire horses required to pull its carts and early ploughs. Two of these stone structures, named the Quadrangle and the Coach House, were ultimately retrofitted to serve as recording studios.

Kingsley is among the most colorful people in this book, having witnessed the evolution of the English recording industry and its related technologies firsthand. His first band, The Charles Kingsley Combo, was recorded and produced by none other than Joe Meek himself. Rockfield began in the early sixties when Kingsley and his brother, Charles, decided to make their own recordings. In 1965, it became the first residential studio in the world when a group from New York called Elephant's Memory came there to record.

The Coach House control room. *Photo courtesy of Rockfield Studios*

Since its opening, Charles and Kingsley have relied on their own ingenuity (with the kind help of friends) to keep it safely ahead of the pack over the years. To get the acoustics right, they have relied on intuition and experimentation rather than formulaic, mathematical principles. Clearly, one of the reasons Rockfield has able to stay ahead of its competition is partly due to Kingsley's stubbornness to remain utterly original.

Throughout its entire history, Rockfield has been family owned and operated. In addition to Charles and Kingsley, Kingsley's daughter Lisa handles the day to day operations of the facility, including bookings. Rockfield continues to usher in the twenty-first century by remaining attractive to innovative artists like Starsailor, Spiritualized, and Super Furry Animals. Despite the studio's past and current success, Kingsley Ward feels that the industry as a whole is currently in the doldrums.

I'm really glad to have you in my book.

Yeah, there was an hour-long program on BBC television, quite well produced, actually, so we're doing quite well, aren't we? The other thing is that we've been in a Japanese newspaper, it's got ten million circulation and they want to do a whole thing on this place. I have no idea how they know about us in Japan, but there you are.

I know that you started out recording with your brother in the sixties. Tell me about this.

Well, my brother's name is Charles and I'm Kingsley. We had a group in 1961 called the "Charles Kingsley Combo" [laughs].

Sounds like Jazz to me.

And we hooked up with a guy in London called Joe Meek.

The legend, the myth.

I used to call for Joe Meek at RGM Sound in North London at 4 Holloway Road. I even remember the telephone number, 94074. I knew Joe quite well, because he came from twelve miles from us. We had the same sound as another band he had, the Tornadoes, so he took an interest. A few months after that record was released, we turned up at his place with the identical sounding group! Frightened him to death [laughs manically]! He took us on.

What kind of music was it?

Oh, it was just a plain rock group. Everyone in the sixties just did covers, didn't they? We were a rock 'n' roll band with an organ, like Johnny and the Hurricanes. You remember Johnny and the Hurricanes? Well, we copied them. Not like a guitar based band, but with an organ: same sound as them exactly.

You can't bring up Joe Meek and expect me not to ask you about that. Can you tell me about some of your experiences with him?

Well, we had two records out. One in America on Dot records in 1962 by a group called the Thunderbolts. The name of the record was *The Lost Planet*. Then a couple of years after that, we changed our name to the Charles Kingsley Creation and we recorded with Joe Meek for EMI. We had a record and it received a lot of airplay. I knew Joe Meek for quite some time, ever since he set up his studio, and he was really clever.

What made him so clever?

I just thought he could do more with two microphones than a major producer could do with an SSL console. He was far cleverer than the producers in his day and certainly more original. So that's how we started with him, we used to go up and down to London. Because we lived far away in Wales, it took four hours to get to London. At the time we were farmers you see, and if you're a farmer, you have to milk the cows in the morning. So we hated getting up at four in the morning to milk the cows so we could be in London by ten o'clock; it was really difficult for us.

In 1960, before we had Joe Meek, I bought a little tape recorder with a Ferro graph, and a little EMI tape recorder. We would record in my mother's front room and we used the corridor outside as a little control room. My brother would write the songs, and I did the business and the technical side. He was the songwriter and I would operate all the equipment. In 1961 we used to run rock shows in Wales and we used to put all these different bands on; kind of promoting them. Then, through playing with these local bands, this guy called Danny Rivers said he was going to call on Joe Meek, who I didn't know much about to be honest with you. So we had our little tape that we made in 1960 [laughs] that sounded similar to the Tornadoes and I went to London and off to Joe Meek's place with my tape. So that's how I got to meet Joe Meek and he took us on and that's how that got going.

But we thought, because we were interested in recording and liked to see how he did it, that we'd set up a little studio to do our own demos in. So in 1962, up in the attic where we live at Rockfield, in a place called Ambeley Court, Charles and I set up a little studio up in the attic.

How did you choose the name Rockfield?

When we first got going, between 1962 and 1967, it was called Future Sounds, Ltd. Joe Meek's company was called RGM Sound, and everybody was "something" Sound. We thought, since we had new, revolutionary ideas being in the country, "We'll call ourselves Future Sound [laughs]!"

The Quadrangle control room. *Photo courtesy of Rockfield Studios*

Then Dave Edmunds walked into the studio one day in 1967 and said "I've got a brilliant name for your studio." I said, "What's that?" He said, "Rockfield," because there is a rock field just down the road from us about a half-mile away. As he came up the motorway and looked at the sign that said, "Rockfield, turn left," it was obvious that we couldn't see the wood for the trees. We never saw it. So that's what we did, we called it Rockfield.

One of the bedroom accommodations at Rockfield. *Photo courtesy of Rockfield Studios*

So you've lived at Rockfield your whole life?

Yeah, since 1958. We started to do our own demos and we got better and better. We had our own little studio going by 1962, even though we were recording with Joe Meek until 1965.

Can you tell me how Joe Meek may have influenced your recording techniques?

We watched how he did things to a degree; he knew how to mic a drum kit up, things like that. It was mono in those days, there was no such thing as stereo. But by 1965, we then had a proper studio going here. We had gone past the stage where we were doing lots of little local bands. We had a proper recording studio with big recording equipment in here.

What kind of equipment?

We had EMI TR90 and a big Philips tape machine. A friend of mine, Dougie Ross, who's dead now, had six of them. He bought them from a company called Philips Records in London, a big studio. They were stereo; now we had two stereo tape machines. An EMI TR 90, and a massive Philips tape machine.

That's some pretty serious equipment.

Yes, it was very advanced at the time. In 1965, the important thing was we had a band come over from New York. I can't remember how they came to be with us, but they were called Elephant's Memory. That was the first time we ever had people stay at the premises. So in 1965, that made us the world's first residential recording studio when we moved from the attic down to a loft, a granary really, above the stables. Then we started to record other bands, such as the Interns, who had a deal in London with Philips, I think.

So at this point in time did you throw in the towel with your band and try to make this your career?

In 1966, I was making a record with a band from Cardiff called Sudden People. There was this cover song by Donny Halibut called "A Little Piece of Lemon" and I wanted a guitar to play in it. My brother was a guitarist, but he wasn't good enough to play in it. So this band from Cardiff said "We know this great guitarist whose name is Dave Edmunds." I hadn't heard of him. I said, "If he's any good, bring him up," because we didn't know anyone else. So in 1966, Dave Edmunds came up and played guitar on this record I was making. And he was a phenomenal guitarist, well ahead of us, you know.

Different kind of style?

Bloody different everything [laughs]! He was a really good guitarist, and he knew a lot more than us about guitar playing and things. And he had a good image. So we took Dave Edmunds on and we worked with him. Then we met a guy from Cardiff called Andy Fairweather Low who was with a band called the Sect Maniacs. Following that he formed a band called the Amen Corner. Andy was only sixteen or seventeen at the time and he had a really good band with a sax player. At the same time, there was another really good band called The Silence from Harringford, they became Mott the Hoople [laughs]! So during the period of 1966 through 1968, there was Dave Edmunds here, there was this band called The Silence which actually became Mott The Hoople, and there was Andy Fairweather Low, who became very famous as a pop singer and then played with Eric Clapton for years as a guitarist.

And this all happened through word of mouth? You weren't doing any promotion around your studio? These people were finding you.

No, no. Exactly right. So we now have first class bands recording here. We never had a big hit by the way, but we were definitely doing good things.

Kingsley, can you recall some of your recording techniques from way back then?

Well, we only had a six-channel mixer. When I first met Edmunds we'd never heard a stereo record, neither of us; we never recorded one. But Dave Edmunds set his band Love Sculpture up, and we made a stereo record. I forget what it was called now. We had a simple little mixing console, but it was enough to make a really good record. When Dave Edmunds and I played it back, we stood in a room, put the lights out,

Coach House exterior. *Photo courtesy of Rockfield Studios*

and with two speakers stuck up, the voice came out in the middle. We couldn't believe it [laughs]! We just stood in awe at this stereo record! The drums were on one side, the bass was coming out, and the voice was in the middle, you see, because we made sure the voice went to the left and the right hand track. We just split the voice up so it came in both channels, causing it to end up in the middle. We nearly died of a heart attack when we heard the record back!

Wow, that must have been great.

Yeah, so that was in the 1960s. That was funny, it was. You should have seen our faces, oh, dear! Then we did all the phase in with Dave Edmunds in 1967, I think it was.

Still, at this time it was only track to track, there were no 4-tracks or 8-tracks or any of that yet. And we did all the phase in stuff and backwards guitar business, but we had to do it on two machines, one running backwards. And Dave Edmunds had to learn the guitar bit backwards to play it forwards.

So what made you want to do this? You just flipped the reel around?

Exactly, yes. I think that Small Faces record, *Itchycoo Park*, had come out, that was covered in phase in. So we did phase in as well and we did it by having two tape machines locked together. We use to alter the tape path with match sticks and it would go in and out of phase.

Are there any techniques that carried through to this point from your experience with Joe Meek?

The funny thing that Joe Meek always said to us was, "When you sing, sing with a smile on your face." We thought it sounded stupid. But he said sing with a smile on your face, and right against the microphone. He had a pop shield, really tight, with I don't know what it was, I think a U47, I'm not sure now. He made my brother sing right up against it with a smile on his face. We noticed in those days, that all the records were happy records in pop, weren't they? Whether it was Buddy Holly or anybody else in the '50s or '60s, they had that sound about them, didn't they? They weren't down sort of records or miserable.

Absolutely. It was a happy time for pop music.

Aye, and he was right because if you smile into a microphone, even if it was for no reason, your voice sounded better! I'd never heard of it before [laughs]! Isn't that funny? Oh, dear! We did learn a bit from Joe Meek, but he was only mono, you know, track to track. I sold him a lot of equipment.

And Edmunds came back from America in 1970. We sat in the control room, and he said "I have a brilliant idea for a record, it'll be all the rage in America. It's called *I Hear You Knocking*. He did it as Dave Edmunds, because Love Sculpture no longer existed as a group. I think *I Hear You Knocking* was released in late '70 or '71; I'm not sure.

Tell me what was involved with that conversion to the stable. How did you do that?

Well, we had a proper control room and a proper long studio with a reasonably high roof. When we got the studio in 1968 to '69, we just met a guy called Gus Dudgeon; Gus was a friend of ours. He wasn't exactly famous then, but he was about to become very famous. Gus Dudgeon was looking at the studio and said "Why don't you put a low ceiling down the bottom end of it? It's much better for separation." These were things we just didn't know. So we split the studio up into two. We had the high bit at the one end, and the very low bit at the other, because Gus said it would be better to control the sound. He was absolutely right, by the way.

For the control room area, we just made sure we had loads of carpet on the walls, no reflection anywhere; that was quite easy to do really, because it wasn't that important. Not in 1968. Then when Dave Edmunds came back in 1970, it was around the same time Black Sabbath turned up with Ozzy, who was very young at the time. Roger Bain was down rehearsing to do the *Paranoid* record.

What kind of equipment are you on at this point?

We had a Rosser now. By this time, my friend, Dougie Rosser in Swansea, who I'd met in 1964 and bought some machines from, had built a proper console for us. So we now had a really nice console. It wasn't huge, I think it had about 20 channels or something, and we were 8-track because in 1968 we bought an eight track machine.

So by 1969, we now had a really nice studio with these two big old valve machines; we still had the Philips, the TR-90, we had other machines, and we now had the eight track Levers-Rich and a Rosser console. We also had a studio with a low end and a high end.

And mixing to stereo on your older decks that were earlier used for tracking?

Yes, we'd moved on. We came from mono track to track in the early sixties, to stereo in the middle sixties, to 8-track in the late sixties. *I Hear You Knocking* went to number one, and was there for seven weeks. It sold three million in the UK, I think, which was pretty good, wasn't it?

It put you right on the map, didn't it?

Slightly, and then all of a sudden we became inundated with people coming down here.

It sounds like you were really connected with people from an early point.

Yeah, we had lots of people down here early on. Black Sabbath became huge, obviously. They would have nothing to do with us as such, but I remember them starting down here with Ozzy and all that rehearsing with Roger Bain for *Paranoid*. I knew them very well. Of course Mott The Hoople became huge, Dave Edmunds was huge, Andy Fairweather Low, he was huge, they were all huge.

The Quadrangle at Rockfield. *Photo courtesy of Rockfield Studios*

Do you think early on there was a draw to get out into the country versus recording in a large metropolis like London?

I'll tell you something, in the sixties, we knew a lot of people in London, and they said, "You'll never, ever be successful in the country, because everything happens in London. You'll never do it." They more or less said that we were wasting our time, really. They got that completely wrong, didn't they?

Yeah, and you folks really defined the residential, "get out of the metro" way of thinking. All the other residential studios came later.

There was nothing, there was only us. From 1962 to '70 or '71, there was only us. We're the world's first by miles. And then Todd Rundgren turned up with a band called Foghat in the early seventies. I learned a lot from Todd Rundgren about ambient mic'ing and things. Todd was producing Foghat and he was good. He put the drums in a big, live ambient room using distant mic'ing techniques. We would typically close mic things until he came along and we learned distant mic'ing from him to be honest about it. You learn from different people as you go along, don't you?

In 1970 we went from 8-track to 16-track and in 1973, I think the 24-track Studers came in. In 1974, we built another big studio at Rockfield, so we had two studios altogether. They both had Rosser mixers in them, much bigger consoles while both studios had 16 or 24-track tape machines.

So you built up another room at this point just to keep up with demand, because you had enough business to keep two rooms going?

Yeah. We had massive publicity and everyone was talking about Rockfield.

Now when you built the second studio, what advice or help did you get?

Well, we'd learned a lot by now; we'd always built our studios by ourselves so that was fine. The new one that we'd got going is now called the Quadrangle, because it's built in a big stable quadrangle. The other, original studio is called the Coach House.

Then Queen turned up in 1974. We did the *A Sheer Heart Attack* record, and in late '74 they came back to do *A Night At The Opera*, which had "Bohemian Rhapsody" of course.

So Queen liked working there, obviously.

Yeah. Then in 1975, we did the big Rush albums. You know, *A Farewell to Kings* and *Hemispheres*. And at the same time we did Iggy Pop's *Soldiers* and all these other trendy bands. We were on a big roll.

I've heard stories about the making of "Bohemian Rhapsody" how Roy Thomas Baker pushed the 24-track format so hard that they almost lost the entire recording as the tape got stretched too thin before a transfer was achieved to save it?

That's right, that's right. It had so many edges in it. They were going in and out. They couldn't find the original tape! There were so many overdubs there that we had to transfer from 24-track to 24-track to start overdubbing again! The tape was getting bit up.

We're at about 1974 and you've just recorded one of the most important Rock 'n' Roll records of all-time, "Bohemian Rhapsody". Now Rockfield is even more famous?

Yeah, yeah, we never looked back after that. We were huge, just rockin' on.

This is now a serious business operation. How did you adapt to operating at such an advanced level?

Well, you've got maintenance departments, chef's apartments, waitresses, and everything, as we do now. It's like running a hotel, a restaurant, and a technical studio in one go. I can't think of any other studios during that point in time that were as advanced and well equipped as Rockfield to look after internationally successful artists to such a degree, especially in a country location. We were the only one, by miles.

So tell me what you're seeing in the mid- to late seventies. You're witnessing technology changing on a massive scale. How did it influence your direction?

Yeah, it was all changing. The really big changes happened when the computers and automated capabilities came with SSL, it was about the late seventies, I think. SSL turned up with this automated console, which we never had by the way. I think that was the beginning of big changes because it was no longer "hands-on" and you could make the record as you heard it. The bloody computer did it for you; it would memorize your every move. It wasn't a big step forward; I thought it was a big step backward, actually.

So the recording became less of a performance and more of an automated procedure.

Absolutely, that's it. You've got it.

Glancing at your client list, you've always been on the "cutting edge" of pop music. Even back in the seventies, working with Dave Edmunds and Queen, these people at the time were innovators in their respective genres. Then you look forward to the eighties with groups like Echo and The Bunnymen, The Damned, the nineties with Oasis, and even now, with Supergrass, Starsailor, the list goes on. I wonder if you've ever gone after a specific genre or if these artists were naturally drawn to Rockfield?

No, no; they find us, and they just turn up. We got a band called Black Bed in at the moment, they're pretty good; all eighteen year olds. Chris Hughes is producing them. So, there we are.

So tell me how you enjoy things these days? Are you keeping busy?

Well, I did all the engineering between 1961 up until the early seventies. I was the main engineer here until 1973. And my brother was out and about doing other things; it was a joint effort, really.

Do you still like to be involved on the ground level with things?

Yeah, we go out there and see what's going on.

Alternate view of the Quadrangle control room. *Photo courtesy of Rockfield Studios*

That's neat you've been able to maintain such a passion for it over the years.

Yeah, about forty-two years. A long time, isn't it?

Can you describe your current set up?

We have two studios, sixteen apartments, a chef and waitresses, and a maintenance department.

How have the studios you have changed over the years? Are they relatively the same, and in the same locations?

Identical, yeah. The only real difference is that we bought the world's first Neve VR, which was delivered in late '88 or in 1989. And we bought another big Neve VR, but we got rid of both of them two years ago.

And you got an MCI now, right?

We went back to vintage; gone back in a big loop. We've now got MCI, API, Neve and vintage Neve, and also all the original Rosser modules, when we took the consoles apart. So each studio's got a vintage console and we've got loads of vintage equipment around it. We've got Pro Tools at the end of it.

So we got rid of all the big consoles, we don't have them anymore. And everybody says that the best thing that we'd done is installing the best sounding consoles, which are the ones built in the seventies because they're much more direct and don't have as much stuff in them. They don't do so much, but they have a much simpler circuit diagram inside and the sound is better altogether. So we've got the best of the past and the future [laughs]. We've gone backwards to go forwards. Rockfield is so far behind that it's in front!

We described the studio a little bit, but can you describe your environment, starting with the part of Wales that you're in?

Oh, we just live in a green valley, it's a farm with grass and cows and things. It's rural, very rural, with meadows and a valley. You know Rolls Royce, the big manufacturing firm? Well, in 1870 to 1920, the Rolls family owned it. In those days, you had these massive horses called shire horses that used to pull all the old carts and ploughs; it was all horse-drawn. That's where we get these big stables from. And this place was Lord Llangattock's; his son was Charles Stuart Rolls, the founder of Rolls-Royce, you see.

That's beautiful. You have the studios and lots of beautiful grounds if folks want to hike or whatever. What villages are close by if clients want to go into town or go for a drink at a pub?

Well, the village of Rockfield is a half a mile away, and Monmouth is about seven miles away. There are about 7,000 people living in Monmouth. They're used to having all these famous people going around, and nobody takes a notice, you see.

Rockfield Studios is surrounded by the beauty of the Monmouth, Wales region. *Photo courtesy of Rockfield Studios*

Where are things going now?

Well, to start, the music business is at the bone of its ass, it's the worst I've ever seen it in forty-two years. The major companies are like sheep, they're all following one another and they've no money anymore. I think it's the end of the big studio business.

But you're still doing great records, and attracting the best artists. I see a lot of other studios slowing down, and it seems you still have the latest and greatest.

We're top three now in the world. There's Oceanway in Los Angeles, there's Abbey Road where the Beatles recorded, and there's us. The rest don't really come into it, not to be rude. Possibly Electric Ladyland and Hit Factory in New York [Author's note: this interview was conducted prior to the sale of Hit Factory New York].

What types of producers are you attracting now?

Well, something old, something new. In this business, something borrowed that makes you blue [laughs]!! It changes so fast now, you know. Most of the A&R people at the record companies are very young now. They don't even know the producers like we're used to, like the big producers of the past: they don't even know them. I think a lot of these producers are finding it difficult now because they are getting on in age. Of course they wouldn't know about these big studios and legendary groups. They don't know what you're talking about. It's the end of an era, really. The best times in the music business was between 1954 with advent of Elvis and the Memphis stuff and I think the last great period of innovation was between 1977 and 1979 with the punk period. After that it has just been bumping around.

Roselane East

Drew Hofmann, Owner

The live room at Roselane East. Control room to left and Robert Johnson mural on ceiling. *Photo by George Moore, courtesy of Roselane East*

Roselane Studios East, designed by world-renowned studio designer and architect Michael Cronin, is a masterpiece sonically and visually. Once the studio infrastructure was completed, Drew Hofmann, the studio's owner, commissioned the interior to be painted in painstaking, breathtaking detail: it took over two years to complete the artistic finishing details alone, a dimension that was equally as important as the acoustic qualities of the facility, according to Hoffman.

Roselane Studios East, located in Wildwood Crest, New Jersey, has a motto: Awakening the Creative Spirit. Nothing could be closer to the truth. On walking into Roselane East, one is immediately awe-struck by the artwork. The level of detail and beauty is staggering, a visual feast in every room. Although it is not enormous when it comes to size, Roselane East ranks exceptionally high on the scale when it comes to vibe and character.

Hofmann went to the Mississippi Delta to research the artistic origins of some of the blues-oriented artwork he had seen in various places around the country. Subsequently, he began appreciating and acquiring the work of folk artists such as Calvin Livingston, Jimmy Lee Sudduth, Richard Burnside, Sybil Gibson, and Mose Tulliver, while learning about the lore and legend of seminal Delta blues figures such as Robert Johnson, Junior Wells, and John Lee Hooker.

Inside Roselane East, the artwork and history of the Mississippi Delta are pervasive. But outside, right on Drew's front porch, is the worldwide capital of Doo-Wop and the location of one of the world's most beautiful beaches: Wildwood, New Jersey. Wildwood has been a Rock 'n' Roll town since the '50s; Bill Haley and His Comets performed their live debut of "Rock Around the Clock" at the HofBrau Hotel on Oak and Atlantic avenues in 1954. Chubby Checker was doing "The Twist" at Wildwood's Rainbow Club almost a month before he appeared on Dick Clark's nationally syndicated television show, launching a national craze and sending the song skyrocketing to Number 1 on the Billboard charts. It is easy to see how Wildwood may have been the inspiration for such hits as The Drifters' "Under the Boardwalk".

Owner Drew Hofmann. *Photo by George Moore, courtesy of Roselane East*

Recently, Wildwood has staked its claim as the "Birthplace of Rock 'n' Roll", with a brand new convention center and a whole town that has been renovated to fit the doo-wop theme. The vibe is palpable throughout town, and this provides the perfect backdrop for Hofmann's studio.

What makes Roselane East so special?

Aside from being sonically superior, our studio is filled with unique décor including custom woodwork from Bangalor, India, and extensive mural work by well-known House Of Blues artists Brent Spears, Scott Guion, Jon Bok, and Andrew Wood. Second, our location in Wildwood, New Jersey, is two blocks away from one of the nicest beaches in the world.

Can you tell me about Wildwood?

We have the biggest beaches I have ever seen in my life, bigger than California; it's ten miles long. Wildwood itself is a rock 'n' roll town that has recently experienced an amazing resurgence. Originally, Wildwood was known for The Platters, the Spinners, Motown, and Dick Clark. I built this studio before the recent resurgence here in Wildwood, so I guess you could say my timing was good.

They've expanded considerably and put a lot of money into the town. There's now a brand new multimillion dollar Convention Hall facility right on the boardwalk. It has an unusual design and has brought a lot of business to town. Actually, the entire town has been renovated in a distinct sixties retro fashion. You have national chains like Wawa, Pizza Hut, and Harley Davidson remodeling their exteriors to fit in with the theme, and it's cool. You also have these nostalgic designs being laid out in brick mosaic on the streets, for example in one intersection, there's a Gibson Flying V. It has all happened in the last few years and it's all over the place.

Do you have restaurants and everything nearby?

There are many happening restaurants here in Wildwood, including Russo's Italian restaurant. We're also two miles from Cape May, which has some of the nicest restaurants in New Jersey. In Cape May, there's The Lobster House, The Washington Inn, The Merion Inn, and many others.

Where are you from originally?

I'm from Philadelphia and moved to Wildwood when I was ten years old. My parents got me right into taking drum lessons. I started playing clubs here in the early '80s, when clubs were pretty big down here. In 1980, when I was about twenty, I auditioned to play with Rex Smith and ended up going on tour with him, playing alongside Cheap Trick, The Cars, Eddie Money, Ted Nugent, and many others.

What was it like growing up around here?

Winters were kind of quiet, but I loved growing up on the boardwalk. I grew up in the Convention Hall that was on Fun Pier. We had apartments inside, literally right on the boardwalk. I would walk out of the kitchen, walk through the hallway, hop over a counter, and right on the boardwalk.

What made you want to get more into recording and production?

Well, I wanted to not just be a performer, but also a composer and a creator. So I went to Philadelphia Music Academy where I studied jazz percussion, composition, and classical music. I just wanted to learn composition and be able to understand harmony and theory.

Did you always want to open a studio up in Wildwood?

Well, this was originally just going to be just my own personal studio. When I came back from the West Coast, I had been playing and doing a lot of sessions. I just wanted my own studio. I actually considered building a facility in Florida, but my friend Michael Cronin told me, "Look, you are two blocks from the beach!" He convinced me that I really had a great location and that it would be a great draw.

Detail of artwork by Brent Spears, made from local artifacts in Wildwood, New Jersey. *Photo by Jeff Touzeau, courtesy of Hummingbird Media*

Wildwood features the longest boardwalk in the world. Pictured is the famous Morey's Piers. *Photo by Jeff Touzeau, courtesy of Hummingbird Media*

This is the beach that is only two blocks from Roselane East. Wildwood features miles of the best beaches found on the Jersey Cape. *Photo by Jeff Touzeau, courtesy of Hummingbird Media*

How did you decide where to put the structure and how long did it take to get going?

It actually only took six months for the guys to come in and build the interior and repurpose the structure, which was originally a garage that sits behind a house I own. The people who came out and built this studio had built the best studios in Nashville: Michael Cronin designed Blackbird and also reworked Gary Belz' studios House of Blues and East Iris. The art phase, once it had begun, was much more time consuming than the building phase.

I have never see a studio with these kinds of murals or this level of artistic visual detail.

It's really over the top. It took two years to do it, to get all the people together. Gary Belz tipped me off to Michael Cronin and the other artists, and we have all since become great friends.

Why all this art? What got you so stoked about it?

For whatever reason, I decided to go on a mission to the Mississippi Delta; I walked down dirt roads in Mississippi to find many of these folk artists. They are each unique in their gifts and use many unusual techniques in their work; Brent Spears, for example often uses this orange shellac technique over his artwork, enhancing the depth and adding a reddish hue. Something else which I find inspiring is the intense detail of Andrew's relief castings.

Can you recall some of the details of the art phase and how it went down?

After I brought in Brent, he painted these pastel balls in the control room. I wasn't comfortable with it initially, but he was like "Don't worry, it's not going to look like Jumbo's clown room. Wait 'till I'm done." When he completed it, it was amazing and you could really see what he was going for. The intricate designs of these black dots, which continue all around the wall, unifies the entire room.

Then, in the middle of the job, I told Brent I wanted him to paint this Robert Johnson thing, and he said, "Well, I know just the guy to do all that." So we called Scott up in New Orleans, and he was down here in two days. He ended up painting the adjacent walls and the Tahitian tattoo. He also did the ceiling mural with Robert Johnson and all that. I've got pictures of him up on the scaffolding.

How did you feel after the live room had been completed?

Well, as it was being painted, I left the artists alone because I didn't want to bother or distract them. I was very hands-off throughout the process and I decided to let them do what they do best. When I finally saw it, I was surprised and thrilled.

How long did it take for the facility to be painted overall?

Two years. We kept changing and adding things. Brent painted the bathroom in a couple days, did the other two rooms in a few days, did the control room in a few days, and did the machine room in about a week and a half. After that was all done, he shellaced all of it. But even after all that was done, it still wasn't complete and there was a lot more detail needed.

I notice that literally all of the doors in your facility have elaborate artwork. Can you tell me about them?

All the doors were painted by Scott Guion and Brent Spears. I wanted to have interesting artwork on the doors because I thought it would add even more to the vibe we've got here.

This is the ceiling of the isolation booth, featuring the "Crystal Ball" surrounded by angels. *Photo by Jeff Touzeau, courtesy of Hummingbird Media*

Roselane East features a collection of exquisitely hand painted doors. *Photo by George Moore, courtesy of Roselane East*

The control room main equipment racks, housed in painted cabinetry. *Photo by George Moore, courtesy of Roselane East*

Where did you find this "bottle cap" piece of art on the wall?

This was in Brent Spears' living room. It's a bunch of broken car reflectors and juice caps. Brent can, and has, made art out of anything: bits of license plates, bent and rebent cans, you name it!

Tell me about the vocal booth.

When Scott painted the roof, he employed another unusual technique by using sandpaper to give it this nice, unusual tattered effect. The Indian flower, which appears in the iso booth, was done by Scott Guion, and it sort of shrouds the whole booth, giving it a very organic and welcoming sort of feeling. I think this makes for a more inspiring vocal booth and creates a unique vibe or mojo, whatever you want to call it.

Is this Strat hand painted?

Yeah, I had Brent paint the pickguard.

With so much artwork in here, lighting must play an important role. What are your objectives with lighting?

Well, I can totally control the lighting dynamically and I can have up to sixteen "scenes". I wanted to be able to create a customized lighting mood for any artist that walked through that door. I can have a custom setting for any kind of style that comes in. We have multiple scenes here that can enable me to totally change the vibe in an instant. I have six different zones to change the lighting mood of the studio and I also have incandescent track lighting.

Brent Spears artwork on the west wall, opposite entry door of live room. *Photo by George Moore, courtesy of Roselane East*

Machine room/snare room ceiling, featuring a custom painted mural. *Photo by George Moore, courtesy of Roselane East*

Did the artists help you spec out the lighting?

I specced it all out. I picked everything and worked with the electricians directly. I knew exactly what I wanted and that I wanted to be able to create all these different lighting moods. We have other unusual lighting around; for example, in our African room upstairs, we have Swvorsky crystals in the lighting fixtures, a design that throws an interesting gobo pattern.

Let's switch to some technical sound aspects. You have a variety of tape formats here. What was the thinking behind this?

We want to satisfy everybody and not miss a trick. Somebody is bound to come in and say, "Why don't you have this?" We have everything, including an Otari MX-80 2" machine for those who prefer analog. We use five digital formats including Pro Tools, RADAR 24, Nuendo, Logic, and Digital Performer, and we're planning to pick up an analog machine from ATR services to mix to.

What are some of your other technical strengths here, equipment-wise?

You'll also find Matchless amps, ZVX, Voodoo Labs, Maxon, Guyatone, and Hao effects pedals. Also, we have access to over 230 microphones via an arrangement with Blackbird Studio. They have the best mic selection I've ever seen. We have a

The innerTUBE Audio "Mag-mic". This high-end mic was a flashlight in a former life. *Photo by George Moore, courtesy of Roselane East*

View of racks in control room from alternate angle, looking towards the isolation booth. *Photo by George Moore, courtesy of Roselane East*

huge collection of vintage keyboards, including the D-50 and a Prophet 5, like Alan Parsons used. Also, as a big Rush fan, I've got a JD 800 right over there.

This is one of the more unusual mics I have ever seen. What is this?

It is a Maglite flashlight with a Neumann U87 put into it by Innertube Audio. It is one of the best sounding mics in the world. It seems to be a little more open sounding than the standard Neumann U-87.

You have an incredible snare drum collection. Can you tell me about that?

Yes. This studio features unique and boutique drums that I endorse or play, including Rocket Shells, Pork Pie, Dunnett Classic, and Truth Custom Drums. These Brady drums, from Australia, are solid pieces of tree that they just bore out. They are called block shells with unique woods and sound amazing. We just did an album with a band called Orange Sky from Trinidad. Jeff Glixman was the engineer, he did all the Kansas albums and has done some AC/DC. He came here and was floored by the studio; co-producer Phil Ehart loved the plethora of snare drums available.

If you had to add it all up, is there a certain profile of artist that you think fits Roselane East and works best here?

I like the fact that I can switch gears and that it's totally flexible to suit any music style. Also, since it's a mix/edit studio, we can track anywhere and bring things back here. I have done lots of acoustic work in here, and strings seem to work well. The first session, in fact, was a three-person string section including a member of the Philadelphia Orchestra. They did "All of My Love" by Led Zeppelin, and it was amazing.

What are your future plans?

I will be working with Carl Tatz of Nashville to perfect the monitoring environment even further. Coming in 2005 will be a second studio: Roselane West in Lake Arrowhead, California, just an hour from Los Angeles. We have just surveyed a location and are now working on plans as we speak. This will also be a high-end facility, but will exist in a more resort-like environment. Also, we are in the process of obtaining a commercial real estate space for a new facility we want to build in Las Vegas. So we're going to have three studios, or hubs, in key locations.

Detail of live room interior, featuring Robert Johnson mural on ceiling. *Photo by George Moore, courtesy of Roselane East*

Countertop detail of rack space in control room. *Photo by George Moore, courtesy of Roselane East*

Painted door found on interior of restroom at Roselane East. *Photo by George Moore, courtesy of Roselane East*

Interior of restroom at Roselane East. *Photo by George Moore, courtesy of Roselane East*

Sawmills Studio

John Cornfield, Producer/Engineer

Sawmills Studio sits on its own tidal creek near the village of Golant, in Cornwall, England. *Photo by Kevin Stanthorpe, courtesy of Sawmills*

Sawmills Studio rests in a secluded location on the banks of its own tidal creek off the River Fowey, in Cornwall, England. Cornwall is situated on the far southwest tip of the country; it has a warm climate, beautiful beaches, stunning coastline, and miles of unspoiled natural countryside. The studio itself, housed in a water-driven sawmill from the 1700s, is situated about a mile from the sea in its own private tidal creek surrounded by wildlife and natural woodland.

The studio is accessible only by boat and only when the tide is in, discouraging unwelcome guests from dropping by. The structure itself is an old sawmill and the site on which it is built dates back to 1066, when it first appears in the Domesday book. Over the years, the River Fowey has been a venerable source of inspiration for many artists and writers. It is along these banks and among its many creeks where Kenneth Grahame was inspired to write *The Wind In The Willows*; the sawmill itself was once a domicile and writing refuge for Denys Val Baker, a champion of Cornwall's creative spirit and author of fourteen novels and hundreds of short stories.

Sawmills began its tenure as a residential recording facility in 1974 when Tony Cox, who did many arrangements for Yes, bought the romantic old building and converted it into a sound studio. Jerry Boys, the famous Abbey Road engineer, was soon drawn to the facility and began engineering and producing artists there, including Steeleye Span and others. Since Dennis Smith, the current owner, became involved in 1983, Sawmills has been host to many groundbreaking acts including XTC, The Stone Roses (*Fool's Gold* was recorded from scratch there), Oasis, Supergrass, and Muse.

While the interiors and technical areas of Sawmills are compelling, the exterior grounds provide their own unique aural ambience. The tidal creek, located directly in front of the control room, creates a kind of natural amphitheater when the tide is out. In fact, Supergrass' song "Hollow Little Reign" was recorded entirely outside.

John Cornfield is currently a partner in Sawmills and its resident producer. He has lived in the Cornwall region his entire life and naturally became associated with Sawmills over the years due to his innate technical abilities, his strong interest in music, and his overall love for the area. Beginning his career as a techni-

Sawmills Studio as it appeared a century ago. The grounds are mentioned in the Domesday book, dating back to the eleventh century. *Photo courtesy of Sawmills*

All the contents of Sawmills, including the console and grand piano, have arrived via pontoon, as pictured here. *Photo by Kevin Stanthorpe, courtesy of Sawmills*

cian for an electronics company, he eventually became noticed as a maintenance engineer before finally coming into his own as a producer.

John, could you walk me through how you landed in this business, and ultimately at Sawmills?

It was more by chance than anything else, as these things usually are. I used to work for a local clay company as an electronics technician and there was a guy who worked in the workshop underneath, played in a local band, and he couldn't get his guitar pedal fixed anywhere. He was about to throw it in the bin. So I fixed it for him and he asked me "Do you fancy going to a gig?" So I went along and ended up fixing the band's equipment and lighting.

So you weren't actually a musician and started right out on the technical side?

Yeah, I came through the other side of it, being into bands all the time, being into sound and always building my own high fi's, PA systems for school bands, and lighting rigs for school bands.

So you certainly had an interest not only in the electronics, but also the music coming into things?

Oh, definitely. That was my driving force. When I worked for the electronics company, I spent my time building speakers, PA cabinets, power amps, hooking up multi-cables and stage boxes, and stuff like that.

This was roughly what years?

We'd be looking at about 1978 through 1984, when I arrived here.

So Sawmills was the first proper studio environment you'd been in? You were doing live sound prior to that?

Well, I was doing live sound to start with, just going out with my own PA that I built myself, out of boxes, soldering it all together because I had no money.

Were there a lot of trips doing sound into London?

No, no, just here in Devon and Cornwall, really. And then I started doing demos for some of the local bands.

So you had a portable home recording rig you'd set up on location?

In anybody's home [laughs]! I'd just bring my van around, just set up in their room and run the multi-core out, they'd play in the garage, and I'd sit in their kitchen or their front room and record it. Then I went into a demo studio, an 8-track facility, and I ran that for about four, five years while still doing the day job.

This is one of the beautiful views clients will find if they walk along the river Fowey towards the village.
Photo by Kevin Stanthorpe, courtesy of Sawmills

Is that where you cut your teeth into recording higher level bands and improving your engineering abilities?

Well, I was only ever working on local bands there; by the time I got there the studio was about to close down. It was going to upgrade, but they hung on to an old multi-track for too long and the building just sat empty. So then I got to know Simon, who owned the Sawmills at that time, and never looked back, really.

So you knew about Sawmills all along, right? Has it always had a very prominent reputation?

Yeah, I knew about it. When it started, I think around 1974, they used to do bands like Steeleye Span and Steve Strange, quite a few old folk bands used to come down here amongst many others.

Didn't Jerry Boys, the famous Abbey Road engineer, work there? He's really into folk.

Yes, many of these kinds of bands worked with Jerry Boys.

When you started at Sawmills, can you describe what it was like?

Well, Jerry and Tony had just left; Tony wanted to be nearer London to work on a new project and Jerry went up to start Livingston Studios around 1980. This place kind of closed down as a commercial venture around 1979/1980, and Tony and Jerry took most of the gear with them. They left the desk, the multi-track, and the plate, that was about it.

That was the Trident desk, right?

No, that was before the Trident; it was a Sound Techniques originally. When I started here I had more of a maintenance and engineering role. We gradually built the studio back up, got a couple more bits running. We replaced the desk because the old Sound Techniques board was really shot. And we eventually replaced the tape machine and, as the business grew, gradually picked up quality items of outboard as we came across them.

You had to really start from the ground up, rebuilding Sawmills' reputation, getting all new equipment. Was it sort of a long run before you felt it was going to be a viable, successful business again?

Well, I was still working at my day job when business started to pick up gradually after Dennis Smith became involved in the mid-'80s. Up until then, I was working here whilst I had a regular full-time job.

The control room at Sawmills, which retains a decidedly "homey" feel in contrast to the more typical "clinical" studio environments.
Photo by Kevin Stanthorpe, courtesy of Sawmills

This photo is taken from the bridge; the water in the creek is typically very still, creating crisp reflections of the surroundings.
Photo by Kevin Stanthorpe, courtesy of Sawmills

So you'd be doing this during the day, and doing the Sawmills thing in the night/weekends? How did that work?

Yeah, so I used to start work at 7:30 in the morning, work till half past three in the afternoon, then come down here and start a session here at 4:00 which I'd run to 2:00 sometimes 3:00, put my head down for an hour or so, and get up and start the next day.

Wow, burning both ends of the candle as they say.

Yep, and it hasn't changed much since [laughs].

Can you give me a brief rundown of the studio's ownership?

Well, the mill was originally owned by Tony Cox who built the place with his wife Leslie Duncan. They built the studio in 1974. Tony Cox cut his teeth doing the musical arrangements for Yes. And his wife, Leslie Duncan, was an artist in her own right. Jerry Boys came in as studio manager and tape op engineer for Tony and generally managed the place. The property was bought by Simon Fraser after Tony and Jerry left in 1979. Simon Fraser was a local musician who had done some engineering here. He moved his family into the house and was kind of using the studio as the toy in the basement if you like. It lay dormant in commercial terms for about four years, with just odd local sessions.

How many structures are actually on the grounds?

There is one main building, the Mill House, with three stories. Then there are three log cabins which were originally used for accommodation, but are now used as engineer's accommodation, workshop, and office. We have three further outhouses that are mainly used for storage.

Was Sawmills associated primarily with the folk scene in the 1970s? Was this the genre that was predominantly recorded there?

Not really. There were all sorts of genres coming through here. It's just that at the time, the folk acts happened to be the ones achieving a heightened profile.

When you landed there, what were some of the specific technical things you had to do to get things into shape? How much work did you have to do?

Initially, it was a bit of an electronic sort out; because Simon had been maintaining the place himself and he hadn't a clue really. So initially it was a lot of electrical stuff and cleaning and refurbishing kit that had suffered ten years of general wear and tear.

When Dennis Smith came in as Simon's partner in about 1983, he brought with him the Trident desk and loads of contacts and enthusiasm. We gutted the control room out; totally rewired it. We also put quite of a lot of acoustic treatment in the control room. I'd had Dennis' 8-track Teac tape machine and Raindirk desk in a demo studio at a little place called Roach.

Dennis knew Martin Griffin, who ran Roach studios, because Dennis used to mix live and in the studio and happened to have mixed an album there. I got to know Simon through Martin, because the studios are a twenty minute drive from each other. Since Martin valued the fact that I could fix things, he told Simon and I came down to Sawmills and fixed a couple of things; just odd bits and pieces, but the repairs made a difference. It was also Martin that put Dennis and Simon together at just about the same time.

So you've always been good with tape machines, consoles, any kind of gear.

Yes, I've always been technically minded. I'd been doing the maintaining and engineering over the years, and I've moved on to producing in the past ten years. I spend all my time producing records now.

When did the first really serious records start coming into Sawmills? When did the Stone Roses "Fools Gold" come in?

When did it feel like some real momentum was building?

It was about '85 or '86 when New Model Army came in. The album was *Thunder and Consolation*. It started getting played on the radio and people were buying it. I thought "Hey, this is good!" The Stone Roses came in a little later in '89.

Was New Model Army an interesting group to record and were you into this genre?

I can't say I was a New Model Army fan before that, because I hadn't really heard of them. I was kind of into their rock and we got on well. I actually did an album before that for Justin's girlfriend Jules, who got some money from EMI to do an album. She's a punk poetess. So she writes and recites poetry. Rob and Justin from New Model Army were going to DO the music for it, so that's when I first met them. They really liked what I was doing and the sounds that I was getting, which is why they decided to come down to do the demos for the next album. They were signed to EMI records and it helped that Dennis had been talking to the label, just promoting the facility. They liked the demos so much that they scrapped a lot of the recording that they subsequently did with Tom Dowd, up in The Manor. So we started touching up the demos down here and sorting bits out with Tom Dowd down here. It was quite bizarre, really [laughs]. He was a real legendary producer.

The live room benefits from natural light, providing exceptional views across the tidal creek. *Photo by Kevin Stanthorpe, courtesy of Sawmills*

The two small outbuildings contain a workshop and an office. *Photo by Kevin Stanthorpe, courtesy of Sawmills*

Can you talk about working with The Stone Roses and John Leckie? Was "Fools Gold" just remixes that you had done there?

No, they were recorded from scratch. Leckie was producing. That was two weeks in August, 1989.

What was it like working with John Leckie?

Fun. I'd done some stuff with him before, The Dukes of Stratosphear.

He told me that The Dukes of Stratosphear was a fun session and that it was full of jokes, bizarre sound effects, and laughing.

Fucking hilarious. For sound effects, we were making all kinds of stuff up; sawing up bits of wood, throwing stones in the creek, amazing. Then we mixed it all together. It was the *Psonic Psunspot* record. I don't know where they did the first few tracks. But these were brilliant sessions; it took three weeks to record and mix.

By this point, was production and engineering a full time gig?

By this point, yes, I'd walked out of my old job.

Did you have a staff at Sawmills? What was the infrastructure like?

Well, Simon Fraser owned Sawmills and had been doing the administration. His wife, Serena, had been doing the cooking for the bands and I was doing everything else. That was it, until Dennis brought in new equipment around 1985 and just raised the level of the facility on a technical and public awareness basis. We had a new cook and assistants then, before New Model Army started using the place. In 1990, Simon moved out and Ruth Taylor moved in. Ruth was responsible for a lot of the day to day stuff that Simon had been dealing with. She was also doing all the cooking and housekeeping. In fact, it was just Ruth and I doing everything in those days. Ruth still manages the site and deals with all the administration, but has the assistance of a cook and housekeeper now. We also have a resident engineer as well as a maintenance engineer and a guy that looks after the grounds and property maintenance.

Sawmills has been from the outset primarily a residential place? Bands don't typically set up shop there for a day and come home, right?

Yeah, there's no road. The only way in and out is by boat. We don't have a road into this place at all. You can come through the woods, walk down the riverbank or you can get a boat when the tide's in. The creek is tidal, so you only have six hours of tide, then six hours dry.

No neighbors whatsoever for miles??

Yep.

What about towns? What do you do if you want to go out for a beer or something?

A ten minute walk through the woods will get you to the village of Golant, where there is a riverside pub and a hotel. That's the village.

That's it?

Yeah, If we want something a little livelier, we jump in the boat and go down river. We have two motor launches, so we jump in the boat and go down to the Town of Fowey, an old Cornish fishing town where you've got restaurants, seven or eight pubs, gift shops.

Touristy and historic??

Yeah, it's very old and very picturesque. A recent survey suggested that Fowey was among the top three places in Britain that people would most like to live in. It's very popular in the summer. Although it's just a half mile upriver in our little creek, you'd hardly know it was there since we're just surrounded by trees and water.

I would think that your natural surroundings are part of your clients' decision making process to record there.

Very much so. It's far enough away from London that it discourages the record companies from dropping in every five minutes. The problem is, when they do get here, they don't want to leave.

We use the whole premises for recording. Not just inside, but outside too. We record outside on the grass, using the ambience of the creek, which is like a natural amphitheater. And that's literally just outside the control room. We've got tie lines running around everywhere; we set up mics in hallways and different rooms and record out in the open.

Does any particular session come to mind that you've recorded outside?

Something that you've heard of would be Supergrass. Their second album, *In it for the Money*, a track called "Hollow Little Reign"; this was all done outside. And there's a track "Tonight", of which parts were done outside. In general, quite a lot of the brass on the album was done out in the creek. In fact, if you listen very carefully between tracks one and two, you can actually hear the ducks!

How many albums have you done with Supergrass at Sawmills?

I've done three with them. They love it here.

How do you run a typical session? Do you track then mix, or do all the tracking first?

I try to avoid going tracking mixing, tracking mixing. If the rough mixes sound good, they end up on the record anyway. I usually get all the recording done and have a stint at mixing towards the end of the session.

Can you walk me through the layout of the building?

It's quite self-contained, really. Once you get off the boat, you land on the jetty. We have a floating pontoon. That's the way most people see the place for the first time, from the water. Or our clients arrive in the little village of Golant, they phone us up to say they're there, they back their van down the slip way, we turn up with our twenty foot dory, we load the equipment in, then we set off down the river.

Do bands typically bring in their own gear? You have a huge equipment list.

There's always their backline gear. They always bring loads of guitar amps and all that sort of stuff. I always tell them to bring everything because you never know what might sound good.

We then unpack all the gear, wheel it on the path through the garden, and we end up in the control room, which is the first place you come to. The main entrance is to the right of the desk. You basically have to wheel in the gear straight through behind the desk into the live room. The live room's not huge, the control room is quite small; but it all works.

So there's one live room, a control room, and an iso booth?

We've got three isolation booths within the live room, and one main room where there's the Hammond, the Rhodes, the Wurly, the grand Piano, and the drum kit.

How do you record drums? I'm thinking of Reni's kit from the Stone Roses, The Supergrass drumming, New Model Army, these kits sound great. What's your approach?

It depends on the drummer, the style, and what kind of kit. I cover my ass, to be quite honest. I get a lot of close mics on everything and ensure that that's all sounding good. Then I'll have a set of ambient mics, sort of a three mic drum sound.

What are some of your favorite mics?

I do seem to have become set on a few particular mics at the moment. I just sort of play around until I find the combination that works. I use a 57 on the snare, 57 on the bottom of the toms, 421s on the top of the toms, RE20 inside the bass drum, D12 or D25 outside the bass drum, 414 overheads, 451 hats, KM84 on the snare along with a 57.

When you recorded New Model Army, were they pretty much playing live, or were there a lot of overdubs? Sounds extremely tight.

Oh, totally live. Nearly everybody who comes here just sets up and plays it live. Absolutely. That's just the way I like to do it as well. I get bored doing it bit by bit.

Recording often takes place on this stretch of lawn outside the building during the summer months as bands take advantage of the famous creek ambience. *Photo by Kevin Stanthorpe, courtesy of Sawmills*

How was it recording Oasis?

I did *Definitely Maybe* and they were still on the up and up. They weren't anybody and I didn't see what all the fuss was all about to be quite honest. They came down here with an engineer called Anjali Dutt, who had been engineering for them in London. She had never used a split console before, so I engineered and set up the backing tracks, recording the bass, drums, and guitars for the entire album in the first three days. And then I kind of left them to it.

Do you live near Sawmills?

Yeah, about five minutes away. I can fall out of bed and get here in ten minutes.

Can you walk me through the history of the structure? What do you know about the building itself?

Apparently the site, before the building was here, was mentioned in the Domesday book, back in 1066 for some reason. The little creek used to be Bodmin's harbor and landing place from the sea. Bodmin is a nearby town, some six miles inland. This place used to be their port if you like, and apparently there used to be a track that went from here all the way to Bodmin before there were roads, which is why this place is actually known as Bodman Pill. Then they built a sawmill here in the late 1700s which was water driven. There was a big water wheel on the side of the building. The whole building is built completely cockeyed, which actually serves the current purpose quite well!

How about the ceilings inside? What kind of height do you have?

Not much; it's not massive.

The kitchen and living area is spacious and comfortable. There are seven bedrooms, many with views across the water. *Photo by Kevin Stanthorpe, courtesy of Sawmills*

And it's a three story structure?

Yes. It's sort of built in the side of the hills, because it's in a valley. Three stories are in the front, and there are two stories in the back. They had big saw benches powered by a massive waterwheel at the side of the building.

I believe it was a sawmill up until the 1920s, then at some point it got converted into a residential accommodation. During WWII, it was requisitioned by the U.S. Army in preparation for the D-Day landings after which it went back into disuse for about ten years. Then, in the late '60s, early '70s, a writer named Dennis Val Baker bought the place and moved his family up here. He wrote a book called *Up the Creek* about the place and the people here.

Where do you see things going for Sawmills over the next two or three years?

Well, hopefully we'll keep going on the up. We're pretty well booked up at the moment. Also, over the years, we've done a number of production deals that have enjoyed success. Supergrass was one band that kicked off as a production deal here. The most successful act to come out of here as a production deal though is Muse, which was developed from the very beginning here. We put out two in-house related limited edition EPs on our own in-house label, Dangerous Records, which contained seven of the first album's songs and five of them were singles. We're still involved with them contractually. They're huge around the world now and just starting to break in the States. They're a very special band with a potentially huge future and they come from down here in the west country. We hope to continue building our reputation as talent spotters and developers of great bands. Not many studios can claim that! We have two more acts in the pipeline as we speak. The Needles and Nixon and the Burn. Watch out for them.

Is your business seasonal?

The summer is usually a bit quieter because most bands are touring, but we've actually had a pretty busy summer. It's usually pretty busy all year round, really.

Is the region most beautiful during any particular season?

Spring into summer I think is probably the best time, when the leaves are getting back on the trees. The again, autumn into winter is pretty amazing as well.

When a big band like Supergrass comes, do they lock out the place for a month?

It's usually three, four or five-week stints most of the time, but you do sort of a lot of week-in week-out. A day here and a day there can require a lot of gear shifting.

I could see how long stretches of recording sessions would enable the artists to really focus in on what they are doing without distraction, getting deep into the material.

Absolutely, yeah. I've done a lot of work in London this year, and it just drives me up the wall. I just hate being there from the start. It makes us like animals. But sometimes this place gets so busy that I can't always get in. But I've been working at Battersea in London, and it's a nice facility. The people are good and the studios are very clean.

I know you have 2" 24-track and you also have 64-track digital. Are you using both formats interchangeably?

The 2" we don't use that often, to be quite honest. But occasionally we'll get a band in that prefers to do it on tape. So I'll parallel record it and then I'll switch between the two for the band, and they always choose the Soundscape system. I don't tell them which is which.

So you A/B it, and they pick the Soundscape.

And then you tell them which was the tape, and they say, "Let me have another listen!"

So what about Supergrass? Aren't those guys analog?

Well, for the first two recordings, we only had 2". We didn't have the Soundscape. From then on, we've run on Soundscape. I mean we have an MTR 90 here, which is a pretty generic machine. It doesn't really have a lot of character. When I was up at Helioscentric the other day, we did record stuff on the 2" 16-track Ampex, which sounded great.

That's the MM1200?

Yeah. MM1200 16 track 2". I think some of these machines add character, but THE MTR 90 doesn't. It just tends to takes the transients off and dulls them up a bit.

What about the preamps on the Trident? Do you use those?

We've actually modified a lot of them. The Trident's own mic amps are alright when you have a pretty healthy signal coming down the mic, but as soon as you've got to wind the gain up much past 40, it tends to lose its edge a bit. It gets narrow and noisier. So we built our own mic amps so it will work for the higher gain stuff.

Do you find yourself mixing in Pro Tools or on the Trident?

I still mix on the desk. I don't use Pro Tools by the way. I have done some internal mixing, and I have done a couple of albums mixing within the computer. It's all right if you have time to do it. It takes longer to get the sound, whereas most of the stuff is right on the board. It's just more hands on, isn't it? Mixing with the mouse drives you up the fucking wall after awhile. But of course, the plus side of it, it is totally recallable. There's no total recall on this desk, and once you print it, you've done it. I always print stems, so you can go back into Soundscape and tweak it, which invariably is what we end up doing.

And you're mixing down to the ATR?

Yeah, we mix to the ATR 102, which we use occasionally, and straight back into the Soundscape system.

How involved are you in the mastering process? What are your views on mastering in general?

Generally, I tend to get quite anal about making sure that what I've stuck out at the end of the day will go onto an album just by lifting the level. So I tend to sort of master as I go. My mix is with master limiters in circuit, so I can hear what's going to happen if it gets cranked up to full CD level. But I'm often monitoring at full CD level, so I know what's going to happen. Then when it comes to mastering, I'll basically take out the final stage limiter and send that for mastering, just so they feel like they've got something to do. Because otherwise they don't feel like they should be there. That's my take on mastering. But occasionally you can get a really good guy on the job, and you say "Fucking hell, that sounds good!" I started using John Davis at Alchemy Mastering, they've only recently got going. He's good, really rock 'n roll. He kind of cranks it up, gets his hands dirty and really kind of goes for it. It's good that he does, because a lot of the time, these guys can get really prissy about it.

Looking from the bridge along the river towards Golant, Sawmills' nearest village. *Photo by Kevin Stanthorpe, courtesy of Sawmills*

Winterwood Studios

Eric Schabacker, Owner

Picture of one of Winterwood's three garden areas beside the oak-sided main building. *Courtesy of Richard Leo Johnson/Atlantic Archives*

Eric Schabacker traversed a long and successful road as a musician, promoter, producer, engineer, and studio owner before he ultimately came to Winterwood Studios, just outside of Eureka Springs, Arkansas, nestled in the Ozark mountains. If tranquility and inspiration are the primary drivers of creativity, the environment at Winterwood provides a rich well of these qualities for its artists. The technical areas of the studio, combined with Schabacker's applied knowledge of classic and digital recording methods, make this an ideal location for any artist who is ready to document the performance of a lifetime.

Winterwood Estate is set on eighty-five acres and consists of a B&B complex and the recording studio, both of which Eric and his wife Sativa own and operate. Most of Winterwood's recording clients take advantage of the accommodations, which are perched on the side of a mountain with huge windows overlooking the 25,000-acre Beaver Lake. To access Winterwood

Estate itself, you must access a two-mile driveway before you are greeted with a beautiful, imposing stone and wrought iron gateway. On entering the grounds, a cascading waterfall becomes immediately visible off a natural Ozark limestone bluff before the lakeside cottage finally appears, serving as the guest residence.

Eureka Springs, which is less than thirty minutes away, isn't just a pretty location to live and work nearby; the entire town, which was built in the Victorian style, is listed on the National Register of Historic Places. It was originally settled in 1897 and the springs themselves were widely believed to offer renewed health and elusive cures for disease. The town's narrow tree-lined streets are adorned with Victorian gingerbread homes, hand-hewn stone hotels, bathhouses, and churches. Eureka Springs is a nice accompaniment to the serenity of Winterwood Estate, offering a great selection of restaurants, art, and shopping.

Winterwood Studio is located on the floor below the living area in the estate's main building. It is built in Adirondack style, consisting of three rooms, a control room, and a piano room. Like many others in this book, Eric had done his tour of windowless, bunker-like studios, and on building Winterwood, which is built in the side of a mountain, one of his primary goals was to have as many windows overlooking the Ozarks and Beaver Lake as possible. He wanted to bring the outdoors, which in his case is one of the most beautiful natural environs in the United States, indoors.

Throughout his career, Mr. Schabacker has remained on the early adoption stage of recording technology. In the late sixties, he was the first studio in Florida to offer 1" 8-track recording, which provided unprecedented flexibility and superior fidelity. Today, his technical set up remains high fidelity, but reflects the ergonomic economies that the digital recording revolution has been able to provide. Schabacker likes to think of Winterwood as a perfect place to compose, arrange, and record, kind of like a writer's alcove in the mountains.

Can you describe your background and how you ultimately arrived at Winterwood? Walk me through the evolution.

My interest in recording probably started in the mid-'50s. I think that the first recording device I played with was a wire recorder, then I graduated from that into a mono reel to reel tape recorder. Like most kids, I enjoyed giggling and farting into the microphone, listening to it, and getting a good laugh. From there I saw stereo evolve, which was called binaural at that time.

Most of the early tape machines were only playback and it was hard to find anything to record on. Well, I put my hands on such a device, called a Viking. Eventually, while in high school, I ventured into the principle's office and suggested to him that it would be a wonderful idea if they made recordings of the glee club concert that year and that I was the guy to do it. So I took my two Electrovoice 664 microphones and the Viking into the gymnasium and recorded it and had my first record made. And then I went ahead and sold them to the parents and

Eric T. Schabacker at one of the studio's twin Steinway pianos. *Courtesy of Allen Smith*

I kept all the money except a dollar an album, which I gave to the school; that was a good deal for me.

So you were making money in recording even before you graduated.

Yeah, I was. I did the same thing the second year when the school asked me to make a 7" disk, 33 1/3 rpm, that would insert on the front inside cover of the year book. I had made all of the recordings in secret, because I didn't want to blow the impact of the yearbook, you know? So finally, before I got out of high school, I recorded my first rock and roll band, called the Moon Glows.

Were you like the geeky kid having all the recording equipment?

Oh, yeah, I guess I was a geek by most standards. Anyway, after I went to college near Orlando, I got into a band called The Starfires and we began to gig; I played guitar. It was pretty much a three-chord "Louie Louie" type stuff, but I knew how to sell it and get jobs. We tied in with a local radio station, WLOF, and we were almost a household name. So eventually, I took the five piece band into a local FM station where we recorded an entire album using two microphones live on an Ampex 350 mono machine.

After we got the records back, I waited till Christmas break or Spring break or something and went to New York City looking for a record deal. This was back in the days when you could actually get heard.

How was the reception?

Nobody seemed to be particularly interested in the group, but Capital Records did start talking a little bit. The lights came on when they told me how much they wanted to pay me, because it was nothing. I was used to selling records in high school where I'd make three bucks a record. And this was in a time when records were selling for five dollars a piece. I would sell the records, pay my costs, give a buck to the school and I'd still have 3 dollars left! Having seen this, I said "Okay, I'm going to just start my own label." So I went back to Florida and opened up my own little company, Tener Records.

So this is the first iteration of Eric the Producer?

More of the promoter at this point. When I was in the city, somehow I ran across this fellow in New York City by the name of Stuart Hemingway, who was an arranger/recording guy. I sent him this song I wrote and he got a bunch of studio people together along with our singer, Suzanne Goddard, who was quite good. They recorded at the same studio where Bob Crew and Four Seasons were recording. It was a three or four track studio at the time, located in a hotel from what I can recall. I got the product back in Florida and we put out our first release, a 45 called "Anything Can Happen" by Suzanne Goddard.

And we really worked the record the best that we knew how. We got a hold of distributors all across the country and we hired independent promoters, or I should say robbers [laughs], but we were learning. Despite all our efforts, we never sold any records and if we did we sure never got paid for them.

So were you going to hang it up at this point?

No, we kept going. There was another fellow from New York that was a black producer named Sticks Evans and he had an artist that he put out on a little label up there by the name of Paul Sindab. I ran across this master somehow, did a lease arrangement and then went to New York. I cut four more sides, mostly as an observer, with Sticks Evans as the producer. We did four sides in I think three hours.

Anyway, we took that record and started another label at that point, our R&B label, called Hype Records. There were a number of releases; I think thirteen or fourteen in all from various people.

That's a pretty good run considering you'd never done this before.

Yeah, but we pretty much came to the conclusion that we're pretty much burning money here, so we pulled the plug on it. Since my group was still going, and since I had a record label with artists, the next natural thing to do was to start a booking agency. My group had so many jobs that we couldn't take them, so we just threw them all into the pot and started a booking agency.

How did the booking agency evolve?

There was a dear friend of mine by the name of Bob Johnson who was a bass player in one of the local bands called the

A massive stone and wrought iron gate welcomes recording artists and guests to Winterwood Estate. *Courtesy of Eric T. Schabacker*

A meandering stairway leads to the suspension bridge, summer kitchen, and lean-to. *Courtesy of Eric T. Schabacker*

Swinging Temptations. So I set Bob up as a booking agent and we called it the Bee Jay booking agency and we got a bumblebee as our logo.

This is all while you are still in college, correct?

Yes. I have an office building just off campus, about three blocks, and I'm walking between classes back and forth to the office. I'm the only kid at the school at the time who was allowed to have a telephone in his bedroom.

Were you able to keep your expenses generally at bay with this company?

Most of the time; it was up and down but most of the time we actually could. The first thing I realized after running the agency for just a little while was that if the bands had any sort of recordings they were more likely to get booked than if they didn't have any at all.

We put together a recording of all our artists and mailed it out to all the fraternities, sororities, and high schools in the state of Florida and they didn't even know it was coming; they just got it in the mail. All of a sudden the phones started ringing.

So there's a huge level of interest generated right out of the gate like that?

Absolutely. It'd never been done before; we absolutely nailed it. So we started doing that for a couple of years and then I decided "Well I think I'm going to go ahead and open a little teeny studio." The purpose was to feed my own little songwriting habit and also to make these demos for the booking agency.

Like a primitive version of a project studio.

Yeah, I guess it was. We moved to a place directly across the street from the railroad tracks, to a place that had a tin roof; and it rains a lot in Florida! So if a train came or if it rained, we would have to deal with that and stop the tape.

It was a tiny little room; we put a little window at one end and made a control room. We got a Synchron condenser mic and ran it into a Bozak mixer that we had which only had one output. We ran that into a Crown four-track four-channel 1/4" tape machine. So we got three more mixers, screwed them together. So now we were 40 in and 4 out [laughs]! We also got a little unit that was called a Space Expander, a new spring reverb unit. It was during that time that Jimmy Page came in just for the fun of it.

When was this?

I'm going to say '66. He was in a group called the Yardbirds. He had appeared with the Yardbirds at a roller skating rink called Kemps Coliseum. After the show, they all came over to the studio and we all drank a bunch of beers together and sat around and showed them the studio and that kind of stuff.

How did you get Jimmy Page into your studio?

I told him there was going to be a little beer party at the studio across the street, so we walked across the street, through an empty field, over the railroad tracks, down an embankment, and we were right there at the studio.

So one thing led to another, and I got pretty friendly with the same radio station that had been pumping us over the years. One of the guys there was a guy by the name of Bill Vermillion and another was named Jim Ivy. They're both jocks and Jim sells Ampex equipment on the side. Finally, I get my hands on an AG 440 1" 8-track. We billed ourselves as the first 8-track studio in Florida.

Pretty state of the art stuff at the time.

That beat out Criteria. We were still using our Bozak mixers but we were now 8-track. So we got an Ampex MR-70 series 2-track, which had specs that went way beyond the AG 440. Bill Vermillion from the radio station would come over now and then to do a little engineering. He was mechanically inclined and he was the one who kept the gear going.

When did you finally outgrow this facility? Presumably your 8-track set up led to more work?

It did. From there we moved across town to another warehouse actually owned by the same landlord. It was beautiful; it was a long, long open warehouse that was shared with other people.

There was an almost paper-thin wooden wall between our section of the building, which was in the front of the warehouse, and the back part of the building which housed everybody else. Directly behind was a Goodyear tire distributor and they had a bunch of big garage doors that they left open because the warehouse was hot. So if you opened the street door and came into our studio, a draft would be created and that wall would move.

Now, we had an upright piano up against the wall, and at one time we had this gospel group in. There was this little old lady sitting down playing the piano and somebody in the back, they were unloading tires and rolling them off the truck. One of them got away and it rolled across and slammed into the wall directly behind the piano. It hit the wall and the piano bounced out about an inch from the wall while the person was playing. And she stood up and thought it was Jesus.

An inspirational studio moment.

Yes. Meanwhile, Bill, who had broken many groups at the radio station by now, is doing more and more engineering. We now had an ElectroDyne console with equalizers on every channel, and we picked up an EMT plate reverb of one kind or another. We had the AG-440, the MR-70 2-track, and an MR-70 4-track machine. We stayed in that building all the way from about 1969 or 1970 up to 1977.

Okay.

We were tied in with a progressive radio station called WORJ. Bee Jay Recording Studios did a series of live concerts from artists that included Emmy Lou Harris, Gary Wright, The

Four desks are set ergonomically in a rectangular control room. A picture window towards the right offers a lake view.
Courtesy of Eric T. Schabacker

Atlanta Rhythm Section, Leo Kottke, and others. Also during that time we had other artists like James Brown come in, and Mickey Rooney came in and did some voice-overs.

So how did the booking agency manage its growth?

Well, we made a decision that by the mid-'70s, the agency had pretty much peaked out. We had gone about as far as we were going to go in that and we were just going to repeat ourselves. My heart was really in the studio; it always had been. So the decision was made: let's go ahead and sell the agency and let's go for the studio. So after placing an ad, I sold it to a fellow by the name of John Bird, and he still runs that agency today.

As far as the studio, we decided to hire a fellow by the name of Bob Todrank from Nashville to help us. None of us had ever built a studio, we didn't know what to do. We bought the property, built the buildings and put in two studios that took up almost 7,000 square feet. We had a 32 input console built by Sphere, expandable to 40. Then we picked up a Stephens tape machine and a 32-track 2" machine, expandable to 40 on 2".

So when we came online and we finally announced ourselves to the world, we put ourselves out there as being the first 32-track automated studio in the United States and nobody challenged us, so we really believed it was true.

What year was this?

That was in the fall of 1977.

What was your first success at the new studio?

It was by an English artist called Long John Baldry, who was residing in Canada at the time and it went gold in Canada. It charted in the United States but never went big. The album was called *Baldry's Out* and that referred to his getting out of an asylum. Just as an aside, he had a big band at one time over in England, and his piano player, Reggie somebody-or-other, decided to quit and start his own band so he took the John name from Long John and the Elton name from a trombone player in the band and there was Elton John.

The B Studio is one of three digital recording rooms at Winterwood Recording Studios. All three studios and the Piano Room are interconnected by video. *Courtesy of Eric T. Schabacker*

So was it exciting to have your first gold record even if it was from Canada?

Yeah, and I think that's when the newspaper came in and they said "How does it feel to be an overnight success?" and I said "Well, since it took about seventeen years I'd say it's been a pretty long night." But then the next group I think that came in I think was Blackfoot, then Molly Hatchet. I was reading Billboard one night before I went to sleep and I read about this group, Molly Hatchet. I called their manager, and I said "Why don't you come on down and record." And they said "Well, who have you been recording?" and I said "I'll make you a deal, come on down, I'll give you three days. If you don't like it we'll burn the tapes and if you like it then we'll talk."

We cut almost all their albums after that. The next one was *Flirting With Disaster*, which must have gone quadruple platinum by now.

So you're legitimately on the map now.

Oh yeah, and then we start bringing them in from Europe and we did Krokus, from Switzerland. Then Judas Priest, Gladys Knight, Lynyrd Skynyrd, it was coming together, and I had a really good understanding of the music business by then because I'd written and authored so many contracts myself and I knew what publishing contracts were and I knew what recording contracts were.

But after a while, I felt like I had achieved my dream and that there just wasn't any place to go except to continue doing the same thing. I was also beginning to see that my equipment was beginning to be outdated. During this time there was a fellow by the name of Jon Phelps who had gone up to a recording workshop up in Ohio. I knew him, and he came to me and asked if he could rent my off-hours in at a discount and start a recording school. So I said "Okay," and it just so happened that he didn't have a curriculum or any teachers.

He was a one-man show.

So our staff went ahead and helped him develop the curriculum. Our staff taught most of it for the first year and a half and then it got so busy and so much of a conflict that he had to go on somewhere else because he wanted to get his school bigger and I wanted to make records. Full Sail Recording Workshop. But what a lot of people don't know is that early, early Full Sail graduates will recall being taught at Bee Jay Studios.

And you helped Jon Phelps get off the ground.

Oh, absolutely. No doubt about it.

So where do things lead with Bee Jay studio?

Well, at this point, I'm not so sure I really want to make another investment on more equipment and I was also beginning to see some of the groups I was doing business with on a downhill slide.

It was a challenging time in the music industry.

Yeah, and I just didn't know if I was ready to go out and try to rebuild all of the clientele at the same time that I'm rebuilding the studio. You know, I've done it, I've been there. At this point, Criteria was outdoing us. So we decided "Okay, we're going to put it on the market and try and to sell this thing. We ended up selling the studio to a company who wanted to use it primarily as a video operation rather than audio and we sold off all the audio equipment.

Did you sell everything?

Some of it never sold at the price I wanted, so I just put it under my bed. Now it's called "vintage" and I'm using it here at Winterwood.

So when did you finally move to Arkansas?

It was ten years later in '94 that I moved to Arkansas and I'll just say that during that ten-year period where I was not visible I found myself lacking and craving technology. There was no technology around me, so I spent a number of years chasing my boyhood dream of becoming a ham radio operator and I got all my licenses and so on and so forth.

And what drew you to Arkansas?

My mom and dad took us up to the Adirondacks during summers, and during my high school years I'd go up there on my own a little bit when school wasn't in session. I was drawn very much to the mountains and the Adirondacks and all that

The 25,000 acre Beaver Lake, as seen from the B&B veranda. *Courtesy of Eric T. Schabacker*

The Piano Room, with its twin Steinways, is accented by Schabacker's many gold record awards. *Courtesy of Eric T. Schabacker*

way of life. After being in Florida for a number of years, with the flatlands and the heat and not knowing what season it was, things got to be pretty boring. I finally got to the point of being burned out on Orlando: tired of the crime, tired of standing in line, tired of the heat, tired of everything. I had been out in Arkansas strictly by accident years before and had discovered the Ozarks, a mountainous region in northwest Arkansas and southwest Missouri. I started vacationing out here in the early '90s and was attracted to the area. I bought some property on a lake and I actually just left my house in Florida pretty much furnished and just walked away.

I built a house in Arkansas, and I really didn't have much intention at all to put in a studio or anything until the foundation was built. The first building that was built is what is now called Winterwood Lakeside Cottage, which is now a bed and breakfast. I lived in that for two years, then I started building what we call the main

The under counter outboard gear racks are handmade from local oak and hold vintage Pultecs and other outboard gear. *Courtesy of Eric T. Schabacker*

Winterwood is the perfect environment for a songwriter to not only record, but create. *Photo courtesy of Eric T. Schabacker*

The veranda of the main building offers exceptional views of the forest and lake. *Courtesy of Eric T. Schabacker*

house. Now the main house actually is two buildings, except they're connect by what appears to be an open-air breezeway that has been enclosed.

The reason for that is because in the Adirondacks, if you've ever been up there, you'll find that a lot of the homes are referred to as camps, and I wanted to steal the idea. So after the main building was built, I said to myself, "Eh, I guess I'll put in a studio." [Laughs.] Once again, it was just going to be for myself and my own little songwriting habit, which I'd always done off and on over the years.

I wonder if being by the lake sort of brought out your songwriting?

No, frustration did. My marriage wasn't going well and I just started writing.

What did the studio comprise of?

It comprised simply of a control room, a little teeny studio, and a break room. I don't know why I wanted to have a break room, but I wired it for headphones and microphones in case I wanted to use that as an iso booth or whatever. And that was it.

Then I started getting some equipment in, and of course when I wasn't looking, Jeff, everything went from analog to digital. I'm saying "What is this stuff?" I was reading all the manuals and trying to figure out all this stuff. The first devices I got were Akai's.

So the ten years you were out between '83 and '93 a lot of technological changes occurred.

Massive amounts. And I was completely, honestly in the dark. I didn't have an awful lot of computer skills either, other than knowing how to type on Microsoft Word or WordPerfect. I bought a Yamaha 02R and still had some great microphones left over from Florida, Neumanns and Sennheisers, DBX-160 compressors [laughs]. I picked up the Mackie HDR-2496. I'm beginning to record some of my friends out here. I record some of my friends, and then more friends, then people are calling me, here we go again.

So it was like déjà vu?

I started getting groups coming in here and working with them, producing them, and engineering them, now that I'm beginning to understand this digital stuff.

What was it like waking up to all this digital technology versus the silky analog experiences you must have had?

I make an analogy of analog and digital very much the way I do canned peas and fresh peas. If you are brought up on canned peas or analog music and that's all you've ever known, chances are you're not going to like fresh peas. However, there's a whole generation out there that was brought up the other way around, and they prefer fresh peas. They prefer digital. As far as, is it warm enough or is it not warm enough, is there a digital harshness or whatever. That's all engineer talk.

And it's all above the average listener, right?

Exactly. It's all above the consumer who doesn't have the monitors or the ears to really care. And now, you know, can have your cake and eat it, too. You can record using the digital format. There's all kind of devices and plug-ins to give it the analog sound. I took my ATR-100 Ampex out of Bee Jay and converted it from 1/4" to 1/2" tape and sometimes I'll mix onto that.

I very much like the visual that digital recording offers, particularly when I'm mixing. I like to be able to see when a

The living room area in the guest cottage B&B opens to a deck overlooking Beaver Lake and the Ozarks. *Courtesy of Allen Smith*

part is going to come, especially if I'm mixing something that I'm not familiar with. The thing that I hate the most about the digital revolution is that the musicians now are getting accustomed to what can be done digitally and so they're just playing sloppy. In the old days, if you got a bad cut you had to go back and play it again and play it right. I actually had a mandolin player come in one time as a back up musician to an artist who brought him in and he just started jamming basically from the beginning of the song all the way to the end and when he was done he turned to me and said "There, you've got enough to work with." I said, "Uh oh."

He had the intention of having you comp it all up in Nuendo?

Yeah. Am I now the musician? Am I the mandolin player? He should go back out there and play.

So the whole mentality has changed now.

Yeah, it really has.

Can you describe the studio at Winterwood?

The recording rooms are situated in the main building on Winterwood Estate. It is built in Adirondack style, right on the side of a mountain. All in all, we have three studios, a piano room, and the control room. Basically, the idea was to create an environment that could accommodate any combination of different instruments and have the ability to achieve any number of different results. We typically use Studio A to track entire bands or rhythm sections. Because of its harder surfaces, Studio A also has a concrete floor, which makes it ideal for tracking drums. Studio B has these hinged wall panels that work well for changing room acoustics, and it's "sonic hue" can be changed from cool to warm in an instant. This room works great for guitars, brass, and wind instruments. Studio C, which has two iso booths off it, is the smallest, but ironically it is used the most. Crow Johnson's CD, *Hearsay*, was cut entirely in this room.

One of the most striking rooms we have is our piano room, which has 26' vaulted ceilings and is made entirely of angled wooden walls. We have our twin Steinways in here, and they sound incredible.

Our control room is comfortable and acoustically correct. I have to say, one of the best features, and most important to me, is the picture window we have that overlooks Beaver Lake and the surrounding forest. Finally, we have a musician's lounge that gets used once tracking is wrapped up.

What were your critical needs when building the facility?

Well, our proximity to the mountain demanded an unconventional design that would accommodate both our space and traffic flow. Since there are six rooms spread out over two and a half levels within a private residence, there was a concern regarding the segregation of clients and family members. So we created a special client entrance and created double floating walls separating the residence and technical rooms. One of my key objectives throughout the design was to create an environment that offered as many views as possible of the Ozark's natural beauty. After being stuck in windowless studios for more than thirty-five years, it was essential to build a studio where I could bring the outdoors inside. All but one of our six rooms offer breathtaking views of Beaver Lake, the forest or private garden areas. We tried to add calming aesthetic touches throughout, like off Studio A, where you will find stained glass and double French doors leading to a fountained garden.

For my control room, aesthetics played a huge role. Essentially, I threw away what was considered to be proven acoustical design methods, choosing to include this huge picture window on the right side of the room. I simply refused to hide the beautiful view I knew was out there. If I do experience any oddball reflections during mixing, I just throw up heavy drapes that alleviate the problem.

A couple of other key considerations for me were being able to access equipment and patching easily without being a contortionist. To that end, I have four long desks that create a rectangle which the engineer sits within in the control room. Another key feature of my control room is that the walls are totally movable. They are all non-supportive, so I can unscrew them, move them aside, change traps, whatever. The room is totally flexible.

What kind of acts seem to be best suited for Winterwood?

We do plenty of major national acts, but it is also perfectly suited for developmental projects for writers and the like. If a group doesn't have all their arrangements or ideas together by the time they want to record, Winterwood is an ideal place to finish that process, then lay it all down. Since the cottage is a stand alone business, it draws its own guests who may or may not have recording plans of their own. There are actually a number of people out here who aren't in the "business", but have talent and want to record.

How has your recording technique changed over the last decade or so?

When Winterwood Studios first came online, I had three Akai hard drive recorders that were linked up to a Yamaha O2R digital board. I mixed directly into Steinberg's Wavelab, using both inboard and outboard effects and dynamics. This method provided a nice analog, tactile feel, but didn't provide sufficient multi-track editing capabilities. Also, of course, there were no outboard recall faculties. Soon after, I got a Mackie HDR 24/96, and this opened up a new world of editing for me, and also provided a new way to back up recorded material. Most of all, it's my approach to editing and mixing that has changed in the last decade. With regard to editing, we all know that it is possible to edit the hair off a gnat, stretch time, create harmonies out of thin air, put a singer on key and a rhythm section on the beat. That is all wonderful stuff and I have done it all. The biggest challenge today is to use this sort of magic only when needed and not to get too cute. As far as tracking, my only change is that I don't feel limited anymore in the number of tracks; the number and placement of room mics, for example.

Do you primarily attract artist or vacationers? How does it feel wearing two different business hats?

Winterwood Estate, as a whole, attracts more individuals to its lakeside B&B than it does to its studio. Running two businesses at the same time doesn't seem to be very difficult, since they are located so close to one another, share the same office, and have the same phone number. My wife Sativa is an excellent hostess; when she's not maintaining the cottage or welcoming guests, she's helping set up or strike sessions or helping with a myriad of other needs.

With Winterwood being in such a rural location, do you ever feel removed from the "scene"?

No. When I ran Bee Jay Studios in Orlando, it was important for groups in those days to hit the clubs and do their thing. I'm a little tired of all that now and enjoy being away from it. Perhaps it's only one man's perspective, but I really feel there are a growing number of artists that are taking their music much more seriously than ever before and I think these are the ones who would rather come to a place like Winterwood where they can concentrate on being their best.

One of three cozy bedrooms at Winterwood Estate. *Courtesy of Allen Smith*

One of only a few rooms with a ceiling less than twenty-six feet high, the formal dining room is adorned with a sixteenth century Italian mosaic depicting Christ's breaking of the bread. *Courtesy of Richard Leo Johnson/Atlantic Archives*

View from the deck looking out to Beaver Lake. *Courtesy of Richard Leo Johnson/Atlantic Archives*

The eighty-five acre Winterwood Estate encompasses six buildings and a three quarter mile shoreline on Beaver Lake in the Ozark Mountains of Northwest Arkansas. *Courtesy of Eric T. Schabacker*

Praise for *Making Tracks:*
Unique Recording Studio Environments

For me, this book is a celebration of a recording style that I was beginning to think was dying out. Although home computers have made the recording of professional quality music available to all, the atmosphere, superlative equipment, and engineering expertise – combined with sheer dedication – of these facilities indicate how some of the greatest albums in Rock history were recorded. Perhaps more than recorded. In these environments, it must be clear that there is some extra quality that can be added to the development as well as the execution of the music. I think it might be called magic...

— Nick Mason, best selling author and founding member of Pink Floyd.

This book captures the essence of all the places we work in and will appeal to anyone with an interest in music and recording. It covers many of the wonderful hidden places where recordings are made, combining just the right amount of technical information and crazy real life stories about the recording world.

— John Leckie, Producer (Radiohead, Muse, XTC)